The Conversation of Faith and Reason

Modern Catholic Thought from Hermes to Benedict XVI

Aidan Nichols, OP

HillenbrandBooks

Chicago / Mundelein, Illinois

The Conversation of Faith and Reason: Catholic Thought from Hermes to Benedict XVI, North American Edition © 2011 Archdiocese of Chicago: Liturgy Training Publications, 3949 South Racine Avenue, Chicago IL 60609; 1-800-933-1800, fax 1-800-933-7094, e-mail orders@ltp.org. All rights reserved. See our Web site at www.ltp.org.

First published in 2009 under the title *From Hermes to Benedict XVI* by Gracewing Publishing, Leominster, England. © 2009 Aidan Nichols OP

Hillenbrand Books is an imprint of Liturgy Training Publications (LTP) and the Liturgical Institute at the University of Saint Mary of the Lake (USML). The imprint is focused on contemporary and classical theological thought concerning the liturgy of the Catholic Church. Available at bookstores everywhere, through LTP by calling 1-800-933-1800, or visiting www.ltp.org. Further information about the **Hillenbrand Books** publishing program is available from the University of Saint Mary of the Lake/Mundelein Seminary, 1000 East Maple Avenue, Mundelein, IL 60060 (847-837-4542), on the web at www.usml.edu/liturgicalinstitute, or e-mail litinst@usml.edu.

Cover art: Wikimedia/E. H. Graben

Printed in the United States of America.

Library of Congress Control Number: 2011923999

ISBN 978-1-59525-034-6

HCFR

Contents

Foreword iv

Preface ix

Chapter 1: Introduction   1

Chapter 2: A Kantian Beginning: Georg Hermes   22

Chapter 3: A Catholic Hegel? Anton Günther   42

Chapter 4: The Response of Fideism: Louis Bautain   60

Chapter 5: Magisterial Interventions: Gregory XVI and Pius IX   73

Chapter 6: Return to the Schoolmen: Joseph Kleutgen and Leo XIII   102

Chapter 7: Embodying the Leonine Project: Etienne Gilson   121

Chapter 8: The Philosophy of Action: Maurice Blondel   133

Chapter 9: The Dispute over Apologetics: From Blondel to Balthasar   151

Chapter 10: A Synthetic Outcome? John Paul II's Letter *Fides et Ratio*   172

Chapter 11: From Cracow to Regensburg: Benedict XVI   190

Conclusion 207

Bibliography 213

Index 219

Foreword to the North American Edition

The eminent Dominican theologian, Father Aidan Nichols, needs no introduction to North American readers. His *Conversation of Faith and Reason: Modern Catholic Thought from Hermes to Benedict XVI* offers a survey of the main currents of modern Catholic thought that inform Pope John Paul II's 1998 encyclical *Fides et Ratio*. He explores the way in which "reason" and "faith," and their relationship, have been understood by leading Catholic philosophers and theologians since the early 1800s. He writes as both a historical theologian and a dogmatician in the area of fundamental theology. The book therefore belongs in the hands not of those who seek popularized depictions of faith and reason, but rather in the hands of those looking for high-level discussions of how humans come to know, to desire, and to express the truth about God and human beings. With his usual clarity and perspicacity, Nichols explains the views of such thinkers as Georg Hermes, Anton Günther, Louis Bautain, Joseph Kleutgen, Etienne Gilson, Maurice Blondel, Pierre Rousselot, Hans Urs von Balthasar, and Joseph Ratzinger, as well as Magisterial teaching from Trent to *Fides et Ratio*. Such figures as Thomas Aquinas, René Descartes, Immanuel Kant, G. W. F. Hegel, Johann Adam Möhler, John Henry Newman, and Henri Bergson appear in the background and receive fitting attention in the course of Father Nichols's narrative.

 Published in Great Britain in 2009, this book leaves little for a Foreword to add. Even so, I may be permitted to sketch in a few broad brush strokes the cultural situation in which Father Nichols's book appears. No doubt the reader recalls G. K. Chesterton's classic *Orthodoxy*, published now almost exactly one century ago. The third chapter of *Orthodoxy* is titled "The Suicide of Thought" and argues that the denial of God inevitably results in the denial of the ability of reason to arrive at truth. This is because, says Chesterton, "Reason is itself a matter of faith. It is an act of faith to assert that our thoughts have any relation to reality at all."[1] The Christian creed is necessary not

---

1. Gilbert K. Chesterton, *Orthodoxy* (New York: Doubleday, 1990), 33.

only for the truth about God, but also for the truth about human reason. For if we do not understand the universe and ourselves as God's creation, we fatally undermine the grounds upon which we presume the universe to be rationally ordered and thus accessible to reason. If there is no lawgiver, there can be no law.

Chesterton's response to the skepticism of his day calls for brief mention of the philosophy of the Enlightenment. The English philosopher David Hume argued that we can know only what we can empirically observe, and so we cannot even trust the law that every effect must have a cause. We can say only that all the effects that we have personally observed have had a cause. Since we cannot make judgments about the natures of things, we cannot even say that any kind of action is good or bad in itself. For Hume, "good" and "bad" refer to our feelings rather than to an objective standard about the nature of human beings and the acts themselves. Immanuel Kant responds to Hume's skepticism by seeking to defend our ability to make certain kinds of judgments. We can make judgments about how things appear to our minds, even though we cannot make judgments about the nature of things in themselves or about anything that transcends our finite mind (for example, God). Kant adds that the golden rule, Do unto others what you would they do unto you, provides a "categorical" moral imperative. Although each person is his or her own lawgiver, a universal ethic can be deduced from the golden rule.

Behind Hume and Kant stands the work of René Descartes. In his elegantly written *Discourse on the Method of Properly Conducting One's Reason and of Seeking the Truth in the Sciences*, Descartes describes how he fell into profound skepticism about his ability to know any truth, from which he rescued himself by developing a method for finding truth. This first principle of this method, he notes, "was never to accept as true anything that I did not know to be evidently so: that is to say, carefully to avoid precipitancy and prejudice, and to include in my judgments nothing more than what presented itself so clearly and so distinctly to my mind that I might have no occasion to place it in doubt."[2] Commencing by doubting everything, including the evidence of his own senses, he seized upon the one thing that seemed

---

2. René Descartes, *Discourse on Method and the Meditations*, trans. F. E. Sutcliffe (New York: Penguin Books, 1968), 41.

undeniably true: "I think, therefore I am."[3] Descartes supposes that on this basis he can prove the existence of other things and even of God, but later thinkers were not so sure that beginning with one's own cognition provides a basis for knowing truth about realities that have their existence outside one's cognition.

Historians of philosophy assist us in seeing the broader context of the work of Descartes, Hume, and Kant. Professor Richard Popkin points out that Descartes's doubts have affinities with the ancient skepticism of the Pyrrhonists, whose founder was Aenesidemus (100–40 BC). Aenesidemus and his followers, preeminently Sextus Empiricus, criticized another school of skeptics known as the Academics. According to the Academics—see for example Cicero's *Academica* and St. Augustine's *Contra Academicos*—nothing can be known with certitude about reality, and so the wise person must act according to what is probable. The Pyrrhonists considered Academic skepticism to be too dogmatic: on what grounds can we know that nothing can be known? The skepticism of the Pyrrhonists, then, is fully agnostic. Popkin puts it this way: "The Pyrrhonist, then, lives undogmatically, following his natural inclinations, the appearances he is aware of, and the laws and customs of his society, without ever committing himself to any judgment about them."[4] The climate of skepticism (and its opposite, fideism) flourished during the Reformation period and early modern Europe, and Popkin shows that this climate influences not only skeptical thinkers such as Baruch Spinoza, Michel de Montaigne (whose essays were deeply influenced by Sextus Empiricus), and Pierre Bayle but also strongly religious thinkers such as Blaise Pascal.[5]

It may also be helpful to mention the work of Professor Pierre Hadot, another historian of philosophy. As Hadot shows, many philosophers over the centuries (especially ancient philosophers) have under-

---

3. Ibid., 53. See also *Descartes and His Contemporaries: Meditations, Objections, and Replies*, ed. Roger Ariew and Marjorie Grene (Chicago: University of Chicago Press, 1995); Roger Ariew, *Descartes and the Last Scholastics* (Ithaca, NY: Cornell University Press, 1999).

4. Richard H. Popkin, *The History of Scepticism from Erasmus to Spinoza* (Berkeley, CA: University of California Press, 1979), xv.

5. See also Jonathan I. Israel, *Radical Enlightenment: Philosophy and the Making of Modernity 1650-1750* (Oxford: Oxford University Press, 2001); David Sorkin, *The Religious Enlightenment: Protestants, Jews, and Catholics from London to Vienna* (Princeton, NJ: Princeton University Press, 2008).

stood their reasoning to be a kind of spiritual exercise. The healthy practice of reason was thought to enable one to master one's passions and to learn how to die well, so that one might live and die with one's mind and heart set upon the highest realities rather than cleaving to the things that are passing away. From this perspective, the dialectical ascent from sensible things to spiritual realities that Plato (through the discourse of Socrates and Diotima) describes in the *Symposium* is certainly not opposed to belief or faith in a divine creator who judges all human beings after death, a God to whom Plato adverts in Book X of the *Republic*, the *Timaeus*, and elsewhere.[6]

To bring this Foreword up to the present day, we can conclude that when Professors Richard Dawkins and Simon Blackburn argue that reason no longer permits faith in a transcendent God, they do so within a longstanding tradition of skepticism and lay themselves open to the charge of truncating reason. Professor Blackburn exemplifies philosophical skepticism. He argues that although there is no "order of things," no moral order, and no God, ethical relativism cannot be absolute because we know some things with certitude. These truths turn out to be mere platitudes: "Happiness is preferable to misery, and dignity is better than humiliation. It is bad that people suffer, and worse if a culture turns a blind eye to their suffering. Death is worse than life; the attempt to find a common point of view is better than manipulative contempt for it."[7] Professor Dawkins's skepticism is more naïve. *The God Delusion* ends with his excitement that he is living "at a time when humanity is pushing against the limits of understanding. Even better, we may eventually discover that there are no limits."[8] But there could only be unlimited understanding if God exists. Otherwise, to discover that there are no limits would be simply to discover that there has never been any real understanding. Professor Dawkins conflates empirical observation of constantly changing things with judgments of truth.

Father Nichols's *Conversation of Faith and Reason: Modern Catholic Thought From Hermes to Benedict XVI* demonstrates that

---

6. See Pierre Hadot, *Philosophy as a Way of Life: Spiritual Exercises from Socrates to Foucault*, trans. Michael Chase, ed. Arnold I. Davidson (Oxford: Blackwell, 1995).

7. Simon Blackburn, *Being Good: A Short Introduction to Ethics* (Oxford: Oxford University Press, 2001), 134.

8. Richard Dawkins, *The God Delusion* (Boston: Houghton Mifflin, 2006), 374.

Catholic thought about faith and reason has been marked by significant change and equally significant continuity. For good reason, the debates among the Catholic thinkers of this period often involve quite fine distinctions. The fruits of these debates prepare us for giving an account of our faith that avoids skepticism without falling into rationalism. As Chesterton puts the paradox: "Pragmatism is a matter of human needs; and one of the first of human needs is to be something more than a pragmatist."[9]

Matthew Levering
University of Dayton

---

9. Chesterton, *Orthodoxy*, 36. See also David Fergusson's excellent 2008 Gifford Lectures, published as *Faith and Its Critics: A Conversation* (Oxford: Oxford University Press, 2009).

Preface

This book cannot claim to be an exhaustive account of its subject. A complete survey of nineteenth- and twentieth-century Catholic thought on the interrelation of faith and reason would have to take into account writing in several modern European languages absent from these pages—and indeed other authors from the French- and German-speaking worlds with which I am chiefly concerned.[1] And of course, were one writing a study of faith and reason in modern Christianity at large, there would be no shortage of individual Protestant thinkers to report on, just as at the same time there would be no magisterial tradition seeking to elicit (or impose) a "central" consensus against which theses could be compared.[2]

I believe, however, that the figures I describe set in every essential the terms of the debate between faith and reason whose issue, where official Catholicism is concerned, may be found as the twentieth century drew to its close in the encyclical letter *Fides et ratio* (1998) of John Paul II. With the egregious exception of the personal flourish which is that letter's Mariological ending, there is little if anything in the terms of reference of *Fides et ratio* that cannot be sufficiently understood on the basis of the nineteenth- and twentieth century authors whose work I describe. Since the end of the twentieth century it is also necessary to take into account the distinctive thinking on this subject of Pope Benedict XVI, not least in the celebrated Regensburg address which, through careless reading, elicited such unfortunate reactions in the Muslim world.

Compared with the Protestant tradition of thought on that same subject in the same period, the Catholic discussion is rather poorly known in English-speaking countries—its Neo-Scholastic

---

1. The closest to a full overview is probably the three-volume *Christliche Philosophie im katholischen Denken des 19 und 20 Jahrhunderts* published by Verlag Styria at Graz in 1987–1990.

2. See, for example, in the Anglo-Saxon context, A. Plantinga and N. Wolterstorff (eds), *Faith and Rationality* (Notre Dame, IN, 1983); A. Plantinga, *Warranted Christian Belief* (Oxford, 2000); R. Swinburne, *Faith and Reason* (Oxford, 1981); N. Wolterstorff, *Reason within the Bounds of Religion* (Grand Rapids, MI, 1984).

phase partially excepted.³ So I hope this study, though more a series of soundings than a total account leaving nothing to the Day of Judgment, will have some utility, and bear fruit in awakening Anglophone interest in its subject.

In the Conclusion, I attempt an adjudication, singling out from among the various accounts of the faith-reason relationship available within the parameters of Catholicism, an approach which seems well suited both to the demands of theology and to the philosophical needs of the present time.

Blackfriars, Cambridge
Memorial of Saint Justin Martyr

---

3. However, G. McCool, *Catholic Theology in the Nineteenth Century. The Quest for a Unitary Method* (New York, 1987) considers a number of non-Scholastic authors, if more briefly than here. See also the same writer's *From Unity to Pluralism. The Internal Evolution of Thomism* (New York, 1989, 1992) for an account of the twentieth-century fate of the Thomist movement.

Chapter 1

Introduction

A study of the interrelation of faith and reason, even if historical in nature, should surely include some introductory attempt at a definition of terms, albeit of a provisional kind. But how ought one to approach this? After all, the nineteenth- and twentieth-century authors I shall be considering in this course have their own ideas about the act of faith, and about the role of rationality within that act. Am I simply to impose from the outset definitions of my own? Here we have:

A Question of Methodology

We do need some preliminary stab at the definition of terms, and yet the writers to be described have their own versions of such definitions. This suggests the need for a spot of reflection on methodology before we plunge into the deep waters of this study.

Writing as a historical theologian I have no desire to thrust down the authors I shall be describing onto a Procrustean bed of my own devising. On the contrary, I intend to let them speak for themselves, in such a way that they retain their integrity as contributors to an age-long debate. No doubt it would be methodological *naïveté* to suppose that absolute objectivity is ever available in the reading of historic texts. Yet over against all dissuaders, whether Idealist, Marxian or Post-Modern, such absolute objectivity remains for the historian his or her scholarly ideal, however asymptotically approached.

On the other hand, wearing the hat of a fundamental or dogmatic theologian, concerned to found more securely the faith of the Church (in "fundamental" theology), or to apprehend more deeply its teaching (in "dogmatics"), I find I cannot stop there. The materials of historical theology, a *descriptive* discipline, are capable of integration into a new form, given them by the fundamental or dogmatic theologian, who practices a *prescriptive* discipline of his or her own. This prescriptive discipline does not cancel out the descriptive work of historical theology but, rather, relies on it for stimulation and thematic richness. The goal of the prescriptive discipline (in our case, we can call this "fundamental dogmatics") is to enhance the self-understanding of the Church considered as a corporate subject. That goal of fundamental dogmatics cannot be, then, simply to display the self-understanding of various individual thinkers within the Church's membership—although studying the latter is the proper aim of historical theology. The goal of fundamental dogmatics is, by using the work of historical theology, to affirm something valid on behalf of the whole Church.

And here—in seeking to enhance the Church's corporate self-understanding through utilization of the fruits of historical theology—the fundamental dogmatician cannot claim to start from a *tabula rasa*. His or her account will always presuppose the Scriptures and the mind of Tradition through which those Scriptures are read. For Catholic Christians it will also take for granted, at any rate on occasion, the magisterium or teaching authority of the Church insofar as the latter has sought to canonize some particular understanding of an aspect of the Scriptures read in Tradition in the course of Gospel proclamation in the community.

These preliminaries license proceeding now to a first effort at defining the act of faith and the role of reason within it on the basis of those sources recognized as authoritative by fundamental dogmatics in a Catholic perspective: Scripture, Tradition, magisterium.

Defining Faith

In the Greek Testaments—Old and New—the word translated into English as "faith" is *pistis* which in its complete character, for Scripture, includes such qualities as "confidence in God, hope for the realization of his promises, and the adoption of a new life."[1] But none of these qualities are feasible without an accompanying condition which is,

---

1. R. Aubert, *Le Problème de l'acte de foi: données traditionelles et resultants des controverses récentes* (Louvain, 1958, 3rd edition), pp. 3–4. For a brief sketch of the understanding of faith in the Old Testament, with references to key Hebrew terms, see A. Dulles, sj, *The Assurance of Things Hoped For. A Theology of Christian Faith* (New York, 1994), pp. 7–10.

quite simply, *knowledge of what they are*. In the words of Canon Roger Aubert, to whose monumental study of the nature of faith in Catholic theology I shall be referring more than once, "It is to this element of knowledge in *pistis* that in later theology the [notion of the] act of faith and the [ensuing] virtue of faith correspond."[2] Cardinal Avery Dulles points out that, in contrast to the Old Testament where faith is essentially "the appropriate response to God's faithfulness to his covenant promises," the more pronounced emphasis in the New Testament on the *cognitive element in faith* may be linked to the fact that, for that Testament, "the hopes of Israel are . . . surpassingly fulfilled in Christ."[3] Christian faith consists, as does Jewish, of an "acceptance of God's word or promises as true and trustworthy," as well as a "commitment to live accordingly."[4] But if the Old Testament promises are fulfilled in Christ and the Church,[5] then in the Christian dispensation faith gains a wider scope, entailing more demands, epistemic, liturgical, ethical. Specifically New Testament faith involves "acceptance of a divine testimony, announcing to human beings the inauguration of the salvation to which [consciously or otherwise] they aspired, and with this the conditions for appropriating the fruits of the objective event which is their redemption."[6]

Since faith entails accepting an *announcement*, it is said to be, in a Latin tag, *ex auditu*. Faith comes from hearing. It is the welcoming acceptance of a message issuing from Christ and his apostles, an "apostolic preaching" which—according to the Gospels, the Acts of the Apostles, and the New Testament Letters—is confirmed by divine acts. These acts may be outer and public in the form of "signs" of some description, generally or quasi-generally available to alert participants, or they may be inner and altogether personal, invisible movements within the human soul.

To sum up the conclusions so far: for the New Testament, taken very broadly, faith is the reception of a message. This message

---

2. R. Aubert, *Le Problème de l'acte de foi*, op. cit., p. 5.

3. A. Dulles, SJ, *The Assurance of Things Hoped For*, op. cit., p. 17.

4. Ibid., p. 7.

5. For a Christian theology of the Old Testament along these lines, see A. Nichols, OP, *Lovely, Like Jerusalem. The Fulfillment of the Old Testament in Christ and the Church* (San Francisco, 2007), which draws its inspiration from (especially) the biblical theologies of Gabriel Hebert and Jean Daniélou.

6. R. Aubert, *Le Problème de l'acte de foi*, op. cit., p. 6.

concerns divine transformation of the world, and especially of human life. It is confirmed by divine acts. It requires of its recipients a new quality of life, and makes that new life a real possibility for them.

We may add that, in the apostolic literature, *Baptism* is the gateway to such newness of life. The Latin Fathers will call Baptism "the sacrament of faith," since it testifies to both the personal response of the individual and the corporate conviction of the community of redemption, the Church, which that individual is entering. This ecclesial dimension serves to exclude any attempt to resolve the issue of faith and reason by philosophical means alone.

From Scripture to the Fathers

The two most developed theologies within the New Testament corpus, the Pauline and the Johannine, indicate a degree of tension as to how to plot the relation between the vital cognitive dimension of faith and that to which it ultimately points, full intellectual vision of the self-revealing God. Saint Paul emphasized the enigmatic and imperfect character of faith, which can only glimpse its own object remotely, and as mediated by witnesses. This is connected, presumably, to faith's meritorious character as sheer obedience to God (compare Romans 1:5). As with the patriarch Abraham, to whom Paul makes appeal as a type of the Christian believer, faith "justifies" those who were formerly not at rights with God—at any rate when such faith is living and operant in charity.[7] Though it brings about an indwelling of Christ in the heart by the Holy Spirit, faith lacks epistemic transparency. It is not a walking by sight. The Pauline tendency to contrast faith with vision is often continued in the Western Church Fathers and in Latin theology after them.

Saint John, on the other hand, underlined the continuity of faith in its cognitive aspect with such full intellectual vision, treating faith as a principle that allows Christians to experience in some fashion the saving gifts of God. It is a new spiritual faculty of seeing (cf. John 1:14; 11:40; 14:8–9). For this theology, faith is a preliminary apprehension of the beatific vision and thus of eternal life.

---

7. The confessional disputes between Protestants and Catholics about the nature of such justification complicate Pauline exegesis. A classic essay in the Catholic perspective is M.-E. Boismard, "La foi selon S. Paul," *Lumière et Vie 22 (1955), pp. 489–514.*

That explains how John could treat faith and knowledge as quasi-synonymous (cf. John 6:69). Such intellectualism is not an assault on the role of the will. It does not prevent the Johannine literature from holding the highest view of charity, since what we "know and believe" is above all "the love God has for us" in the incarnate Word (1 John 4:16), and this calls for a congruent practice of charity in return (cf. 1 John 3:23).[8] Nevertheless, the Johannine emphasis on the essentially illuminative and mystical character of faith may be said to stand at the origin of typical Eastern Christian reflection on this subject.

These varieties of apostolic understanding are not to be counterposed as though they were contradictory. Within the unity of the Canon of Scripture they cast complementary light. Perhaps one useful way of identifying "classics" in Christian theology, such as the work of Saint Thomas Aquinas, is to establish how this or that theologian does justice to both the Pauline and the Johannine understandings of faith as a cognitive enterprise in the theologian's work. Thus, Thomas defines faith as "the habit of mind whereby eternal life begins in us, causing the mind the assent to things that do not appear,"[9] and this seems a combination of the Pauline ("things that do not appear") with the Johannine ("whereby eternal life begins in us"). More fully Johannine is his statement that "the light of faith causes to see the things that are believed."[10] That more Pauline-inclined scribes could find this excessively "visionary" is suggested by the way some codices acquired a marginal gloss, so that the statement reads ". . . causes us to see that the things believed are credible."[11]

So far nothing has been said about rationality. But, returning to the New Testament, in the First Letter of Saint Peter, the apostle adjured his readers always to be ready to offer an *apologia* (we can translate that "a coherent explanation") to anyone who asks them for a *logos* (which we can translate "a reasoned account") for the "hope" that is in Christians (1 Peter 3:15). *Hope*, we have noted, is a key dimension of the biblical concept of *pistis* though, plainly enough, it is the cognitive dimension of faith with which such epistemic notions as "coherent

---

8. For a full account, see R. Schnackenburg, *The Gospel according to Saint John* (English translation, New York, 1968), pp. 558–575.

9. Thomas Aquinas, *Summa theologiae* IIa.IIae., q. 4, a. 1, corpus.

10. Ibid., ad iii.

11. I take this point from A. Dulles, SJ, *The Assurance of Things Hoped For*, op. cit., p. 238, n. 25.

explanation" or *apologia* and "reasoned account" or *logos*, make primary contact. The early Christian Apologists were exemplary producers of such *apologiae*. That, of course, gives the group of writers called "The Apologists" their collective title. Among their number Justin Martyr provided the most comprehensive principle for our subject when he ascribed the intelligibility of the created order to the eternal Word "of whom all mankind partakes."[12] The Apologists' outlook was widely shared. In some words of the North African ecclesiastical writer Tertullian:

> Reason is a property of God's, since there is nothing which God, the Creator of all things, has not foreseen, arranged, and determined by reason. Furthermore, there is nothing God does not wish to be investigated and understood by reason.[13]

Tertullian's words about Christ's Resurrection, "it is certain because it is impossible," were, in context, an appeal to Aristotle who, in his *Rhetoric* argues that an extraordinary claim, just because it is so out of the ordinary, may turn out to be well-founded.[14] Tertullian, who, quite unjustly, has become for some a symbol of evangelical irrationalism, did not in fact renege on the commitments of the Apologists.

Nor did their project die with them, as we can see from, for instance, Saint Augustine's little treatise *De vera religione*, "On the True Religion."[15] It is not, however, in that treatise but in his Letter 120 to Consentius that Augustine proposed two complementary maxims which will have a great future before them: *Intellige ut credas*, "Understand that you may believe," and *Crede ut intelligas*, "Believe that you may understand."[16] On the one hand, "Understand that you may believe": the basic act of faith would be unworthy of human beings if it lacked a reasonable and prudent character. As Augustine

---

12. Justin, I *Apologia*, 46; cf. II *Apologia* 8–10.

13. Tertullian, *De paenitentia* 1, 2.

14. R. D. Sider, *Ancient Rhetoric and the Art of Tertullian* (Oxford, 1971), pp. 56–59. The proper context for the notorious citation from De paenitentia 5, 4 was already elucidated at the time of the First World War in J. Moffatt, "Tertullian and Aristotle," *Journal of Theological Studies* 17 (1916), pp. 170–171.

15. That their project did not perish could be called in fact the controlling thesis of John Rist's entire study of Augustine, as indeed its sub-title indicates. See J. M. Rist, *Augustine. Ancient Thought Baptized* (Cambridge, 1994). But see especially pp. 41–91.

16. See for this letter, *The Works of Saint Augustine* II/2. Letters 100–155 (Hyde Park, New York, 2003), pp. 129–140.

put it, "Heaven forbid, I say, that we should believe in such a way that we do not accept or seek a rational account, since we could not even believe if we did not have rational souls."[17] On the other hand, "Believe that you may understand": there is a kind of understanding—a more advanced kind of understanding, I shall want in a moment to call it a *contemplative* understanding—for which faith is an epistemic precondition, and this "kind of understanding" Augustine termed in Letter 120 "the fullness and perfection of knowledge, . . . the peak of contemplation, which the apostle calls *face to face.*"[18]

What Augustine meant by "believing" is, at its most intense and comprehensive, a form of religious understanding where, under the enlivening action of charity, faith "expands into a theological elaboration and mystical penetration" of its own object.[19] That explains why Augustine could add to his own words about faith as a precondition of contemplative understanding:

> If an unbeliever asks me for an account of my faith and hope and I see that, before he believes, he cannot grasp it, I give him this very argument by which he may, if possible, see how preposterous it is to demand before faith an account of those things that he cannot grasp.[20]

Augustine's homilies on the Gospel of Saint John gave eloquent expression to the possibility of a mystical deepening in faith through what we might call "drawing by delight."

> Must we assume that the bodily senses have their delights, while the mind is not allowed to have any? But if the soul has no delights, how can Scripture say: "The children of men will take refuge in the shadow of your wings. They will feast on the abundance of your house, and you will give them drink from the river of your delights. For with you is the fountain of life: in your light we shall see light"? Show me a lover and he will understand what I am saying. Show me someone who wants something, someone hungry, someone wandering in this wilderness, thirsting and longing for the fountains of his eternal home, show me such a one and he will know what I mean.[21]

---

17. Ibid., p. 131, = Letter 120, 1 (3).
18. Ibid., = Letter 120, 1 (4).
19. R. Aubert, *Le Problème de l'acte de foi,* op. cit., pp. 22–23.
20. Augustine, *Letters 100–155,* p. 131, = Letter 120, 1 (4).
21. Idem., *Homilia 26 in Joannem,* 4–6, with an internal citation of Psalm 32, 7b-9.

Before leaving Augustine, we should note that even the more modest sort of understanding which makes possible the reasonable and prudent adhesion of faith has, for him, certain moral preliminaries, notable among them humility of heart, itself a mode of love. Thus while, to his mind, faith necessarily involves an exercise of reason—in the course of producing a celebrated definition of the act of faith as "pondering with assent," he explained that "no one believes anything unless he has first thought that it ought to be believed"[22]—still the aspect of *assent* implies a willingness to resolve the "pondering" in a particular direction. Such willingness is, for him, love-directed.

> It is love that asks; it is love that seeks; it is love that knocks; it is love that makes one adhere to revelation, and it is love that maintains the adherence once it is given.[23]

Augustine's approach to the faith-reason relation is broadly paralleled among the Greek divines of the same period, and notably in Theodoret's cumbrously entitled *The Cure of Pagan Maladies, or the Truth of the Gospels proved from Greek Philosophy*, probably written fairly soon after his becoming bishop of Cyr, near Antioch, in 423. Every student, so Theodoret pointed out, has to believe in his teachers before he comes to understand, and yet he or she must also have a measure of understanding before such belief can be rightly exercised.[24]

Later Instances in the History of Doctrine

Resuming the further history of the theology of faith in three giant strides,[25] I move on via the Second Council of Orange in 529, through Thomas Aquinas in the thirteenth century, to the Council of Trent in the middle years of the sixteenth century.[26]

---

22. Idem., *De praedestinatione sanctorum* 2, 5.

23. Idem., *De moribus Ecclesiae* I. 17, 31.

24. Theodoret, *Graecarum affectionum curatio*, Preface. Most of Book I of this work is devoted to the topic of the nature of faith and its relation to reason. The theme could also be followed up, if less programmatically, in, to name only a few of the pertinent Greek fathers and ecclesiastical writers, Origen, Gregory Nazianzen, Pseudo-Denys, Maximus the Confessor.

25. I shall, however, offer some discussion of a figure of importance for this subject between Second Orange and Aquinas, namely Anselm, in the course of Chapter 8, for reasons which should there become clear.

26. An overview of the entire development of the theology of faith up to the later twentieth century, and including sections on authors belonging to the Reformation traditions, may be

Orange II

First, then, the Second Council of Orange, a local council meeting in 529 in southern Gaul under the influence of Augustine's writing. Its decisions, approved by a contemporary pope, Boniface II, but lost to view for some centuries, were later widely accepted in the Latin Church (its canons are cited at both the First and the Second Vatican Councils).[27] If we ask after its authority, a modern ecclesiologist who is also a fundamental theologian responds:

> Although particular councils lack authority to speak to the universal body of the faithful, their decrees have sometimes gained general acceptance by being confirmed through the approval of popes and ecumenical councils or, less formally, through the general consensus of bishops and theologians.[28]

The bishops at Orange sought to exclude the notion that faith can ever be simply the upshot of intellectual reasoning without an engagement of the will. And they had in mind here not just any voluntary self-commitment but one which is the result of divinely originated morally transformative action. Thus the Council's fifth canon runs:

> If anyone says that the increase as well as the beginning of faith and the very desire of faith—by which we believe in Him who justifies the sinner and by which we come to the regeneration of holy baptism—proceeds from our own nature and not from a gift of grace, namely an inspiration of the Holy Spirit changing our will from unbelief to belief and from godlessness to piety, such a man reveals himself in contradiction with the apostolic doctrine . . .[29]

The synod declared the act of faith to be impossible without divine grace acting on the will to give the human being the necessary strength to convert to the new life God offers in the gift of salvation. Its sixth canon reads:

---

found in A. Dulles, sj, *The Assurance of Things Hoped For*, op. cit., pp. 20–169.

27. See G. Fritz, "Orange, Deuxième Concile de," *Dictionnaire de Théologie Catholique* 11. 1 (Paris, 1931), cols. 1087–1103.

28. A. Dulles, sj, *Magisterium. Teacher and Guardian of the Faith* (Naples, FL, 2007), p. 55.

29. English translation from J. Neuner, sj, and J. Dupuis, sj (ed.), *The Christian Faith in the Doctrinal Documents of the Catholic Church* (London 1983, 2nd edition), p. 550. The Latin original is given in H. Denzinger, *Enchiridon symbolorum, definitionum et declarationum de rebus fidei et morum* (37th edition, Freiburg, 1991), 375.

> If anyone says that mercy is divinely conferred upon us when, without God's grace, we believe, will, desire, strive, labor, pray, keep watch, endeavor, request, seek, knock, but does not confess that it is through the infusion and inspiration of the Holy Spirit that we believe, will or are able to do all these things as is required; or if anyone subordinates the help of grace to humility or human obedience, and does not admit that it is the very gift of grace that makes us obedient and humble, he contradicts the apostle . . .[30]

Pauline texts are cited in the close of both of these canons: Orange II represents a moderate version of Augustine's deconstruction of Pelagianism, itself pursued in the light of Saint Paul's letters.

Saint Thomas Aquinas

For his part Thomas Aquinas (*c.*1225–1274) did not renege on the teaching of Orange, formulated as it was in opposition to the Semi-Pelagianism for which the beginning of conversion is entirely a human affair, even though its continuance and completion is not. But Thomas's immediate background was the new Christian humanism of the twelfth century.[31] Its representatives sought to ensure that grace was invoked in favor of an enhanced human spontaneity. That entailed giving thought to the psychology of faith—both as an act and as the way of life thus opened up.[32] Thomas, too, travelled this road.[33] And at a deeper level of analysis than the psychological, divine action impacting on the human will in the genesis of faith should not be taken to suppress the status of faith as a humanly meritorious act, which must mean in some way a *free* act. In the first place, such freedom is a requirement of the God-given dignity which belongs to human beings as made in the divine likeness. And in the second place, for the free act of faith (and the life that flows from it) to be meritbearing mirrors a conviction of both the New Testament writers and the Fathers of the

---

30. English translation from J. Neuner, SJ, and J. Dupuis, SJ (ed.), *The Christian Faith in the Doctrinal Documents of the Catholic Church*, op. cit., pp. 560–561. The corresponding Latin text is found in H. Denzinger, *Enchiridon symbolorum, definitionum et declarationum de rebus fidei et morum*, op. cit., 376.

31. See R. Southern, *Medieval Humanism and Other Studies* (Oxford, 1970).

32. The subject of the enormous labors of Dom O. Lottin, *Psychologie et Morale au moyen âge* (Louvain 1942–1960).

33. Explored in P. Duroux, OP, *La psychologie de la foi chez S. Thomas d'Aquin* (Tournai, 1963).

Church: God rewards those who come to him, both in conversion (justification) and ongoing discipleship (sanctification).

The act of faith will be, then, a free human act that, nevertheless, issues from the enabling activity of God: that is not a contradiction in terms if we think of divine action as itself liberating human freedom from within.[34] This, too, is genuine Saint Paul as we can see if we consult the Letters to the Romans and the Galatians, as those epistles are summed up in the cry, "For freedom Christ has set us free."[35]

Thomas also added a concern with the role of grace not merely in energizing the will but also in enlightening the human intelligence: what in his exceptionally influential treatise on the subject is called *lumen fidei*, the "light of faith," a phrase with marked Johannine resonances in both the Gospel and the First Letter of Saint John. For John, in the Incarnation of the Logos, "the true Light, that enlightens every man, was coming into the world."[36] For Thomas, though faith comes from hearing a herald, an authoritative messagebearer, the habit or disposition of faith is itself infused by God. That is not, he thought, a surprising, much less a contradictory, combination. In a comparison he drew with human understanding in general, there too very different factors are synthesized in a like fashion: "The knowledge of principles comes from the senses, and yet the light whereby the principles are known is innate."[37]

For Thomas, the act of faith is formally an act of the intelligence, raised by the light of faith to a new quality of operation. But this adhesion of mind to the divine self-revelation is itself, he insisted, a work of love, and hence of the will, which freely turns towards the supreme Good under the leading of divine action, thus making faith a praiseworthy human act. Despite his reputation in some twentieth-century quarters as an intellectualist, or even a Christian rationalist, for Thomas the act of faith is prompted by the desire or appetite for

---

34. B. Lonergan, sj, *Grace and Freedom. Operative Grace in the Thought of St. Thomas Aquinas* (London and New York, 1971).

35. Galatians 5:1.

36. John 1:9.

37. Thomas, *In Boethium de Trinitate*, q. 3, a. 1, ad iv. For a thorough discussion of how Thomas views faith in relation to such understanding, see J. I. Jenkins, *Knowledge and Faith in Thomas Aquinas* (Cambridge, 1997).

what the will obscurely apprehends as a promised Good that embodies the ultimate goal of human striving. The endless striving of the human will for the good, in other words for what will truly satisfy it, is, for Thomas, the principal underpinning in human nature of the act of faith.

> One characteristic of faith is that the believer's mind is made up for him by his will, which is moved by its own object, namely the good which draws him to his final goal. Consequently he is engaged by a double object, the good and the true, namely the will's own object and motive, and the object to which the mind assents under the will's influence. The ultimate good attracting and moving the will is both natural and supernatural. As natural it lies within the scope of our natural powers; it is the felicity matching human nature about which philosophers discourse—the contemplative happiness of active wisdom, the practical happiness of active prudence spreading out into the activities of the other moral virtues. As supernatural, it exceeds unaided human nature and cannot be reached by our inherited powers; we cannot think it or wish it of ourselves. We are set on this happiness solely by divine liberality.[38]

This is how divine grace can take hold of us without violation of our integrity.[39] Such attraction of the will for the uncreated Good releases what Scholastic theology came to call the *pius affectus credulitatis*, the "devout inclination to believe." (The last two words of that three word phrase were already to be found, incidentally, at the Second Council of Orange.) As Thomas puts it in his Commentary on Saint Paul's Second Letter to the Corinthians:

> Between knowledge through science and knowledge through faith there is this difference: science shines only on the mind, showing that God is the cause of everything, that he is one and wise, and so forth. Faith enlightens the mind and also warms the affections, telling us not merely that God is first cause but also that he is saviour, redeemer, loving, made flesh for us. Hence the phrase "maketh manifest the savour of his knowledge."[40]

---

38. Thomas, *Quaestiones disputatae de Veritate*, XIV, 2.

39. See Thomas's treatise on faith in the *Summa Theologiae,* IIa. IIae., qq. 1–16, and especially 1–7.

40. Idem., *In Sancti Pauli Epistolam ad Corinthos* II, ii. Lect. 3, with an internal citation of 2 Corinthians 2:14.

In a love which lets reason be captivated, the will actively proposes to the intellect the super-ordinate good to be attained. The affections cannot but follow in what the French call *connaissance savoureuse*.

Especially in his later writings, such as his commentary on the Gospel of Saint John, Thomas regarded as crucial to the act of faith what he terms the "interior instinct and attraction for doctrine."[41] But he never ceased to acknowledge the significance of *humanae rationes*, "human reasons," in leading to faith or sustaining faith. Into this latter category he put such very different considerations as confirmatory miracles on the one hand, and, on the other, arguments for the congruence of dogma with what we know about reality from other sources or, at the least, dogma's non-impossibility: dogma is not self-contradictory, or in flat contradiction to what we genuinely know about the world by other means. Thomas envisaged that there can be, up to a point, on the basis of such "reasons," notably the occurrence of miraculous phenomena, a natural certitude of the fact of revelation,[42]—though the "what" of events wholly beyond the order of created nature is never treated by him save in relation to the "why" or *rationale* of such events for which we must invoke the finality of the Incarnation, which was "to restore all things in Christ, in heaven as on earth."[43] Only the intervention of grace in the workings of the person's mind and will can procure not just this wider vision but also absolute certainty of its veracity through eliciting the act of divine faith. Not that Thomas or any other high medieval writer had a huge amount to say about the question of certitude. That is, for the most part, a later preoccupation which derives from a greater degree of critical sophistication (some would say pseudosophistication) about the human subject as distinct from the object which he or she knows or claims to know.[44] Thomas distin-

---

41. Idem., *In Joannem XV, lectio 5, no. 4*. In *Summa Theologiae* IIa. IIae., q. 2, a. 9, Thomas describes this as "the inner inspiration of God inviting someone to believe." Cf. C. S. Evans, *The Historical Christ and the Jesus of Faith. The Incarnational Narrative as History* (Oxford, 1996), pp. 259–282, where a Reformed philosopher-theologian incorporates this Thomasian text into his account of the inner testimony of the Holy Spirit as knowledge-producing in its grounding of (true) belief in the basic "story-line" of the New Testament.

42. G. Berceville, "Les miracles comme signes de crédibilité chez Thomas d'Aquin," *Mélanges de science religieuse* 53 (1996), pp. 51–64, considers this entire issue from Augustine to Thomas.

43. Ephesians 1:10. Cf. J.-P. Torrell, OP, *Le Christ en ses mystères. La vie et l'oeuvre de Jésus selon saint Thomas d'Aquin* (Paris, 1999), I., pp. 268–270.

44. An example of an early twentieth-century theologian desirous of returning to the older approach is Karl Adam, for whom faith's assent is voluntary since "in the image of Christ is

guished between objective and subjective certainty. No certainty can be objectively greater than revelation's, for the cause of this certainty is God. Faith rests on the divine truth. But as to subjective certainty, inasmuch as faith, owing to its darkness before the final vision, satisfies the human mind less than do some other forms of knowing, it may be regarded as less certain than these. But that is *quoad nos*, "in regard to us." Taken *simpliciter*, "as it is in itself," faith is supremely certain.[45]

In the wake of Renaissance Humanism, people focused more fully on the psychological condition of the knowing agent—his or her consciousness, and in this context, the question about subjective certitude—over against systematic scepticism, above all—achieved a prominence it had rarely possessed in antiquity or in the Middle Ages.[46] In a Religious Order marked by its Renaissance origins, the Baroque Scholastics of the Jesuit School came to specialize in this topic in their treatises on the "analysis of faith," the grounding of faith's certitude. But in a very different period and setting, Newman, too, will be a good example of a theologian or religious writer deeply preoccupied with the question of certitude.[47]

---

encountered that *summum bonum* to which [the will's] nature is directed, and which completes, fulfils, and commits it . . . From the psychological point of view, then, the belief in Christ is an experience of good, wrought by God, and not an *experience of certainty*," *The Christ of Faith* (English translation, New York, 1957), p. 16. Italics original.

45. Thomas, *Summa theologiae IIa*. IIae., q. 4, a. 8, corpus.

46. K. Eschweiler, *Die zwei Wege der neueren Theologie. Georg Hermes*—Matthias Joseph Scheeben. Eine kritische Untersuchung des Problems der theologischen Erkenntnis (Augsburg, 1926), p. 29. In the years immediately following the Council of Trent, the Roman Catechism called faith "the very certain assent by which the mind firmly and constantly assents to God as he discloses his mysteries," *Catechismus ex Decreto Concilii Tridentini I. 2. 2*. It should be noted, however, by way of qualification that ancient scepticism also generated concern with certainty, as in the early writings of Augustine of Hippo.

47. As pointed out in E. Przywara, sj, *Religionsbegründung. Max Scheler—J. H. Newman* (Freiburg, 1923). Przywara's account was confirmed by H. M. de Achaval and J. D. Holmes (ed.), *The Theological Papers of John Henry Newman on Faith and Certainty* (Oxford, 1976). In the year of publication of the "Papers" there also appeared W. R. Fey, *Faith and Doubt: The Unfolding of Newman's Thought on Certainty* (Shepherdstown, W.Va., 1976). For the importance of the struggle with scepticism in shaping early modern epistemology, see J. Dewey, *The Quest for Certainty* (New York, 1929). By the late twentieth century, epistemology was likely to be less concerned with rebutting outright scepticism, and more with reflecting on the nature of the knowledge we actually have, and how it is obtained.

The Council of Trent

In that perspective, the Council of Trent might almost be called the last of the medieval Councils of the Church. On the cusp, at any rate, of the late medieval and early modern periods, the Council of Trent echoed a kind of thinking conspicuous in Thomas (but by no means confined to him) in the course of its Decree on Justification, in chapters VI and VII and the relevant canons. Canon 3 anathematized those who say that, without preceding inspiration of the Holy Spirit and without his help, a person can believe, hope, love and repent, as he ought (*sicut oportet*) so that the grace of justification may be granted to him.[48]

The seemingly anodyne phrase "sicut oportet" is actually of some importance. It was added at the insistence of one of the Council's premier theologians the Franciscan Andres de Vega (1498–1549), in order to distinguish between a merely human faith, *fides humana*, based on conjectural reasons whereby we grant to revelation some kind of natural credibility, and a fully evangelical or "divine" faith based on "supernatural testimonies," *testimonia supernaturalia*, leading to acceptance of the Christian message simply "on account of divine authority," *propter auctoritatem divinam*, i.e., on the ground that God the First Truth has spoken.[49] For such "divine faith" grace is indispensable.

Here the word "faith" is not being used univocally but equivocally: these are two discreet though inter-related kinds of human act. Supernatural faith, aroused and assisted by grace, and leading toward God by the way it believes to be true what God has revealed and promised, can alone be called, in the language of Chapter Eight of the Decree, "the beginning, foundation, and root of all justification." So far as authoritative or classical sources for Catholic thought are concerned—Church Fathers, doctors, ecumenical Councils, papal definitions of doctrine, there the position, taken by and large, may be said to stand as the nineteenth century opens.[50]

---

48. N. P. Tanner, SJ (ed.), *Decrees of the Ecumenical Councils.* II. Trent to Vatican II (London and Washington, 1990), p. 679, which provides both the Latin original and the English translation.

49. R. Aubert, *Le problème de l'acte de foi*, op. cit., p. 77.

50. Baroque Scholastics in the Jesuit Society, however, refined the "analysis of faith" (i.e., the explanation of the grounding of the certitude of faith), notably by distinguishing more sharply

Defining Reason

That is not to say, of course, that nothing world-shaking had been happening to the second term in our duo: not this time "faith" but "reason," or "rationality."

What do we mean by "reason"? In a highly minimal way, we could perhaps give the term "reason" a gloss like "argumentative inquiry," with the possible addition of "on the basis of, or bearing in mind, first principles, whether presumed or explicit." That I think is the most we can glean from the *Oxford English Dictionary* whose entries under the headings "reason" and "rationality" tend to the tautologous. Reason is what we appeal to when we pursue rationality by means of argument, rationality what we arrive at through the exercise of argumentative reason. It is obvious that such statements get us no further forward, though the reference to "first principles, whether presumed or explicit," is worth keeping hold of. A minimal definition of reason might manage with just that alone, on which more anon.

If, however, we wish to give a fuller account of what reason or rationality may be we soon find ourselves embroiled in what the ethicist Alasdair MacIntyre dubbed the struggle of "competing" or "contested" rationalities, something especially palpable in the realm of *practical* reason where conflicting kinds of justification for alternative courses of action, or sometimes the same course of action, are plainly on offer. As MacIntyre puts it, by way of example: "some conceptions of justice appeal to inalienable human rights, others to some notion of social contract, and others again to a standard of utility."[51]

When we move from the arena of practical reason to that of pure or theoretical reason, the situation is hardly improved. In the *Metaphysics,* so MacIntyre notes, Aristotle, with whom MacIntyre is inclined to agree on this point, treats the law of non-contradiction—that X cannot be both p and not p in the same respect—as the foundational law of rational thought. Others have given the same role to the principle of identity, whereby X is X, though one late twentieth-century treatise on logic calls this "according to

---

than had the medieval between natural and supernatural phases in the approach to faith (that will become especially pertinent when the "debate over apologetics" is considered in Chapter 9 below). See on this A. Dulles, sj, *The Assurance of Things Hoped For,* op. cit., pp. 55–58.

51. A. MacIntyre, *Whose Justice? Which Rationality?* (London, 1988), p. 1.

taste either the supreme metaphysical truth or the utmost banality."⁵²
In either case, law of non-contradiction or principle of identity,
acceptance of such laws of logic can only be accounted a necessary
condition of rationality, not a sufficient condition of it, for more must
surely be added, if one is to be justified in ascribing rationality to
modes of inquiry or legitimations of beliefs. Let us call this further
aspect—going beyond the conditions set by the laws of logic—the
"metalogical" aspect of rationality. And here's the rub, not least in
the context of that highly productive, philosophically speaking, eighteenth century which ushers in the period I am to deal with. Simply as
historians of ideas, and without any ecclesiastically motivated partisanship, we need to be aware, that while for the Enlightenment, in
MacIntyre's words:

> Rational justification was to appeal to principles undeniable for any
> rational person and therefore independent of all those social and cultural
> particularities which the Enlightenment thinkers took to be the mere accidental clothing of reason in particular times and places, . . . [yet] both the
> thinkers of the Enlightenment and their successors proved unable to agree
> as to what precisely those principles were which would be found undeniable by all rational persons.⁵³

When we look for accounts of meta-logical rationality and turn to,
for instance, the French Encyclopedists of the eighteenth century or
the Scottish empiricist David Hume in the same period, or slightly
later, the founder of German Idealism, Immanuel Kant, or in England
Jeremy Bentham, the father of Utilitarianism, we soon discover that
their versions of meta-logical rationality differ markedly. Rationalities
are, in MacIntyre's phrase, "tradition-specific." The historian of
thought should acknowledge "the diversity of traditions of inquiry,
each with its own specific mode of rational justification."

Yet, as MacIntyre wisely adds, the philosopher, so as to do
justice to the claims of reason, even modestly defined as with the help
of the Oxford Dictionary, must avoid any assumption that "the differences between rival and [seemingly] incompatible traditions [of rationality] cannot [themselves] be rationally resolved."⁵⁴ In other words:

---

52. W. Hodges, *Logic* (Harmondsworth, 1977), p. 164.
53. A. MacIntyre, *Whose Justice? Which Rationality?*, op. cit., p. 6.
54. Ibid., pp. 9–10.

de facto these philosophical schools may be operating with a variety of meta-logical principles of reason, but we cannot and should not accept that, *de jure,* reason is just up for grabs. If humanity is on a shared search for truth—and this is an assumption of morality, civilization, and the University, it cannot simply be a case of "You pays your money and you takes your choice."

Provisionally, however, there is no alternative to accepting the analogical character of rationality. "Reason" covers a variety of strategies for thought, though all have it in common that they respect logical form and deploy arguments from or to principles. Over and above that minimal definition, what "reason" signifies in fuller terms must be established contextually. A given author's understanding of rationality will emerge from the tasks they set reason, the roles they expect reason to perform, and the resources they allow it. The family resemblance between rationalities—itself a consequence of the minimum "core" definition taken together with the comparability of such tasks, roles and resources—justifies the use of the term "reason" *tout court.*

Ultimately, though, some more architectonic account is needed. In the perspective of philosophy, that would necessarily take the form of some (future) adjudication of epistemic foundations. Fortunately for the present writer, in the perspective of *theology,* it is possible to suggest a conceptual architecture to house reason the lines of which are simple yet which does the job. That topic can be briefly broached now, but a firm proposal must await the Conclusion to this study.

Faith and Reason in Catholic Thought

In Western Catholic theology where major reference points are Augustine, Thomas and the other high medieval thinkers whose work underlies the Council of Trent, the realm of natural understanding based on reason is not seen as a separate, self-enclosed sphere but as a component—albeit a massive one—within a more comprehensive whole. In its activity, divine grace constitutes a higher principle which overarches natural created reality. In giving access to this higher principle, faith englobes reason without truncating it. Divine grace in its essential supernaturality is not counterposed to the natural experiencing, reasoning and knowing subject as though it were antithetical to that subject in the latter's native modes of moving around the world. Rather, just as nature is ordered to grace, so the life of the mind with its created faculties is in its totality ordered beyond itself with a view to an *expansion of its range,* not a diminution of it. Thus reason and faith are for Catholicism conjoined in a relational unity. The difficulty about faith for post-Renaissance people is that they do not approach their rational and free "I" as naturally ordered beyond itself. Not surprisingly, then, Christian faith, originating in the divine action of revelation, loses for them its proper intelligibility.[55] In an era of intellectual disorientation such as our own (the distinguishing "pathologies" of our time are fundamentalism and relativistic secularism), it is of high importance not only to allow reason to illuminate faith but to let faith steady reason likewise. And in any case, if such mutual help is available, that can only be because human reason has what Scholastics call an "obediential potency" in regard to faith. Of its own intrinsic character, reason enjoys, if not an active *nisus* towards faith, then at any rate a passive capacity to be drawn into faith's *modus operandi*. The only possible explanation for this lies in the being and mind of God from whom all truth, natural and supernatural, derives. Accordingly, my principal epistemological commitment is to the thesis that human rationality shares (in a finite, and therefore incomplete mode) in the reason of God.

    Thus the question, "Is there a universal rationality?"—"defined," as the twentieth-century American philosopher Hilary Putnam, phrases things, "by a set of unchanging 'canons' or 'principles'"[56]—admits only of a differentiated reply. Where divine reason is *bracketed out*, as by the eighteenth-century Enlightenment, the concept of universal rationality, a potential universality of reason only partially actualized in the multiplicity of rationalities, becomes, *pace* MacIntyre, practically unattainable—even in theory! Our concepts of reason *do* develop, shift their emphases, and so become various. In examples drawn from the present book: metaphysical reason, which operates with such principles as causality and "sufficient reason," is not the

---

55. K. Eschweiler, *Die zwei Wege der neueren Theologie,* op. cit., pp. 39–40.
56. H. Putnam, *Reason, Truth and History* (Cambridge, 1981), p. x.

same as the existential reason which lays out the "logic" of action as it unfolds in a human life-project, nor is either of these identical with the aesthetic reason which considers the pattern of epiphanies in the experience of beauty. But where divine reason is *included in,* as with the Catholic intellectual tradition taken by and large, then the variety of modes in which rationality can function is unified—rendered fully universal—in the reason of God himself. Those modes do not, then, approach unity only asymptotically, such that they are destined never to reach it. To the contrary: they are forms of imperfect universality, which have their perfect archetype elsewhere—yet this "elsewhere" is also "here" in that it guarantees their prospective unity in advance and renders what I call above an "architectonic" account of rationality something feasible. A plenary human rationality in act is, one might suggest, the reason of Adam before the Fall: a pure participation (not, of course, an absolute coincidence, impossible to a creature) in the reason of God. There is a covert indication of this in a contemporary philosopher who is far from holding a theological view of these issues when Hilary Putnam writes:

> The very fact that we speak of our different conceptions as different conceptions of *rationality* posits a *Grenzbegriff,* a limit-concept of the ideal truth.[57]

Meanwhile, on a range of issues in ethics, metaphysics, aesthetics, when we are discussing, respectively, the good, the true and the beautiful, Catholic Christians can share intellectually with others (of almost, if not quite, every philosophical persuasion[58]), both by debating within the presuppositions of different rationalities, and by appropriate disputing of the adequacy of those very presuppositions themselves.[59]

As indicated, I shall return to this issue in the Conclusion, assisted, I hope, by the materials surveyed in between. In that "in

---

57. Ibid, p. 216.

58. Even the concept of rationality subjacent to logical positivism can find a possible rapport with the rationale of faith through the notion of the eschatological verification of Christian truth-claims. But I exclude as a hopeless case Postmodernism of the anarchist variety: compare the remarks on the relative "merits" of Kantian and Nietzschean hegemony in the Conclusion to this book.

59. Those in the logic-dominated mainstream of Anglo-American philosophy might prefer the word "premises" here to my somewhat Collingwoodian term "presuppositions." There is clearly a difference between these. Premises have to be stated; presuppositions may remain tacit. Yet the general idea remains the same.

between," the lion's share of this book, we shall be looking at a variety of Catholic thinkers of the nineteenth and twentieth centuries who, in my opinion, still have something worth hearing to say on these issues—as well as the critiques to which these thinkers were sometimes subject, in the name of the wider corporate Church.

Chapter 2

A Kantian Beginning: Georg Hermes

I now call to the witness box the first of the thinkers to be surveyed: Georg Hermes, who figures in most Catholic accounts of the vagaries of the faith-reason relationship, and whom I present here under the rubric "A Kantian Beginning."

WHY HERMES?

This thinker is a good place to begin not least because of his crucial chronological position. As a (sort of) Kantian, Hermes represents a key theological response to the first modernity, that is: to the eighteenth-century Enlightenment.

The ruling principle of Enlightenment modernity is that the human being, whether as individual person or as species, is an end in itself, and the only court of appeal for the evaluation of reality.[1] That was Kant's own answer to his own question, *Was ist Aufklärung?*: "What is Enlightenment?" In a word, enlightenment means anthropocentrism. It is "man's release from his self-caused immaturity, primarily *in matters of religion,*" a liberation which will come about through using intelligence autonomously, that is, without dependence on any putatively higher guidance.[2] What is nonetheless religiously interesting in Kant's position is that he sought to find an opening in this monis-

---

1. This generalization naturally requires nuancing for a host of different writers in a variety of situations: see J. Schmidt, "What is Enlightenment? A Question, its Context, and Some Consequences," in idem. (ed.), *What is Enlightenment? Eighteenth Century Answers and Twentieth Century Questions* (Berkeley, CA, 1996), pp. 1–44.

2. I. Kant, "What is Enlightenment?," in C. J. Friedrich (ed.), *Immanuel Kant's Moral and Political Writings* (New York, 1949), pp. 138–139. The emphasis is original.

tically anthropic world-view for an approach to God—an approach which works by way of practical reason, not theoretical reason. (In the previous chapter, reference was made to the Protean character of the concept of reason: the sense to be given those terms in a Kantian context will emerge in the course of expounding the philosophical claims in which they find concrete embodiment.) It is an approach which can find a place for religion within the limits of reason, so long as we treat the divine as a postulate we need for the successful functioning of freedom in the moral life.[3]

Over against both rationalism—which explicates reality by reference to principles that prescind from immediate experience,[4] and empiricism—the mandatory and exclusive appeal to such experience, Kant's philosophy struck out on a new path. Its aim was to establish the conditions of possibility of objective knowledge. In Kant's hands, that turned out to mean: theoretical reason must accept the limiting of possible experience to the realm of the sheer appearance of things, eliminating thereby any recognition of metaphysics as *Wissenschaft*, genuine, well-founded knowledge. In Kant's practical philosophy, on the other hand, not only does he claim to re-found ethics, the grounding of morals, which for him is a series of postulates on the part of practical reason. He also regards such practical reason as re-opening a way to metaphysics—in affirmations of the existence of God, the freedom of the will and personal immortality. By this means we are able to reach the supra-phenomenal level, not, however, through knowledge but through a morally necessary act of philosophical faith.

As the later history of classical German philosophy would show, to start with man, focused on the nature and limits of subjectivity, spirit, selfhood, did not mean necessarily to end there.

---

3. Kant's writings on a "religion within the limits of reason alone" are gathered together in English translation in A. Wood and G. DiGiovanni (ed.), *Immanuel Kant, Religion and Rational Theology* (Cambridge, 1996).

4. A further defining characteristic of rationalism, even when, as with Leibniz and Wolff, the work of believing Christians, is its strict prescinding—when philosophically at work—from principles drawn out of revelation. But this hardly contrasts it with empiricism, so here can be left to one side.

Hermes against His Background

The background is *institutionally* the beginning of a new phase in Catholic intellectual life in the German-speaking lands after the demise of the pre-Revolutionary *Germania sacra*.[5] The lifetime of Georg Hermes,[6] a farmer's son, born in Westphalia in 1775, dying in 1831, coincided with the greatest shock German Catholicism had known since the time of Luther—namely, the massive disruption of church life which followed the decision in 1803 of the various civil authorities in the old *Reich*, under pressure from the militarily triumphant French, to secularize *Germania sacra*. "Sacred Germany," consisting of twenty-three prince-bishoprics and forty-four prince abbacies, had hitherto been responsible, not only for administration and the enforcement of law but also for educational, philanthropic and cultural activities generally, over some ten thousand square kilometers of territory with about three million inhabitants.[7] Whereas the intellectual life of Protestant Germany was concentrated in a small number of major universities, such as Halle and Jena, the intellectual life of Catholic Germany was diffused among a huge number of sites: notably the courts of the ecclesiastical princes, the monasteries and the *Stiften* or collegiate churches. The suppression of the Society of Jesus in 1773 was already a set back for tertiary education, at any rate in the south, where older university foundations had been entrusted to the Jesuits since the Counter-Reformation, but ways and means could be found—for example, by an enterprising prince-bishop at Dillingen—to carry on. In comparison, the secularization attendant on the ending of the German *ancien régime* was more a body blow than a pinprick. Of the eighteen pre-Revolutionary Catholic universities only four survived, and these had to accept a change of status whereby Protestantism received parity of status with Catholicism.[8] The secularization of these entities created an institutional vacuum, and the

---

5. For a short overview of nineteenth-century German church history, see A. Dru, *The Church in the Nineteenth Century: Germany 1800–1918* (London, 1963).

6. The main source of information for Hermes' life is W. Esser, *Denkschrift auf Georg Hermes* (Cologne, 1832).

7. K. Schatz, *Zwischen Säkularisation und Zweitem Vatikanum. Der Weg des deutschen Katholizismus im 19. und 20. Jahrhundert* (Frankfurt, 1986), p. 15.

8. The four were Würzburg, Landshut (later transferred to Munich), Freiburg and Breslau: see ibid., p. 26.

need for a new beginning for theological life. (Hermes, for instance, was little exposed to patristic or even medieval theology and seems to have been, to a considerable degree, an auto-didact.[9])

Such a new beginning was not eased by the reserved attitude towards the Catholic Church on the part of elites in the German states in the post-Revolutionary, post-Napoleonic, period. This was true even of those states which were nominally Catholic though the reorganization in 1803, confirmed at the 1815 Vienna Congress, had in fact transferred hundreds of thousands of Catholics for the first time to the tender mercies of historically anti-Catholic sovereignties, notably Prussia. In fact only three Catholic states remained: Bavaria, Austria and the tiny principality of Hohenzollern-Sigmaringen; they had thirty-six Protestant counterparts.

The background is marked *intellectually* by the decline of the influence of the "empirical rationalism" of Gottfried Wilhelm von Leibniz and Johann Christian Wolff—figures on the cusp of inherited Christian Scholasticism and Enlightenment novelties, and the rise of alternative philosophies more purely *aufklärisch* in inspiration. Hermes, already in his late twenties when the "holy Roman empire of the German nation" was brought to its end, represents the often positive reception which the German Enlightenment, less deistic than its British counterpart, and certainly less anti-clerical than its French, enjoyed in much of *Germania sacra*.[10] While a great deal of work remains to be done in excavating the theologies left behind by German Catholicism in the eighteenth century,[11] the theology, both philosophical and dogmatic, of the opening years of the nineteenth century is somewhat better known. That is owing to the interest aroused in

---

9. D. J. Dietrich, *The Goethezeit and the Metamorphosis of Catholic Theology in the Age of Idealism* (Berne, 1979), p. 46.

10. H. Maier, "Die Katholiken und die Aufklärung," in *Aufklärung im katholischen Deutschland* (Hamburg, 1993), pp. 40–53. That is not to say that all Enlightenment figures proved equally acceptable to a Catholic audience. Hermes had studied the rationalizing but apologetically robust theology, strongly Wolff-influenced, of the Jesuit Benedikt Stattler (1728–1797). Had he appreciated positively Stattler's three-volume study *Anti-Kant* (Munich, 1788), the title of which speaks for itself, his intellectual (and posthumous) history would have been very different.

11. Some light is thrown by K. Eschweiler, "Die Philosophie der spänischen Spätscholastik auf den deutschen Universitäten des XVIII Jahrhunderts," in *Gesämmelte Aufsätze zur Kulturgeschichte Spaniens* 1 (1928), pp. 251–325, which stresses the continuing, if declining, role of the Baroque Scholasticism of Francisco Suárez and his co-nationals. For a wider casting of the net, see R. Haass, *Die geistige Haltung der katholischen Universitäten Deutschlands im 18. Jahrhundert. Ein Beitrag zur Geschichte der Aufklärung* (Freiburg, 1952).

historians by its pivotal status, as the German lands moved into the post-Revolutionary era, with the first stirrings of Romanticism and the nineteenth-century Catholic revival. Where Hermes differed from his contemporaries was in the more radical (but not by any means fully comprehensive) character of his adhesion to the thought of Kant.

At the same time, there is also a significant *political* background. Hermes' cause became embroiled with a specifically nineteenth-century issue. How could the civil power in Prussia overcome the moral resistance of its newly acquired Catholic population to full integration in a civic order at once Protestant and authoritarian in type?[12] With the later nineteenth-century mobilization of the Catholic laity, not least through Ultramontanism with its emphasis on a Catholic press, Catholic trade unions and even Catholic political parties, this became much more difficult. It was easier in the early decades of that century, whose watchword in the German-speaking lands was *Staatskirchentum*: "state-churchness."

Hermes and the Place of Kant

Basic to any attempt to introduce Hermesianism must be an account of how Hermes accepted what we can call Kant's "fundamental project." Kant, the tenor of whose interventions has already been sketched in preliminary fashion above, was without question, at the end of the *ancien régime,* the great philosophical doctor of Brandenburg-Prussia. Specifically, Hermes, a priest professor in the academies of the northern Rhineland, hitherto a series of prince-bishoprics but now under Prussian rule, responded warmly to Kant's project of "going beyond knowledge," *as Wis en aufheben,* "in order to make room for faith," *um zum Glauben Platz zu bekommen*[13] — to make room for faith, namely, by re-locating faith in the context of the life of practical reason whose postulates, according to Kant's critique of the same, included the existence of God and the immortality of the soul as well as the freedom of the human will.

---

12. On the background of the Prussian State's relations with Catholicism, still useful is G. Goyau, *L'Allemagne religieuse. Le Catholicisme [1800–1848]* (Paris, 1905; 1923, 6th edition), I., pp. 93–97, 143–150.

13. I. Kant, *Kritik der reinen Vernunft* (2nd edition, 1787), B xxx.

As a newly ordained priest teaching at a Gymnasium in Münster, Hermes had been introduced to the critical method of Kant (and its prolongation in the thought of Fichte, the founder of "subjective idealism") by his friend Ferdinand Überwasser (1752–1812), lecturer in philosophy at the Münster Akademie where Hermes would join the staff as lecturer in dogmatics in 1807. With Hermes' promotion in 1820 from this rather provincial academy (later, however, made a university) to the University of Bonn, he found a platform from which he could reach a wider audience.[14] This prestigious University had been created in 1786 at the height of rationalist fervor and (for a time) revolutionary expectations. Owing to its 1818–1819 re-foundation, with both Protestant and Catholic theological faculties, by the Kingdom of Prussia, Hermes would be not only a priest-academic but a civil servant.

In point of fact, by the time Hermes reached the acme of his professional career, theological interest, even among Protestants, was seeping away from Kant, by whom it had been only moderately enthused. It was shifting instead toward the post-Kantians Fichte, Schelling and Hegel who were deemed more obvious dialogue-partners owing to their attempts to integrate religion (or at least ethics) with thinking rather more organically than had Kant himself.[15] However, the continuing importance of Kant's thought, which in Neo-Kantianism enjoyed a massive revival in the later nineteenth century and has never since lost its place in the sun, even in Anglo-American philosophy, suggests that Hermes had taste, albeit of a metaphysically austere kind.

Hermes' Own Project

Hermes' starting point—manifest in both his early treatise, the 1807 *Untersuchung über die innere Wahrheit des Christentums,* and his masterwork, the 1819 *Philosophical Introduction to Catholic Theology*[16]—was

---

14. K. Eschweiler, *Die zwei Wege der neueren Theologie* op. cit., p. 22. In Eschweiler's judgment, such was the influence of (Protestant and Catholic) anti-rationalist thinkers—notably Johann Georg Hamann, Friedrich Jacobi, Johann Michael Sailer—in *Münsterland* that without the Prussian government's appointment of Hermes to Bonn his work might have been still-born, ibid., pp. 21–22.

15. T. Fliethmann, *Vernünftig glauben. Die Theorie der Theologie bei Georg Hermes* (Würzburg, 1997), p. 25.

16. G. Hermes, *Einleitung in die christkatholische Theologie, Erster Teil: Philosophische Einleitung* (Münster, 1819). This work was republished at Frankfurt in 1967 in photographic reproduction.

criticism of the state of the late Baroque intellectual culture in Western Catholicism at the end of the *ancien régime*. Hermes distinguished between the content of the received theology and its form. The latter—the form—was in his estimation woefully lacking. The methodology proper to theology had become unclear.[17] Theology—formally or methodically speaking—had fallen behind the standards of scientific self-scrutiny represented by the European Enlightenment, above all in its especially rigorous Kantian version. This was true not least of theology's philosophical underpinnings. As one twentieth-century writer put it. "A hazy philosophical syncretism is the signature of the apologetic work of Catholicism in the eighteenth century."[18]

Hermes was concerned, then, not with the content of theology but with the manner of the representation and grounding of that content. For him, theological content issues from divine revelation, in precisely the way classical dogmatics indicates, and as such cannot be adapted to the measure of the *Zeitgeist* which, on the contrary, is invited to be adapted to it. What can and should be adapted, however, is the fundamental manner in which the truth claims of Christianity are asserted. The systems of thought in which theology allows itself to be embodied are not supra-temporal. Rather, they derive from an indefinitely variable task of representing the truth theology harbors in a plausible or arguable way, given the state of scientific discourse in some particular time. For Hermes, ever conscious of Enlightenment critics, the specific forms that intellectual doubt take in any given period vis-à-vis revealed religion are what should compel theology to develop an appropriate systematic guise. Hence, the so-called method of "positive doubt" to which such theologians of the Roman school as Giovanni Perrone objected; the First Vatican Council would later go

---

17. In the contemporary German Protestant context, this appears to have been the view of F.D.E. Schleiermacher likewise. "In his day, not unlike our own, theology as an intellectual discipline was poorly defined, its tasks and methods anything but self-evident": thus R. Crouter, *Friedrich Schleiermacher. Between Enlightenment and Romanticism* (Cambridge, 2005), p. 208. Pedagogic disarray stemmed in part from uncertainty as to how best to inter-relate, in the modern period, the various university faculties (including philosophy, law, theology, arts). The most notable contributor to this debate was Kant, but Schelling, Fichte, and Schleiermacher were notable participants. See C. E. McClelland, *State, Society and University in Germany, 1700–1914* (Cambridge, 1980).

18. K. Eschweiler, *Die zwei Wege der neueren Theologie*, op. cit., p. 75.

out of its way to declare unwarranted the deliberate adoption of doubt about the faith on whatever grounds.[19] *Bene dubitare* might be Thomas Aquinas's advice to philosophical searchers;[20] but would he have said the same about students of *sacra doctrina?* What, however, for Hermes cannot be doubted is a supernaturally practical faith, since this can be justified before the bar of reason and thus is genuine *Wissen,* well-founded knowing. In the foreword to his "philosophical introduction," Hermes explains how he came to adopt the method of doubt and analysis.[21] But this is not the stuff of mere autobiography. He generalizes and prescribes. Any contemporary teacher of religion should know that he does not know in order to seek with zeal the knowledge he lacks; he must wander through all the paths of the labyrinth of doubt so as to be able to accompany the doubter on all his ways.[22]

On the supposition that Kantianism had identified the peculiar difficulties modernity finds in the idea of a historic revelation, then, Hermes crafted his system in answer to the Kantian, or Kantian-style, questioning of theology.[23] Evidently, Hermes would have had no time for the concept of "Christian philosophy" which later in this study will come prominently into view.

The Distinction between "Philosophical" and "Positive" Theology in Hermes' Work

Hermes asserts that the method of grounding theology can only be (a revelation-independent) philosophy, since philosophy, whose general medium of argumentation is reason, is the *Grundwissenschaft*—the essential epistemic foundation—of every positive science of whatever kind. "All knowledge which has opened the way for man on the basis

---

19. H. W. Schwedt, "Georg Hermes," art. cit., p. 232. Hermes appears to have used the term in a Fichtean sense according to which lack of a sufficient grounding of some proposition renders impossible a firm decision in its favor. Theoretical reason is not moved to a determination—but practical reason may be.

20. Thomas, *Sententia super Metaphysicam [Aristotelis]*, Liber III, I. 1.

21. G. Hermes, *Einleitung in die christkatholische Theologie, Erster Teil: Philosophische Einleitung*, op. cit., pp. v–ix.

22. Ibid., p. xv.

23. Ibid., pp. 74–80.

of his nature alone is philosophical."[24] Dogmatics, then, can have no axiomatic founding propositions of its own, no native *Grundsätze* from which its discipline can proceed in deductive fashion. It may, however, have principles for the organizing of its own contents—principles which enable it to clarify its materials internally, for the benefit of studious believers, though not to defend them externally, to those who are operating by reason alone. These internal principles of scientific theology, the *Erkenntnisprinzipien* as Hermes calls them, are master in their own house. They are not beholden to philosophical reason, but they must be appropriately related to it. The theologian must explore the "inner relation of the *Erkenntnisprinzipien* of Christian and Catholic theology to the overall capacity of man for truth."[25] Where this connection is left unmade, faith remains unwarranted. Hermes recognizes, of course, that many people lack the mental or educational capacity for immersion in philosophy. The "unlettered believer" relies on the "devout pastor," his parish priest. But in so relying, the simple faithful (so Hermes argues) assume precisely that their pastors have tested rationally the claims of revelation and found them convincing.[26] "Proofs and defenses" are what the theology of revelation is all about: how else did Thomas or Scotus treat of it, or, for that matter, Augustine, Basil, and Gregory Nazianzen among the Fathers, Justin and Clement of Alexandria among the earliest Christian writers?[27]

Not surprisingly, given these convictions, Hermes' *Einleitung in die christkatholische Theologie* falls conveniently into two parts. The "Philosophical Introduction," which comes first both in literary design and date of composition, has already been mentioned and will engage the lion's share of our attention hereafter. The "Positive Introduction" to theology, the *Positive Einleitung*, follows, again in both senses: literary and chronological. Dating from 1829, it is a treatise on the principles of Catholic dogmatics, principles taken to constitute inner-theological rationality. Quite simply, those principles for Hermes are: the biblical Canon, oral Tradition, and the ecclesiastical magisterium. They control the presentation of a content which Hermes articulates as a diptych: "theoretical positive theology," which treats

---

24. Ibid., p. xx.
25. Ibid., p. 3.
26. Ibid., p. xxi.
27. Ibid., p. xxii.

three doctrinal themes—God, the relation of the world to God and the relation of man to God and constitutes dogmatics, and "practical positive theology," which treats two themes—duties toward God and duties toward human beings and constitutes the moral theological sequel to dogmatics. The content of Hermes' doctrinal theology, organized along these lines, is not greatly different from that of the standard theological works in use in his day. Though his doctrine of grace is somewhat minimalizing, Hermes has no general plan to reduce positive theology to the modest proportions—in a later Neo-Kantian generation, Rudolf Bultmann will call these *demythologized* proportions—of a "religion of reason" in the Kantian sense. Furthermore, though ethics is Hermes' key to the warranting of revelation, his presentation of the content of that revelation is far from merely ethical in character. At his hands, dogma is not ethicized in the manner of Bultmann's fellow-Lutheran Albrecht Ritschl, or Ritschl's successors Hermann Schulz and Adolf von Harnack. Only in a very limited sense, then, can Hermesianism be regarded as an instance of what German Protestant historians of ideas call *Vermittlungstheologie*: the chronologically first and intellectually prime example of which is the thought of F. D. E. Schleiermacher, who sought to mediate between (*vermitteln*) the Pietistic Christianity of his forebears and the enlightened Romanticism of his contemporaries.[28]

However, a form can be noted of what we might term "doxological reductionism." Hermes treats man and human happiness as the aim of creation. The First Vatican Council would declare that aim to be, rather, the glory of God.[29]

Still, the primary difference Hermesianism makes comes not so much with the *Positive Einleitung* as with the companion

---

28. A comparison of Hermes' two part *Einleitung* with Schleiermacher's proposal for re-structuring theological life in *Brief Outline on the Study of Theology* (English translation, Richmond, VA, 1966) would show great differences, and similarities, too. "Far from seeking to demonstrate the truth of Christian teaching [contrast Hermes], philosophical theology" for Schleiermacher might be paraphrased as "philosophical reflection on the form and content of a religion in its givenness," R. Crouter, *Friedrich Schleiermacher*, op. cit., p. 212. On the other hand, Schleiermacher's opposition to any mixing of philosophy and dogmatics, itself a form of historical theology—see, for instance, the introductions to both the first (1821–1822) and, especially, the last (1830–1831) edition of "The Christian Faith"—parallels Hermes' division, more than distinction, of philosophical and positive theology.

29. For a summary of the Council's teaching in regard to the three figures who occupy chapters 2, 3 and 4 of this book, see the last section of chapter 5.

"philosophical introduction" to theology, the *Philosophische Einleitung*. This is where we find Hermes explaining how faith is systematically grounded in relation to reason. Since Kant's religion of reason is unacceptable—it could only lead to the wholesale mutilation of dogmatic thought—another philosophical foundation must be laid, but this can only be, given Kant's mirroring of the *Zeitgeist*, by pressing Kantian criticism in some rather different direction from Kant himself. What this amounts to, as we shall see, is a somewhat cavalier treatment of Kantian positions. Yet what remains intact is the typically Kantian primacy accorded to practical rather than theoretical reason in the religious domain. Hermes remarks with pride:

> I have philosophized, not in terms of any of the celebrated philosophical systems which have done Germany honor one after another over the last thirty years, but in my own manner, and I have had—almost exclusively—recourse to those systems only when I had to dispute for the defense of my own [philosophy] and the foundations for theology for which it furnishes proof.[30]

Specifically, he has, on this limited basis, made appeal to the philosophies "I treasure most," namely, those of Kant and Fichte, though he admits in a footnote he has not made use of Fichte's principal works, but only the minor essays—unspecified—which Fichte wrote for the "general public."[31] That will be Fichte on moral experience as man's share in the supreme reality, the ultimate "I"—a unique free activity that seeks to realize itself in perfect self-awareness.

Granted the structure and content of Hermes' bipartite "introduction" to theology, he might well be in mind when a modern historian of early nineteenth-century Catholic thought reports:

> Catholic theologians realized that philosophical principles could not be used to derive positive Christianity with its emphasis on the reconciliation of man with God, but that philosophy could help with analyzing the signs of revelation in order to ensure that these could support belief.

---

30. G. Hermes, *Einleitung in die christkatholische Theologie. Erster Teil: Philosophische Einleitung*, op. cit., p. ix.

31. Ibid. That probably refers to, in particular, "The Vocation of Man" (1800); "On the Nature of the Scholar" (1804), and "Addresses to the German Nation" (1808), the latter of which called for a new form of German education to regenerate the intellectual world.

Philosophical analysis was to illuminate the terrain on which the penetration of human by divine freedom could happen.[32]

How, then, did Hermes deal with that crucial question of post-Cartesian thought, "What can I know?"

HERMES' THEORY OF KNOWLEDGE

Were Hermes more consistently Kantian, he would, we might suppose, recognize the fundamental heterogeneity of mind and things, and like the supporters of "transcendental philosophy" in the Kantianized Scholasticism of the twentieth century, declare it to be unclear what the "correspondence" of mind with extra-mental reality might mean. But, like the classical Scholastics, he holds that truth is indeed correspondence, such that mind must be able in principle to be "adequated" with extra-mental reality: brought into full agreement, *Übereinstimmung*, with it.[33] We *should* be able to affirm the unconditional objectivity of all that we know. Unfortunately, for claims to such "adequation" to be confirmed, the knowing subject, for Hermes, has to be conscious of certainty in the matter, and for him an internal criterion of such certainty is necessity. I can only be really certain of something if I see that it has to be so, and can only be so. Yet what kind of necessity can be ascribed to perceptual experience save a merely subjective necessity of supposing things to be as they appear?[34] Moreover, without the application of such concepts as being, substance, and the properties of substance, no perceived object could be understood. But all such conceptually thoughtful reworking of perception still remains in the realm of subjectivity, on the near side of the cleft between mind and the reality of things. Whether in fact "something" we claim to be known *is* appropriately conceptualized by us: precisely that is the question. In leaving us hanging in this respect, Kantianism, or rather Kant's critique of pure reason, is really no more than a representation

---

32. D. J. Dietrich, *The Goethezeit and the Metamorphosis of Catholic Theology in the Age of Idealism*, op. cit., p. 9.

33. G. Hermes, *Einleitung in die christkatholische Theologie. Erster Teil: Philosophische Einleitung*, op. cit., p. 84. "I take truth to be the harmonious correspondence of knowledge with what is known."

34. Ibid., p. 191.

of cognitive consciousness, and thus furnishes nothing beyond an account of the would-be knowing self to which an inner and an outer world *appears*.

Hermes' Use of Constructive Reason

On this, it might be thought attenuated—since recognizably Kantian—basis, Hermes proposes that constructive reason can nonetheless build up, if minimally, a rational picture of the "I," the world, and of God. How does that work?[35] Well, awareness of an inner world, however elusive its status, gives us the concept of the "I" as a bearer of inner conditions, the character of which fluctuates in time, thus showing, to Hermes' satisfaction at least, that such internal changes in us are modifications of a substance, namely, the human self.[36] So far as the *outer* world is concerned, the ground of sensuous perceived objects can only be an—admittedly unknown—"substantivity": my attempt to render Hermes' deliberately vague term *Wesenhaftigkeit*.[37] Finally, on God: the ultimate ground of change in the conditions of the inner and outer world cannot be things even in their substantivity: for then things would have to be as they are forever, in which case there would be no change at the level of phenomena. The series of finite causes must be, then, upheld by a primordial cause which is not a member of this series. Such an *Urursache* must be completely grounded in itself without contingent properties of any kind.[38] In other words, for Hermes a phenomenally changing world makes God necessary to reason. From the order and purposiveness of the functioning of the causal series in dependence on this primordial cause Hermes further deduces the main divine attributes which he identifies as: power, knowledge and goodness.[39] If we ask what is the end-goal of the entire functioning order, Hermes proposes optimistically that it is the happiness of

---

35. For his explanation of his constructive method, see ibid., pp. 269–277.
36. Ibid., pp. 279–319.
37. Ibid., pp. 320–340.
38. Ibid., pp. 340–413.
39. Ibid., pp. 451–469. As Herman Schwedt comments, "the proposition about a ground here becomes the central principle of truth, and not just a mere form of thought, as with Kant," "Georg Hermes (1175–1831), seine Schule und seine wichtigsten Gegner," in E. Coreth et al., (ed.), *Christliche Philosophie im katholischen Denken des 19. und 20. Jahrhundert. 1. Neue Ansätze im 19. Jahrhundert* (Graz, 1987), p. 229. Cited below as "Georg Hermes."

man, a happiness to arise from awareness of man's freely achieved ethical excellence. The ethical blessedness of man, as lord of the world, is the unique sublime goal of the visible creation.

For a thinker who holds that perceptual knowledge is only of phenomena, this must be accounted an ingenious extraction of a quart from a pint pot. Though Hermes sought valiantly to appropriate the Kantian critiques, Kant himself would surely have regarded his thought as a relapse into metaphysics, even if, from a Scholastic standpoint, metaphysics of a half-hearted sort. We cannot but think of phenomena as causally grounded: reason unavoidably projects thinking along this trajectory. That is, as Hermes puts it, *unsere Wirklichkeit*, reality so far as we are concerned.[40] We have already noted that Hermes does not present himself as an *interpreter* of Kant. Rather, he claims to philosophize "in his own manner," even though, as he confesses, Kant (along with Fichte) is the philosophical writer he prizes most.

Not that there is a complete absence of shared outlook in fundamental ontology. In the second edition of the *Critique of Pure Reason* Kant added a "refutation of idealism"—which may seem odd, granted that "transcendental idealism" was his name for his own philosophy. But Kant had in mind the "empirical idealism" of George Berkeley, the view that "empirical" objects are "nothing but perceptions: the world of science has no reality beyond the experience of the observer."[41] Kant's writing wavers between subjectivism, which focuses on the perceiver's point of view, and objectivism, which insists that any point of view is always in and on a *given* world. His re-writing of the first *Critique* emphasizes the objective. As the historian of modern German philosophy Paul Gorner has pointed out, the "refutation of idealism" proposes an argument to the effect that awareness of the temporal succession of mental states presupposes direct awareness of something external . . . and yet Kant explicitly denies that this amounts to a

---

40. G. Hermes, *Einleitung in die christkatholische Theologie. Erster Teil: Philosophische Einleitung*, op. cit., p. 191. A "physically" inescapable "having to hold as real," a *Für-wirklich-halten-Müssen* which is what Hermes means by his phrase *Für-wahr-Halten*, trumps, in the context of pure reason, any voluntary "accepting as true," *Für-wahr [An]nehmen*. The objection of Neo-Scholastics like Joseph Kleutgen (see chapter 6 below) was that such a formulation, involving a distinction in psychology rather than metaphysics, showed Hermes had no more achieved the hoped-for transition from appearance to being than had Kant.

41. R. Scruton, *Kant* (Oxford, 1982), p. 44.

causal proof of an external world.⁴² Causal laws hold only of the "world of appearances." *A fortiori,* they hold exclusively of events in time. Kant would have scolded Hermes for following a logic of illusion. When metaphysical thinking pursues the nature of the soul, or the world as a totality, or God as perfect being, it "transgresses the limits of experience," dealing with concepts to which no "intuitions" (that is, items in sensuous experience) correspond. For Kant this cannot generate knowledge. It leads "not towards truth, but towards fallacy."⁴³ In Kant's distinctive vocabulary, the understanding is "nothing but the faculty of combining *a priori,* and of bringing the manifold of given representations [of sensuous appearance, q. v.] under the unity of apperception."⁴⁴ That is fatal for a "cataphatic" or affirmative account of the divine. For Kant:

> [W]e cannot represent God adequately because the interpretative role of the pure concepts of the understanding does not legitimately extend to the realm of the transcendent. So if we are to talk of God we cannot say anything that positively describes Him. Moreover, the theology which issues from this position must contest the statements of any theology which does make dogmatic positive assertions about God. In short, Kant's theology is a negative theology.⁴⁵

And the Australian analyst of modern philosophy Kevin Hart, here cited, goes on to comment: "If Kant develops a negative theology, it is one which answers not to the ineffability of God's *essence* but to our inability to know that God *exists.*"⁴⁶ This makes of it a different kettle of fish from the kind of negative theology which the Greek patristic tradition had learned, in the wake of the devout Jewish philosopher Philo of Alexandria. That was a negative theology which invited mystical appreciation by arousing longing for the eschatological vision of God. Unlike Kant's, it was designed to bring on, not put off. Furthermore, the negative theology of the Fathers was always accompanied, in some way or other, by an affirmative counterpart. Typically,

---

42. P. Gorner, *Heidegger's "Being and Time": An Introduction* (Cambridge, 2007), p. 50.
43. R. Scuton, *Kant,* op. cit., p. 41.
44. I. Kant, *Kritik der reinen Vernunft,* op. cit., B 134.
45. K. Hart, *The Trespass of the Sign. Deconstruction, Theology and Philosophy* (New York, 2000, 2nd edition), p. 224.
46. Ibid., p. 225.

affirmative theology works up to God as Cause of all being and its perfections, a "way of ascent" which gives us some glimpse of the divine attributes and their "names." Critics of Kant have often considered his *Diktat* that the principle of causality must stop short with "appearances" an arbitrary stipulation. Hermes was evidently among them, even if he also imported the subjectivism of the *Critique of Pure Reason* by effectively conceding that causal reasoning is—perhaps *merely*—the inevitable human point of view. Hermes' favored epistemological vocabulary, a combination of *Fürwahrhalten* ("holding as true") and *Fürwahrnehmen* ("taking as true"), had in the ears of not a few readers an uncomfortable suggestion of *als ob*—"as if."

Grounding Belief in Revelation through Practical Reason

So far everything has been in the realm of philosophical ontology, or, if one prefers, rational theology: Hermes would have called it a critical *theologia naturalis*. As yet, Hermes has said nothing to show the well-groundedness of belief in revelation as such. The way to do so for Hermes is to invoke the idea of action, specifically of an ethical kind. In cognitive judgments about truth certainty will elude us, but what of ethical judgments about how human beings should behave? Reason, declares Hermes, will never lead to error in what it must *do*: that is, in its mode of functioning as practical reason where on the basis of duty or obligation we take a moral judgment as absolutely binding. This reflects Kantianism. For Kant, moral conscience—*sittliches Gewissen*—is in itself unconditional and necessary. Purely hypothetical imperatives ("If you would be happy, fulfilled, or successful as a human being, do this or that") never attain the status of the moral as such. Only in the command *du sollst*—thou ought, come what may—does ethical reason oblige the human will in the latter's freedom to act. Such freedom is for Kant a fact given directly with the moral conscience itself. And the commands such conscience registers are sovereign and inescapable. They are, then, implicitly religious. Religion for Kant is "the knowledge of all our duties as divine commands."[47]

---

47. K. Eschweiler, *Die zwei Wege der neueren Theologie*, op. cit., p. 64.

Such an approach, so Hermes considers, is eminently suited to the truth-claims of Christian revelation. What makes him say that? Two considerations do so. Firstly, this approach is congruent with the truth-claims of revelation whose appeal to history cannot be demonstrated except through investigation of the moral consequences of the life, death, and resurrection of Christ—precisely what most occupied (according to Hermes) the minds of the New Testament writers. Positive theology, which sets forth revelation's content, presupposes the historical certainty of the facts on which it reposes: such historical certainty cannot in any case be demonstrated theoretically, even by Scholastics, but it may, as Hermes proposes to show, be found demonstrable in practice—by ascertaining, precisely, the moral consequences of the life of Christ, his death and resurrection, and the diffusion of his Spirit.[48] People's moral lives have been progressively altered, not just as individuals but as contributors to moral culture in the corporate sense, and a cause must be assigned for this. Such a cause *is* assigned when dogmatics speaks of a divine intervention in history in the economies of the Son and the Holy Spirit.

There is also a second way in which an approach to revelation based on practical reason may be deemed congruent with Christianity, and this concerns the nature of the act of faith, which, like moral action, is essentially free. The act of faith is foundational to theological epistemology. Faith is the subjective appropriation of revelation—it is what corresponds in me as a subject to revelation outside me as an object. This act of faith is said in Catholic doctrine to be not only a rational but also a *free* action, and as such belongs more naturally to practical reason, concerned as this is with ethical choice, than it does to reason of a pure or theoretical kind. Unfortunately, as we shall see in the following section, entitled "The Upshot," there was a serious flaw in Hermes' treatment of this theme.

Hermes holds that practical reason generates three anthropological postulates: first, man is intelligent in a morally pertinent way; second, he is free (these two together—intelligence and

---

48. After nearly six hundred pages dealing with the "historical or outer truth" of the New Testament revelation, Hermes seeks to show in less than ten pages that the content of the New Testament Scriptures is necessarily bound up with man's fulfillment of his moral duties: G. Hermes, *Einleitung in die christkatholische Theologie. Zweiter Teil: Positive Einleitung* (Münster, 1829), pp. 37–614; 615–623.

freedom—constitute his ethical dignity), but third, he is capable of sympathy and benevolence which make me able—in principle—to recognize the dignity of others and seek to further it.[49] To the consequent command of practical reason to defend and enhance human worth wherever found, by whatever means, are attached notes of universal validity and necessity. The formal parallel with Kant's categorical imperative to "universalize one's maxims" springs to the eye,[50] and yet it is precisely from here that Hermes proceeds to his proof of Christian revelation. (The status of the *Old* Testament revelation is secured, for Hermes, only via the authentification of the status of the *New*.)

How does his proof work? As already stated, there is a command of practical reason to forward the dignity of other persons by every possible means. The facts of moral evil make it plain that human beings do not, actually, observe the exceptionless norm which binds us to forward each other's dignity. The question then arises as to how the divine aim in the world order can be achieved under the existing conditions of human sinfulness. The rationally known attributes of God—power, knowledge, goodness—do not of themselves show us how God stands vis-à-vis sinners. What they *do* show, however, is that God as *Urursache* is perfectly capable of being the cause of a revelation, and its symptomatic signs. It is not alien to a "critical *theologia naturalis*" to suppose that God *could* offer, in the urgent circumstances that are humanity's, a revelation in and through history, a revelation attested by special signs indicative of divine action. It need not be contrary to a critical *theologia naturalis* to allow for God introducing into human consciousness, through prophecy, representations of a plan for salvaging the world, and bringing about, through miracle, sensuous changes in the phenomenal world so as to indicate that the *Urursache* is directly at work in—so Hermes would add—an "abbreviated" version of its statistically normal operation.

But it is one thing to allow that this *could* happen, and quite another to accept that it actually *has* happened in the events set forth in

---

49. G. Hermes, *Einleitung in die christkatholische Theologie. Erster Teil: Philosophische Einleitung*, op. cit., p. 221.

50. "Act as if the maxim of your action were to become through your will a universal law of nature": thus H. J. Paton, *The Moral Law, or the Categorical Imperative: A Study in Kant's Moral Philosophy* (London, 1958, 3rd edition), p. 84.

the biblical narrative. Why should we credit the claim that the origin of the Church is a miraculously attested prophetic transformation of human awareness? Hermes' answer runs: Because practical reason urges it, when it finds that what the revelation offers is invaluable assistance, of a kind available by no other means, assistance in leading the moral life in a state of reconciliation with God, receiving from him fresh resources for ethical living—living of a kind that at all points forwards the dignity of others. If we ask what such resources might be, we could do worse, in an English context, than to cite George Eliot's attempt to work her way toward a concept of God defined in relation to the moral life, what she termed: "the idea of a God . . . who will pour new life into our too languid love, and give firmness to our vacillating purpose."[51] That is, surely, one way of describing redemptive grace.

THE UPSHOT

Thus for Hermes the moral content of revelation is the source of its compellingness for reason, which can only be then, a compellingness for practical reason.[52] Hermes does not propose that revelation is reducible to its moral content (the *Positive Einleitung* shows as much, not to mention the posthumous dogmatics). But revelation's moral content is to Hermes' mind revelation's identifying mark. The flaw in Hermes' account was that while moral freedom is the *punctum insertionis* of revelation into the human condition, the human mind is not, on his view, free to withhold its assent to that revelation. Practical reason finds the truthclaims of revelation *absolutely compelling*. This is the famous *Vernunftsglaube* (the "faith of reason") to which the "faith of the heart" (*Herzensglaube*) can only follow at a second stage, by a voluntary act of self-commitment in trust and love.[53] That would not suffice the apostolic guardians, for whom both self-commitment and intellectual assent must be free, however sufficient (not coercive) the "motives of credibility" of the latter.

---

51. A. S. Byatt and N. Watten (ed.), *George Eliot. Selected Essays, Poems and Other Writings* (London, 1990), pp. 66–67, cited P. C. Hodgson, *Theology in the Fiction of George Eliot. The Mystery Beneath the Real* (London, 2001), p. 23.

52. Indeed, for Hermes, "the highest achievement of the critical philosophy is the proof that no theoretically necessary reason, either against the reality of supernatural revelation or for it, is to be found," K. Eschweiler, *Die zwei Wege der neueren Theologie*, op. cit., p. 98.

53. A. Dulles, sj, *The Assurance of Things Hoped For,* op. cit., p. 228.

Conclusion

Eighteenth-century Catholic apologists had already drawn attention to what they called the "moral necessity," after the Fall, of supernatural revelation—its necessity in practice—for an adequate grasp of ethical responsibilities: even for those responsibilities that belong to the most fundamental level of human nature, the basic decencies. But *Aufklärer*, enlightened people, took it for granted that this was a message for *hoi polloi*, the uneducated masses. For mature people, they thought, the natural light of human reason and the fact of moral freedom sufficed. No doubt Hermes by his writing and lecturing spoke to such, at least in Germany, and encouraged them to think again.

The Christianity of his followers—the Hermesians—was above all morally serious, didactically engaged. It was distanced from popular piety, sceptical of liturgical richness. Filled with a Kantian sense of duty, it could be considered the ecclesial version of the ethos of the Prussian state official. Hermes was scathing about Romantic apologias based on feeling, a Gothic Catholicism of "dark, never developed and never tested representation."[54] Its champions, borne up on waves of emotion, were unlikely, he considered, to stay the course "amid the dangers and storms of the world."[55] Cultural "agreeableness," *Annehmlichkeit*, was hardly a preoccupation of the Savior who, to the contrary, presented his Gospel as a call to attain perfection, *Vollkommenheit*, and this was an obligation laid on people that should divert them from the pleasures of this earth.[56] Some, if not all, of these features of Hermesianism might be thought to bring it closer to critics of Catholicism, and further away from the Romanticism—or "Restorationism"—which had sealed the conversions to Catholicism of most of the Church's outstanding early nineteenth-century converts. This hardly endeared it at Rome. How Hermes' account of the faith-reason relation came to be found unsatisfactory, not only by some of his theological successors but also by the teaching authority of the Catholic Church, subsequent chapters will show.

---

54. G. Hermes, *Einleitung in die christkatholische Theologie. Erster Teil: Philosophische Einleitung*, op. cit., p. xix.

55. Ibid., p. xxv.

56. Ibid., pp. 25–26.

Chapter 3

A Catholic Hegel? Anton Günther

Life and Background

The Austrian empire, as it emerged from the general European settlement of 1815, enjoyed much more continuity with the pre-Revolutionary cultural system than did the German lands to the north. In this period, "Austria" is to be defined as the multi-ethnic but German-dominated dynastic possessions of the House of Habsburg—to be distinguished, then, from the old German Reich, with its plural and indeed complex set of political authorities, over which the Habsburgs had also presided until its French-imposed end in 1803. Thanks to the survival of Austria's centralized system of bureaucratic administration, Church-State relations, and, within that, the parameters of university theology, were not much different in 1815 from what they had been in 1789. Church and theology were controlled by a civil service which was "Josephinist" in outlook. Taking its cue from the church policies of the last pre-Revolutionary emperor, Joseph II, it sought to limit the independence of the Catholic Church, both in its pastoral action and in its thought, and not least, to minimize the significance of its links with Rome.

By his own independence of mind, and his adhesion to the developing Ultramontane movement, Anton Günther constituted something of a challenge to civil and clerical bureaucracies alike.[1] His

---

1. The biographical facts given here are drawn from P. Wenzel, *Das wissenschaftliche Anliegen des Gütherianismus Ein Beitrag zur Theologiegeschichte des neunzehnten Jahrhunderts* (Essen, 1961). Günther's autobiography stops at 1828 with the publication of his first book. Wenzel was able to press beyond the limits of earlier Old Catholic biographies through having access to hundreds of Günther's letters, preserved at the abbey of St. Paul's without the Walls, Rome, where under the influence of a German monk, Dom Anselm Nickes, the abbot had hoped to create a Roman centre of Güntherianism: a project scotched by the condemnations under Pope Pius IX.

highly original philosophical-theological synthesis expressed itself as a decisive refutation of, on the one hand, Idealism and Romanticism insofar as these are non-Christian, and on the other, Catholicism's long-standing rival in the German lands, which was Protestantism. It sought to impose itself as the definitive Catholic-Christian form of thought. A blacksmith's son from northern Bohemia, Günther paid his own way through Prague University by helping with the teaching. Planning to practice law, his fundamental education was, rather, philosophical. Under the influence of Kant among others, as a student he lost his Catholic faith, compensating for the meaning deficit by exploring the writings of Fichte and Schelling—no bagatelle. As was noted in the previous chapter, by the 1830s if not earlier, philosophical interest in Germany and Austria was shifting away from Kant in favor of the post-Kantians Fichte, Schelling and Hegel, admired not least for their attempts to integrate thinking with religion more organically than had Kant.[2] Idealism sought to overcome what it considered the rationalistic unilateralism of the Enlightenment by retrieving a view of the world as a totality unified by its relation to mind or spirit. In so doing, Idealist philosophy played its part in the genesis of Romanticism, for which the sense realities given in experience function as symbols, symbols of a transcendent order appropriately registered by *das Gemüt*—usually translated "feeling," but the German term enjoys more cognitive weight. For Idealism, reality is "a totality unified by its relation to mind or spirit": such a claim is open to either theistic or pantheistic interpretation, and indeed—as shown by the accusations of atheism to which Fichte was subjected—it is susceptible of atheistic interpretation as well. Nor could any very useful adjudication between these three be expected from Romanticism which lacked the rational tools required. Painted in generous brush-strokes, such is the basic—and, evidently, problematic—context of Günther's emerging thought.

In 1810 Günther arrived in the Austrian capital in the modest role of tutor to the children of an aristocratic family. In his early years in Vienna, he came under the influence of the Romantic Catholic revival there, making the acquaintance of the future Saint Clemens

---

2. T. Fliethmann, *Vernünftig glauben*, op. cit, p. 25.

Maria Hofbauer and his circle,[3] which included the political theorist Adam Müller whose "organic" account of civil society, formed consciously in tradition-minded opposition to Enlightenment ideas of "social contract," was indebted to Romantic-Idealist thinkers—thus suggesting that Catholicism and Idealism could be combined at least at certain points.[4]

Hearkening to these voices, Günther returned to the practice of his ancestral religion. For one who has gone down in the history of the Church as a hübristic arch-speculator, it is striking to note his testimony how re-immersion in Scripture showed him that "no knowledge (*Wissen*), but an act (*Tat*) saved the world."[5] The implications of the incarnation for world history would be a central motif of his thought. After an abortive period as a Jesuit novice, he studied theology privately, and was priested in 1824, when in his late thirties. Günther conceived his priestly apostolate in severely intellectual terms. Much of his time was spent on reviewing works of literature, theology and philosophy but since this was ill-paid employment he earned a living in the censorship office of the imperial government—somewhat ironically, given the fate of his own subsequent writings.

In the German-speaking lands Günther was well thought of by many in Church and academy. Offered a canonry of the cathedral chapter of Vienna in 1847, he received honorary doctorates in theology from the University of Prague in 1849, and that of Munich in 1852. Rumblings south of the Alps, however, were heard later in the 1850s when a Neapolitan philosopher, Giambattista Savarese, thought it necessary to publish a defense of the philosophical heritage of the Church Fathers in the form of an attack on Günther's thought which

---

3. See K. Fleischmann, *Klemens Maria Hofbauer. Sein Leben und seine Zeit* (Graz, 1988). Hofbauer called Günther his "Augustinus": thus A. Bunnell, *Before Infallibility. Liberal Catholicism in Biedermeier Vienna* (London and Toronto, 1990), p. 51.

4. In such works as the 1819 *Von der Notwendigkeit einer theologischen Grundlage der gesamten Staatswissenschaften und der Staatswirtschaft insbesamt* and its 1823 successor *Die innere Staatshaushaltung: systematische dargestellt auf theologische Grundlage* Müller echoed the Romantic-Idealist critique of both the mechanistic model of society implied by enlightened Absolutism and the artificiality of liberal constitutionalism. Favoring their replacement by the idea of a *Ständestaat als Grossfamilie*, his attack on individualistic capitalism has been described as an anticipation of Marx's doctrine of alienation. Thus M. Schwering, "Romantische Theorie der Gesellschaft," in H. Schanz (ed.), *Romantik-Handbuch* (Stuttgart, 1994), pp. 508–540.

5. Cited P. Knoodt, *Anton Günther,* I (Vienna, 1881), p. 104.

he stigmatized as "logical anthropomorphism."⁶ That phrase was not completely inapt, as we shall shortly see.

The Motivation of Günther's Thought

In the ample opportunities for reading contemporary writings which his lifestyle not only permitted but required, Günther came to one principal negative conclusion, and one principal positive one. From copious scanning, his main negative conclusion was this: the chief intellectual error of the age was pantheism.⁷ According to Günther, contemporary pantheism came in many shapes and sizes, but all of them had it in common that they treated the relation between God and the world on some version of the conceptual models of the relation of universal to particular, or substance to accident, or being to appearance. For pantheism, the world is, in one of these three ways, a mini-edition of the divine. Günther's case was arguable. German Idealism, certainly in its Hegelian form, draws much of its dialectic from Neo-Platonism—and Neo-Platonists, unlike Christians, had been unable to envisage the possibility of God-without-a-world. And whereas Christians understood creation to be *ex nihilo*, out of nothing, Neo-Platonists thought it was *de Deo*, out of the substance of God.⁸ Günther considered even conventionally orthodox theology to be, to a degree, guilty of this same intellectual crime. Thanks to its continuation of the patristic inheritance, Scholastic theology repeated the mistake of the Fathers in permitting pantheism-friendly philosophical ideas like participation and analogy so to structure an account of the basic God-world relationship as to mutilate the organism of Christian

---

6. G. Savarese, *Introduzione alla storia critica della filosofia dei SS. Padri ovvero Idea della filosofia Cristiana e patristica* (Naples, 1856), p. 274.

7. Compare the comment of a twentieth-century student: "Rejecting mechanistic rationalism and influenced by moralistic pietism, idealists remained close to Christian thought. But at the same time the *predominant pantheism* inherent in the idealistic systems stimulated the questioning of such major tenets of the historical faith as the reality of a personal and transcendent God as well as of sin . . . [Moreover] Catholics found that in responding to idealism they *simultaneously* entered into dialogue with the romantic thinkers of the era," D. J. Dietrich, *The Goethezeit and the Metamorphosis of Catholic Theology in the Age of Idealism*, op. cit., pp. 19, 23. Italics added.

8. J. Rist, "Augustine of Hippo," in G. R. Evans (ed.), *The Medieval Theologians* (Oxford, 2001), p. 13. This makes a comparison of Augustine and Hegel, both of whom sought to reconcile elements of Neo-Platonism with some version of Christianity, a plausible enterprise—up to a point.

thought. To say the world participates in certain attributes of the divine reality, or that the divine reality can be understood by analogy with certain features of the world: what is this if not a halfway house to the pantheism for which the world is a cut-down God? Günther had no objection to participation language in regard to the realm of grace, but his attitude to its use in the realm of nature is memorably signaled in his posthumously published *Anti-Savarese*. Savarese, he writes, is "a Papageno"—a reference to the comic bird-catcher in Mozart's *The Magic Flute*—who fails to notice the "Pan-pipes which the ancient Scholasticism has hung around his neck."[9]

Hostility to pantheism—thus broadly defined—was the driving force behind much of Günther's work. His 1834 study *Der letzte Symboliker*, "The Last Symbolist," ostensibly an investigation of contemporary Liberal Protestant theology, is chiefly a satire on theological Romanticism, which Günther claims is submerging the Christianity of the German people in a cult of divinized nature.[10] Salvation in Christ should not be presented as merely the noblest form of *Naturleben*.[11] That is the point of its C. S. Lewis-like closing dialogue between two devils specializing in speculation, *Spekulationsteufel*.[12] On the way to this conclusion, however, Günther is able to consider numerous doctrinal topics, and notably the original nature of man, justification, the Church, the sacraments, Tradition and, a favored theme, Christ as the New Adam, *Stammvater der neuen Menschheit*: "the proto-parent of a new humanity." Four years later, in *Juste-Milieus der deutschen Philosophie gegenwärtigen Zeit* ("The Via Medias of Contemporary German Philosophy"), he turned his guns on the Idealist thinkers whom he accused of ill-judged attempts to mediate between contradictory propositions, especially in regard to the simultaneous radical unity and yet radical plurality of the real.[13] The correct mediation between monism—the view that there is only one reality—and

---

9. A. Günther, *Anti-Savarese* (Vienna, 1883), p. 78.

10. By 1848, Günther was naming as public enemy no. 1 ("the first Messiah") Ludwig Feuerbach with his "no salvation outside man." But he still added in second place the erroneous maxim of "no salvation outside mother nature and she is God and outside her is no other." Thus the preface to the second edition of A. Günther, *Die Vorschule der spekulativen Theologie des positiven Christentums* (Vienna, 1846), I. pp. viii–ix.

11. Idem., *Der letzte Symboliker* (Vienna, 1834), p. ix.

12. Ibid., p. 365.

13. Idem., *Juste-Milieus der deutschen Philosophie gegenwärtigen Zeit* (Vienna, 1838).

radical pluralism—the view that there are, ultimately, irreducibly many realities—can only be found in the doctrine of creation which finds its own proper context and culmination in the doctrine of the Trinity.

What of Günther's main positive conclusion? Günther held that for Catholic theology to be renewed in a form suited to his own, or indeed any, age it must be reconstructed as *speculation*—as the modern German philosophers from Fichte onwards had understood that term. By "speculation" Günther meant: meta-logical thinking that originates in the self-reflection of spirit.[14] "Only what knows about its own being comes to knowledge of other being."[15] In its specifically Catholic form, still starting from the departure point of self-consciousness, theology should generate an intellectual totality of its own in which the entirety of traditional Catholic doctrine would be included. That gives us the key to the title of his chief work, the *Vorschule zur spekulativen Theologie des positiven Christentums*, "Preschool for the Speculative Theology of Positive Christianity," of which the first edition, 1828–1829, appeared in fascicules amounting to two volumes of letters between a parish priest, "Peregrinus niger," "The Black Pilgrim," parish priest of Kirchfels ("Rock of the Church") and his nephew who is setting out on the study of theology at the Swiss abbey of Einsiedeln, itself a place of pilgrimage owing to its shrine of the "Black Madonna." A second edition appeared between 1846 and 1848. In each edition, volume one concerns creation and the Trinity, volume two evil, Christology and salvation. The noted Tübingen theologian Franz Anton Staudenmaier commented on the first edition, "Henceforth pantheism should be seen as annihilated."[16]

Consonant with his two main aims—one positive, the other negative—the *Vorschule*—a name which, granted Günther's pervasive sense of humor, should perhaps be translated "The Nursery School"—opens by declaring on its very first page that this most systematic of Günther's treatises, despite the characteristically Late Romantic epistolatory form, will take as its aim to exhibit the

---

14. Thus his *Euristheus und Herakles. Metalogische Kritiken und Meditationen* (Vienna, 1843). In this work, Herakles represents the struggle at once for freedom and *Geist*, aimed at liberating the world from the coils of the concept.

15. A. Günther, *Die Vorschule der spekulativen Theologie des positive Christentums*, op. cit., I., p. 174.

16. Cited by P. Wenzel, *Das wissenschaftliche Anliegen des Güntherianismus*, op. cit., p. 14, from Staudenmaier's review in the (Tübingen) *Theologische Quartalschrift* 14 (1832), p. 99.

self-grounding of the act of faith. On the other hand, in the very next breath Günther makes it plain that his project will be situated at the Antipodes from fideism. The self-grounding of the act of faith requires for its exhibition what he terms "an Ideal reconstruction of Christianity as a world-historical fact"—in other words, showing how this influential phenomenon, Christianity, when its essence as grasped by faith is laid bare, meets all the principal intellectual demands that the self-reflection of spirit entails. The first stage of this apologia —dealt with in volume I of the *Vorschule*[17]—entails the justification of belief in creation, specifically by a *triune* Creator: the divine Trinity.

The way to justify belief in Trinitarian creative agency, so Günther informs his readers, will start from an exploration of the implicates of self-consciousness which are, via the fundamental idea of the "I," the departure-point of all theoretical knowledge. Five years later, in 1833, in the enigmatically entitled *Januskopf für Philosophie und Theologie* ("Janus-head for Philosophy and Theology") he would excoriate all systems based on act of faith not yet reappropriated in reflection, while equally insisting that reason must not be misused in the way the Enlightenment had misused it. Philosophy and theology, he explains, are two "contemplative modes," *Betrachtungsweisen,* of Ideal thought: thought, namely, that arises from the reflective self-thinking of spirit.

For Günther the need of the hour was precisely for an academic undertaking of this kind. He set to work on a comprehensive strategy for the intellectual revivification of the Church. That is attested in his five-volume philosophical diary *Lydia*, named from the woman of Thyateira in the Acts of the Apostles who was Paul's first pupil in Europe.[18] At Günther's hands, Lydia become a symbol of European Christian philosophy which, he thinks, should be Pauline in character, based on acknowledgement of divine transcendence, the notion of creation, and the dualism of nature and spirit. (Güntherianism is, among other things, a revived Paulinism in anthropology: like Paul it works with a picture of man as body and soul together with spirit.) Günther's self-set task was to uncover false tendencies in the intellectual life of the Church—philosophical,

---

17. A. Günther, *Die Vorschule der spekulativen Theologie des positive Christentums,* op. cit., I, p. 97.
18. Acts 16:14–16.

theological, literary and aesthetic. The first and worst of these he had already announced in an article of 1852 to be *Vernunftshass*, "hatred for reason" which, he claimed, had entered Catholicism from Lutheranism, or possibly from Luther's sources in the medieval mystics, and was intensified by the influence of Kant, who in the supra-sensuous realm could find room only for what Günther contemptuously termed "non-knowing"—that is, faith defined *over against* knowledge.[19] (Hence, not surprisingly, Günther's animus against Hermes with whom, somewhat bizarrely, standard histories classify him under the name "semi-rationalists.") In Günther's *oeuvre*, Luther represents a view not only of nature and grace as antithetical but of the human spirit as exclusively "nature," rather than in its qualities as free and reasonable which, actually, raise it quite above natural life, into the sphere of the (in some sense) *super*natural.

NATURE AND SPIRIT IN GÜNTHER'S THOUGHT

In what sense? The terms "nature" and "spirit" are so key to the Güntherian system that his gloss on them must be explained straightaway. "Nature" for Günther means: the unified totality of natural forms from mineral, through vegetable to animal, including there the naturally ensouled body of man. The principle of nature, which principle is for him a single substantial reality, not just a category of thought (we might think of the English locution "Mother Nature"), renders itself individual and external in a multitude of appearing things, striving of its own immanent character ever more to interiorize itself: something especially apparent in distinctively human sense awareness in which nature recognizes its own manner of appearing—namely, in sensuous forms—and thus becomes self-aware. However, such recognition is only *sensuous* knowledge: the self-awareness of nature does not constitute reflection strictly so called; only the self-awareness of spirit deserves that label.

In the human being, living and thinking *by means of concepts* is not, as Christian Scholasticism considers it, a sign of transcending the natural level but, on the contrary, is symptomatic of nature so

---

19. A. Günther, "Ein Wort über den Vernunftshass auf katholischer Gebiet," *Zeitschrift für die gesamte Katholische Theologie* 3 (1852), pp. 53–64.

understood. Conceptual activity mirrors what nature most essentially is: namely, the representation of appearance in which what is universal or general becomes particular and specific in each natural kind of thing. What Günther terms *das begriffliche Denken,* "conceptual thinking," never goes beyond the level of natural reality. By appealing to concepts of kinds of things—humanity, cathood, treeness, or whatever—we never really grasp ontology, the foundational being of things, but remain at the level of an abstract, schematized picturing of what is general or universal in its self-presentation in nature. (This, then, is Günther's take on the problem of "universals" in philosophy.)

However, besides such conceptual understanding, there is another kind of thinking, which belongs properly to spirit, *Geist,* as such. This Ideal, meta-logical thinking is the characteristic product of spirit and issues from the "I": indeed, the thought of the "I," *der Ichgedanke,* is par excellence *the* idea, *die Idee,* of such meta-logical thought. Whoever thinks only in concepts is a naturalist, and can grasp nothing beyond the schemata of nature; whoever thinks in terms of the idea, truly grasps being and is an Idealist, because he or she is thinking on the level of spirit, of selfhood, which level alone is calibrated with the *Urgrund* of things, the divine "I."

Applying this to theology and its epistemic precondition, faith, we reach the following conclusion: conceptual thinking as a product of nature, which is itself *geistlos,* "spiritless," is incapable of raising itself to the divine. Thus when Thomas Aquinas remarks in his *Summa theologiae* that "it is impossible through natural reason, *per rationem naturalem,* to reach a knowledge of the divine persons of the Trinity,"[20] Günther willingly concedes that this is so since by *ratio* Aquinas doubtless means conceptual thought or what, following the cue of the Idealist philosophers, Günther would call *Verstand.* But this does not at all mean that an Ideal kind of meta-logical thinking, which Günther—again, with the Idealist philosophers—terms *Vernunft* cannot come to coincide with the supreme intelligibility of the Holy Trinity, using the more-than-natural capability of spirit. As one twentieth-century critic has commented: "Günther's anthropology is [thus] the foundation of his theory of knowledge and this in turn gives

---

20. Thomas, *Summa theologiae,* Ia., q. 32, a. 1. *A Catholic Hegel? Anton Günther* 57.

us the key for his *Glaubenslehre,* his account of faith."[21] Basically, inasmuch as Ideal thinking entails self-reflection from the departure-point of an "I" that is to natural awareness, invisible, such thinking can itself be termed "faith"—fundamental philosophical faith, of course. Rightly understood, the act of *Christian* faith is a *consummate* act of such meta-logical thought, the *supreme* achievement of reason as *Vernunft.* Of the two imperatives Augustine proposed in his celebrated Letter 120, "Believe that you may understand" and "understand that you may believe," the first—"Believe that you may understand"—can now be dispensed with; it was only ever suitable for an age whose inhabitants were intellectual children. That leaves us with the second Augustinian imperative: "understand that you may believe." Enlightened faith, *erleuchteter Glaube,* is nothing other than "holy knowledge," *heiliges Wissen,* and as such it will be the dominant intellectual power of the future. How so?

Günther's Philosophical-Theological System

To answer this question means providing an overview of Günther's system which he creates partly by building up internal coherence and partly through undertaking a critique of other views. Günther starts out from man, in whom nature and spirit are at one. In the human "I" spiritual reality is disclosed, and the consequent self-understanding of spirit is the climax of philosophy. In his second published work, *Peregrins Gastmahl,* attacking the traditionalism of de Maistre, Lamennais, and de Bonald (more on that in Chapter 4), he remarks that self-consciousness is the only possible departure-point of philosophy. From the "I" a way leads directly to Trinity and creation alike. On the Ideal path both mysteries are proved by *Geist* and so the Creed gains fresh confirmation from reason. Here we begin to see why Savarese stigmatized Güntherianism as "logical anthropomorphism." For Günther, the self-discovery of spirit is decisive for the

---

21. J. Pritz, *Glauben und Wissen bei Anton Günther. Eine Einführung in sein Leben und Werk mit einer Auswahl aus seinen Schriften* (Vienna, 1963), p. 146.

fate of metaphysics since it enables us to grasp that the "I" is the most significant moment in the unfolding of being, the general character of which can now be described as a *striving toward disclosure* or revelation. The being of nature has an inward tendency towards the emergence of consciousness; spiritual being has a like tendency towards the emergence of *self*-consciousness in and as persons.

In this evolutionary process natural substance differentiates itself. It does so first of all by the emergence of the twin poles, or opposite polarities, of receptivity and spontaneity which characterize all conscious inhabiting of environment. Günther calls such inhabiting of environment *Objektivierung,* "objectivization," since here things become objects for each other for the first time. Natural substance differentiates itself second by the emergence of self-consciousness or subjectivity in which spirit comes to possess itself as a principle that illuminates all being, since all the ideas and categories of any metalogical thinking worth the name are born in the "I," which Günther calls the "cradle of spirit." Günther terms this second sort of differentiation "subjectobjectivization," *Subjektobjektivierung.* It is when the subject grasps itself in relation to objects that it can find in its own characteristic categories a new and decisive resource for understanding reality. Günther would have had in mind such notions as unity, uniqueness, difference, identity, finitude, infinity, substance, relation—at any rate when these notions are thought in the light of the self-discovery of spirit. When these notions are so thought, they are treated as qualities of the self (human or divine), denoting features of that selfhood which is paradigmatic for all other approaches to the real. To them we must add of course the notion of spirit itself—self-consciousness, subjectivity, personality, and indeed for that matter community, the fellowship of spirit.

On Günther's view, man, like the Jesus of Chalcedonian Christology, has two natures: not human and divine, as with Jesus, but natural and spiritual, reflecting this two stage prehistory. Each human being is an organic unity of the two kinds of reality involved: *Natur,* "nature," composed of body and soul, and "spirit," *Geist.* That is why we can practice *both* conceptual or natural thinking, suggested by natural forms, *and* meta-logical or spiritual thinking, which re-works conceptual thought-forms in the light of subjectivity. Whoever confuses these two or thinks either of them to be dispensable is, declares Günther, "an ignoramus in his own house."[22]

The most important example of meta-logical thinking is that in which the process of emergence to self-consciousness comes to light as thesis, antithesis, and synthesis: thesis, namely, substance, as yet not fully determined; antithesis, objectivization; and synthesis: subject-objectivization, which is a recovery of unity from out of opposed polarities in the breakthrough to subjecthood. The laborious character of this process highlights the deficient character of created being. But in uncreated being, as the New Testament revelation bears witness, the same kind of processive consciousness is instantiated—the Father generates his living Word with whom he spirates the Holy Spirit, thus becoming the unique Subject that is God the Holy Trinity. Hence Günther's doctrine of the immanent Trinity. The immanent Trinity is the "self-determination of the Absolute" by which the Word of God is constituted the perfect objectification of the Father in a counter-position to the Father's "thesis," and this objectification in the Word, just because it is perfect, then yields synthetically the "Product" of God and his Word, namely, the Holy Spirit, in whom Father and Son find themselves entirely as for each other. This process, by which divine substance becomes Trinity, is not a labor, or if it is, it is an effortless labor of love. In God all takes place in an absolutely positive fashion which can be described precisely by negating what is negative in its human counterpart.

In this self-realization of the Absolute as Trinity lies for Günther nonetheless a *sort* of negativity, though one which, unlike the negativity in created being, in no way denotes deficiency or lack. Inasmuch as the process of the Trinity's coming to be formally excludes any other coefficients of the divine life, that process brings to light what Günther terms the "non-I" in God. The "non-I" in God is that aspect of primordial being which is not taken up into the tri-personal life of God precisely in his subjectivity as the Holy Trinity. It is divine substance insofar as it is not divine subject. With the successful achievement of the Trinitarian processions God's own thinking of his non-I then becomes the presupposition of the creation.

---

22. A. Günther, in *Lydia* 3 (1851), p. 176.

For Günther, to say that creation issues *ex nihilo*, "from nothing," is to say that what must be positive, since based in divine wisdom, in the life-process of the Godhead, arises in a new form from what can only be called absolute negativity inasmuch as it is the negation—in the sense of the formal exclusion—of the absolute triune "I": the negation (in this sense, formal exclusion) of the totally realized subjectivity of the triune God. The creaturely realization of this thought of the divine "non-I" must be sought in the emergent trio of nature, spirit and man, the human being, who as the unity of nature and spirit plays something like the same synthetic role in the world that the Holy Spirit enacts in the life of God. The creative act is thus the beginning of the formation of human beings as natural beings raised to the dignity of personal subjecthood who in that way—through the personalization of nature—become images of the Trinity, despite their origin in the creaturely reflection of the non-I. Owing to creation's basis in the divine "non-I," the same act of creation also founds the maximal contrast of Creator and creature and in that fashion—this is key for Günther—excludes unconditionally pantheism of any kind. Still, since the divine "non-I" is itself divine wisdom, divine thinking, the world as a whole is nonetheless anchored in the life of God, while human subjects, through their mirroring of the process of God's own becoming fully subject as the Holy Trinity, are "rendered capable," in Günther's words, of "being drawn into his divine life and blessedness."[23]

It is to the actualization of this capacity, in the post-Fall situation where nature and spirit in man have been sundered by evil, that the Incarnation and Atonement are ordered. Then it is that the distinctive self-consciousness of the Word, a personal mode of the divine Trinity, is united with the self-consciousness of a man in the unique "I," *Ichheit*, of Jesus Christ who thereby enters human genealogy as the Second Adam, the new father of humanity, and in that office makes plenary satisfaction for all his kin. That is the message of the second volume of *Die Vorschule*.

And the upshot is that the revelation *ad intra*, within the Godhead, of the three divine persons and the revelation *ad extra*, in the world around us, of the tripartite cosmos of nature, spirit and man, are unified in the New Testament claims about a Trinitarian creation—a world that is from the Father, through the Son, in the

---

23. Idem., in *Lydia* 4 (1852), p. 424.

Holy Spirit—and the New Testament promises of the consummation of such a world in the liberation of the children of God. These two revelations are unified in those claims and promises as re-thought speculatively from the starting-point of self-consciousness. The two revelations concerned—the biblical uncreated Trinity and the cosmic created "trinity"—can now be seen as two harmonized modes of the disclosure of absolute being, one mode of which is infinite, the other finite. Günther calls this duo of triads the "Christian-dualist view of the world . . . the doctrine of the tripartite world-whole as a counter-position to the triune Godhead."[24]

This is thanks to the Güntherian theology which its originator describes as at once the "nativity feast of philosophy," which at last is born rather than struggling to be born, and the "Tabor" of science, in which Christ can celebrate his transfiguration anew in the domain of *Wissenschaft*, fully reasonable knowledge. The incarnate Word already inaugurated the salvational fullness of time in history in Judaea, at the start of the common era, and yet he left to the future his establishment of a scientific fullness of time. This is achieved in Günther's system, which its originator—who clearly suffered from no false modesty—identified with the fulfillment of the words of the Savior to his disciples in the Fourth Gospel, "I have many things to say to you, but you cannot bear them now."[25] The facts of the objective revelation have now at last been raised to the level of ideal knowledge—the kind of knowledge typical of spirit.

Günther's Critique of Other Thinkers

As already mentioned, Günther advanced his views partly by a vigorous critique of other men's thought. The overall perspective in which Günther criticizes his predecessors is furnished by the notion of an enduring struggle between the philosophy of the concept, which when dominant is inevitably naturalistic and reaches its climax in Hegel, and the philosophy of the idea, which when dominant permits access to the transcendent. Only in orthodox Christianity, as interpreted by Günther, are concept and idea, nature and spirit, reconciled

---

24. Idem., *Die Vorschule der spekulativen Theologie des positiven Christentums,* op. cit., pp. viii–ix.
25. John 16:12.

one with the other. Outside Israel, or Judaism—the carrier of creation thinking—not least to the Church, there is only some version of pantheism. Ancient conceptual thought even at its best, as in Plato and Aristotle, has no inkling of creation thinking and hence is unserviceable for Neo-dualism, Günther's project. Philosophically minded Church Fathers, like the Scholastics after them, are too indebted to this flawed patrimony to be safe guides. Thomas Aquinas makes a mighty effort, as Günther puts it, to "bind into a single whole" classical philosophy and Christianity, but the consequence is a compromised doctrine of creation, which Günther judges semi-pantheist in type. Moreover, Thomas was content for faith and reason to remain distinct, and even separate. To affirm of the doctrines of faith merely that, at any rate, they can't be shown to be counter-rational, is for Günther a failure of intellectual nerve. Doctrine should be shown to be not only, negatively, not unreasonable, but, more importantly, positively reasonable, too.[26] Christian doctrine is a first sketch of constructive rationality as empowered by the idea. The revealed mysteries are in fact supernaturally furnished primordial truths, which in the providence of God have now—with Güntherianism—attained their own rational mediation. They have become truths of reason as well. Neo-Scholasticism, or what Günther called "repristinated Scholasticism," thus fails to recognize the historic moment in which its own misguided efforts are situated, and its renewal of semipantheist features of ancient Christian thought renders it singularly unhelpful in an age which has seen a reflorescence of pantheism in Idealism and Romanticism.

While the culture of Protestant Germany, emancipated from the authority of the Church as organ of the Holy Spirit, fell increasingly into monism, its neighbor across the Rhine produced a thinker, René Descartes, who by his "cogito ergo sum" pushed open, in Günther's metaphor, the hitherto closed door into the realm of the

---

26. J. Reikerstorfer considers the search for a "positive criterion of reason" to replace the "negative criterion of reason" that is non-contradictoriness to be the real foundation of Günther's enterprise: see his "Anton Günther (1783–1863) und seine Schule," in E. Coreth et al., (ed.), *Christliche Philosophie im katholischen Denkens des 19. und 20. Jahrhunderts, I., Neue Ansätze des 19. Jahrhunderts*, op. cit., p. 268. Cited below as "Anton Günther."

subject. In words I borrow from Etienne Gilson, who will figure in a later chapter of this study.

> [Descartes] set aside from the massacre [of Scholastic cosmology] one substantial form, the human soul, of which, contrary to the Aristotelean conception, he attributed to us a direct intuition, not only with respect to its existence but also regarding its essence.[27]

At the same time Descartes misconceived his own discovery, grasping neither the ontological disclosure made in the "I" nor the now opened up meta-logical path to the ground of thinking.[28] Günther reminds his readers that in 1663 Descartes' writings were placed on the Roman Index of Prohibited Books with the marker *donec corrigantur:* meaning, "until they are corrected." Günther's claim is that he provides this correction, all the more necessary now that Kantianism has renewed the hegemonic claims of merely conceptual thought and completed the separation between speculation and revealed religion. But above all, Günther's enterprise is made necessary by the appearance of Hegelianism, which is the apogee of conceptual pantheism. Hegelianism's chief errors consist in its conceptual—rather than Ideal—starting point, its notion of spirit working as nature—to Günther's mind, sheer contradiction in terms, and its affirmation of a dialectic of the Absolute, which is the blasphemous attempt to write a natural history of God. Though Hegel elected, rightly, to make self-consciousness the supreme vantage-point of philosophy, he took the being of spirit to be not personhood but individuality or particularity, and thus no more than the appearing or revelation of being in general. Hegel's system seems to be the representation of spirit but such spirit in Hegel's work is in fact nothing other than nature, albeit nature masquerading as the dialectically developed expression of absolute spirit.

---

27. E. Gilson, *From Aristotle to Darwin and Back Again. A Journey in Final Causality, Species, and Evolution* (English translation, Notre Dame, IN, 1984), p. 127.

28. A century later, the Neo-Scholastic philosopher and theologian Réginald Garrigou-Lagrange in effect agreed with Günther here. The "I," he wrote, is "*au fond* fatally ontological"—though in his view the ontological conclusion Descartes should have drawn from the cogito concerned being rather than spirit: intelligence is "only intelligible to itself in function of the being it knows directly before knowing itself by reflection," *Le Sens commun, la philosophie de l'être et les formulas dogmatiques* (Paris, 1922, 3rd edition), pp. 138, 139.

Conclusion

Though he was critical of Hegel, Günther drew much from Hegelian philosophy, notably Hegel's notion of nature as the representation of the concept, his view of the propulsive power of negation, and of the place of process in being. Though Günther sought to purify Idealism evangelically in the service of Catholic thought, he also hoped to profit by its advances, above all its sense of the unique status of self-consciousness, and the importance of organic development. In the aftermath of *die Goethezeit* when Idealism and Romanticism formed the intellectual and cultural world of the German-speaking bourgeoisie, Günther spoke in a language that was familiar, despite its difficulty. As such philosophy "sought to solve similar epistemological, anthropological and metaphysical problems" to those addressed by Catholic theology,[29] it was hardly surprising that the integration of the two into a single system was so effortless at his hands.

Günther's disciples who included holders of chairs in the German and Austrian universities and bishops of major sees like Salzburg, Breslau, Trier and Münster, as well as supporters at the Roman court, believed themselves to be opening a new phase in the intellectual life of the Church. Typically, they accepted the sobriquet the "Neo-dualist School," since they emphasized divine transcendence, the doctrine of creation and the dualism of flesh (that is, ensouled body) and spirit, which they considered a datum of Saint Paul's anthropology. The triumvirate Paul, Benedict, Günther, constituted their theological pantheon: Benedict inasmuch as they regarded the Rule of Saint Benedict as reflecting Pauline concerns; and also because, after their expected doctrinal victory, they planned to found a monastery dedicated to the Holy Spirit to serve the spiritual culture of German Catholic learning. The post-Benedictine Religious Orders they considered too wedded to Scholasticism to embrace the new thinking necessary to overcome the twin challenges of philosophical paganism and cultural Protestantism. They would have scorned the plea, entered a century later, of the historian of medieval philosophy

---

29. D. J. Dietrich, *The Goethezeit and the Metamorphosis of Catholic Theology in the Age of Idealism*, op. cit., p. 19.

Etienne Gilson, that Christian philosophy "is necessarily solidary with its past: we arrive too late to claim to change its style."[30]

Pius IX's condemnation of Günther's writings in 1857 did not dent their spirits. Merely, they said, a disciplinary decree inhibiting young theologians from making use of Günther's writings. The rehabilitation of his thought was simply a matter of time. As one told Günther who at the age of seventy-three only had six years to live: "Your Resurrection festival will come as surely as God created the world, and as surely as Christian wisdom and science will have the victory over pagan, and Catholicism over Protestantism."[31] The reiteration of the condemnation by the First Vatican Council in 1869–1870 was thus a shocking blow, which precipitated the flight of a number of leading Güntherian priests and laymen to Old Catholicism. On these vicissitudes there will be more anon.[32]

---

30. E. Gilson, *Le philosophe et la Théologie* (Paris, 1960; 2002), pp. 203–204.
31. Cited P. Wenzel, *Das wissenschaftliche Anliegen des Güntherianismus* (Essen, 1961), p. 46.
32. See Chapter 5, "Magisterial Interventions: Gregory XVI and Pius IX."

Chapter 4

The Response of Fideism: Louis Bautain

Introduction

In the last two chapters we have been looking at thinkers who in the general run of textbooks are described as "semi-rationalists." We now turn our attention to a writer who is customarily seen as a fideist, though possibly here the invocation of "semi" would again be justified. Louis Bautain was born in France at the height of the Revolutionary turmoil, something brought home to one when one reads that the date of marriage of his parents is given as 11th floréal in the year III.[1] So far from thinking—with Hermes—that the rational necessity of Christianity could be proved by the exercise of practical reason, or—with Günther—that an Ideal reconstruction of the act of faith would show it to be the supreme achievement of reason as *Vernunft*, for Bautain there is simply no possibility of a rational reconstruction of revelation either in its grounds (compare Hermes) or in its content (compare Günther). No more did the classical apologetics whose roots lie in early Christian propaganda convince him. No preamble of faith based on objective assessment of the historical evidence for the credibility of Christianity is worth formulating. Nor are we in possession of any epistemic tools for critically evaluating its content. These negative convictions are of course what justify historians of thought in calling Bautain a fideist.

What *can* usefully be written, however, so Bautain thinks, is an essay on the intelligibility of dogma, showing the light which Christian doctrine, once credited, casts on other areas of life and

---

1. P. Poupard, *L'Abbé Louis Bautain* (Tournai, 1961), p. 63, n. 4. This work draws on much unpublished material.

knowledge.[2] This is the point at which the inclusion of the qualifier "semi"—"semi-fideist"—might be deemed justified. For Bautain, the light shed by the content of revelation on the subject matter of the human disciplines, above all philosophy, is the only evidence for the credibility of the fact of revelation there can be. That is: the only form of apologetics Bautain can recognize is one which draws attention to the explanatory power of dogma for a range of areas of human understanding, which stretch from the structure of physical reality to an account of the goals of human life. This limitation did not worry him, because, as we shall see, for him reason of any kind is an inferior faculty, a mere tool which can be set to serve intellectual intuitions, without which the argumentative mind gyrates in a void, deprived of any worthwhile contact with the real. If true, that would explain, of course, the difficulty to which, as I mentioned in the opening chapter, Alisdair MacIntyre has drawn attention: namely, that beyond the level of such basic logical maxims as the principle of non-contradiction and the principle of identity, it seems impossible to gain a philosophical consensus on the question, "To which rational principles should all reasonable people agree?"

Early Life

So who was Bautain? Born in 1796, from a petit-bourgeois Parisian background (his father was a dance master), he secured entry to the prestigious *Lycée impériale*, newly founded by Napoleon, from where he moved on to the well-known *Ecole normale supérieure*, forcing-ground of highflying French bureaucrats. Bautain, who abandoned his ancestral Catholicism at this time, had an unfashionable academic interest: philosophy. The emperor spoke dismissively of philosophers as "ideologues." To his project of rescuing the Revolution for order they were irrelevant or worse. No better might have been expected under the restored Bourbons, but in fact 1815 saw the appointment to the chair of philosophy at the Ecole of Victor Cousin, whose philosophical style (self-described as "Eclecticism") would enjoy enormous influence in France over the next fifty years.

---

2. Ibid., p. 369.

As its name suggests, Eclecticism sought to extract valid elements from all the principal schools and writers in the history of philosophy, often by the simple device of tracing a *via media* between opposing views. Traditional Christianity was viewed with disdain by Cousin and his colleagues—Bautain describes the prevailing attitude as a conviction that all positive religion was a human construction, and dogmas ideas of reason sadly distorted by perfervid imagination.[3] But the philosophical formation he received gave him a good basis in the history of philosophy, notably the ancient Greeks, the rationalists (Descartes, Spinoza, Leibniz), the British empiricists, and Kant. At the same time, he discovered the Achilles heel of Eclecticism: if no satisfactory philosophical system can be built up on the basis of first principles, by what means are the criteria of selection used in Eclecticism to "pick 'n mix" *themselves to be legitimated*? Bautain's experience of academic philosophy left him with the conviction that an ordered evaluation of life and reality—what he termed "wisdom"—is not available except via faith. At a rudimentary level, as we shall see, that might mean philosophical faith, simply, but for any more developed or more comprehensive aim, only a faith that corresponded to the historic Judeo-Christian revelation could—such was his eventual conclusion—suffice.

In the autumn of 1816 Bautain was made lecturer in philosophy at the *Collège royal* in Strasbourg, and a year later received a concurrent appointment to teach philosophy in the faculty of letters at the University there. In this period, Alsace was bilingual, and Bautain set himself to learn German and read the post-Kantian Idealist philosophers scarcely known so early in France proper. Brief personal encounters with Schelling and Hegel ensued. Bautain's delvings into German Idealism—including meetings with the masters—imbued him with the notion that any philosophy worth the name must attempt a total account of the real. His course notes in the years 1818 to 1820, from which some 3,500 manuscript pages survive, show a general if not always highly focused adherence to Kantian and post-Kantian Idealism on which, however, Bautain puts his own spin. To accept reason as a capacity for the Absolute—practical reason drawing

---

3. L. Bautain, *De l'Education publique en France au XIXe siècle* (Paris, 1876), p. 193, cited in ibid., p. 69.

us to the "absolute" or unconditional reality of God by action, theoretical reason drawing us to the same goal by (in the widest sense) scientific inquiry—requires (this was how Bautain understood Hegel and, especially, Schelling) an act of philosophical faith. Few human beings, however, are actually capable of attaining via such an act the level of reason in the exalted meaning Idealism gave it as *Vernunft*, whereas religion to which, under Idealist influence, Bautain shows a new openness, can intimate the truth housed in universal reason by adapting it to human sensibility, presenting it in an anthropomorphic fashion through symbols.[4]

THE MEETING WITH MADELEINE-LOUISE HUMANN

Another meeting, however, was even more consequential than his discovery of the Idealists. During a crisis in his personal life, Bautain was thrown together with a Catholic mystic, Madeleine-Louise Humann, the director of a school for young ladies in Stuttgart. It seems clear that in 1820 Bautain underwent some kind of breakdown, the result in part of the strain involved in his attempts to master some of the most demanding philosophical texts ever written, but also of the contrast between the enthusiastic acclaim with which his lectures were met, on the one hand, and, on the other, of his deep disappointment at the lack of any life-transforming power in the Idealist writings as he experienced them. As he put it, "I began to be disenchanted with this high speculation which, of scarce use except for course- and book-production (*ne servant guère qu' à des cours ou des ouvrages*), has so little influence on real life."[5] While, on medical advice, taking the waters at the celebrated German spa town of Baden-Baden, he ran into Mlle. Humann, whose extant papers show to have been a highly cultured woman with a view of mysticism bearing definite affinities to that of the early fourteenth-century Dominican Meister Eckhart. The philosophical "faith" in which Bautain had found no personal inspiration now yielded to her mystical intuitionism which was explicitly anti-rational in kind.

---

4. P. Poupard, *L'Abbé Louis Bautain*, op cit., pp. 80–83.
5. L. Bautain, *Les Choses de l'autre monde, Journal d'un philosophe* (Paris, 1868), p. 428, cited ibid., p. 87.

For Humann, the truth of any science turns on that of the key idea from which a given discipline develops, but such crucial truths, with their common prototype in the idea of being which they refract in one way or another, are not themselves established by reason, *la raison*. Instead, they are disclosed to intellect, *l'intelligence*. Or rather, they *were* so disclosed to the intellectual eye of man when in the soul's primitive condition it was united to its divine source. Only by asceticism, in an effort to purify the spirit through habitual contemplation, can the human soul become re-attuned to the being which in its origin is divine being, the great "I AM" of God.[6] If truth is what is sought then intuitive evidence is available for the truth of knowledge (in its dependence via the truth of being on divine being itself). But a condition of attaining such intuitively evidenced knowledge is personal relationship with God—some sort of covenant relationship where there is communication from the divine side, and faith—receptivity to that communication—from the human.

In her own version of the ontological argument, associated most famously with Saint Anselm, but found also in, amongst others, Augustine and Descartes, Humann argued that the presence in the human mind of the idea of God creates a presumption that human capacities do indeed include the ability to receive divine communications. However, owing to the spiritual malaise of fallen humanity, which covers our inner eye, as she puts it, with a kind of cataract, God can now only communicate with us mediately—not immediately, then. And "mediately" here turns out to mean through a historic revelation whose organ of communication is spoken language and whose organ of reception is hearing. This is, then, the *fides ex auditu*, the "faith coming from hearing" of the Latin theological tradition to which I drew attention in the introduction to this study.

Humann impressed on Bautain, and the conviction stayed with him, that in our actual state, we have no way other than revelation of attaining the knowledge of God. Proofs of God's existence only have value for minds already enlightened by the *lumen fidei*, the supernatural light of faith, which is subsequently able, along the lines

---

6. "The directing inspiration of Rhenish theology is the inscription of the theology of the blessed union in a certain theory of the mind founded on the distinction between the essence and the powers of the soul": A. de Libera, *La Mystique rhénane d'Albert le Grand à Maître Eckhart* (Paris, 1994), p. 251.

of Saint Paul's celebrated text in the Letter to the Romans, to read off the invisible divine perfections from the visible works of creation. Reason in its argumentative mode is limited for Humann to the comparison of terms. The kind of comparative judgments it makes cannot yield up what she calls the "substantial Absolute": the God who is in her vocabulary, not uninfluenced by Idealism as it was, the "principle of all principles." Reason in its heuristic capacity—its capacity for finding out things—is a degraded faculty which, as Kant did well to show, cannot go beyond the limits of sense experience, the phenomenon.

How, then, we might ask, is one to explain the persistence in a wide range of human cultures untouched by the historic revelation, of myths, forms of cult, symbolic artworks and the like all indicative of at least a confused perception of a divine origin for the world? For answer she refers us to the notion of a primordial revelation to Adam, basis of all subsequent world religions other than the Abrahamic faiths. At the outset of human history there took place—this is the only conclusion one can draw—a primordial revelation which is subsequently present in pagan religions only fitfully and in fragments.[7] The name of this doctrine in nineteenth-century religious thought is "traditionalism"—some of its contemporary exponents, de Maistre, Lamennais, de Bonald, were mentioned in Chapter 3—and, though it left England largely unaffected, a good example of it is Edward Casaubon, the dessicated husband of Dorothea, in George Eliot's *Middlemarch*. Casaubon's doomed project, to which he devoted a lifetime's scholarship, was the "Key of All Mythologies," tracing back all pagan religions from their sacred texts or anthropologists' findings to this common root. But if knowledge of God comes exclusively from either the historic Judeo-Christian revelation or the primordial Adamic revelation, then all attempts to show the autonomous capacity of reason to constitute a preamble of faith are counter-productive. The ravages of rationalism among old-style apologists and new style Hermesians are alike to be deplored. In his treatise *La Morale de l'Evangile comparée à la morale des philosophes* Bautain describes the effect of her message:

---

7. For a "pure" example of traditionalism from a recognized Catholic theologian, see W. F. Hogan, *A. Bonnetty and the Problem of Faith and Reason* (Washington, 1957).

I was neither better nor happier for being more learned... I [now] read the Gospel of Jesus Christ with the desire to find there the truth, and I was seized with a lively admiration, penetrated with a gentle light, which not only enlightened my mind but brought its warmth and life to the depths of my soul. As it were, it raised me from the dead ... I saw man as he is and as he must be: I grasped his past, his present, his future, and I trembled for joy in refinding what religion had taught me from childhood, in feeling faith, hope and joy being born again in my heart. Thus it was that the power and truth of Christianity were demonstrated to me; thus it was that I acquired the conviction that its morality is superior to all human moralities, its dogmas above the opinions of men.[8]

We could find that statement paralleled in many Evangelical writers of the same period, the later 1820s, in England, though an indication of a difference is to be found in the words "I grasped man's past, his present, his future" which suggest more than a religion of piety; they suggest an intellectual project. And so it was.

The Project of the "Philosophy of Wisdom"

Retaining Humann's fideist convictions, including her traditionalism, Bautain now set about developing a Christian philosophy of considerable sophistication, under the rubric "the philosophy of wisdom." What he was doing, so he held, was to re-create the manner of thinking of numerous earlier figures in Christian history, the second-century Saint Justin at their head, who had not distinguished between theology and philosophy but treated Christianity as, quite simply, "the true philosophy," *vera philosophia*.[9] A matching Bautainian apologetics would seek to show that Christian wisdom could contextualize better than any non-Christian philosophy the data presented by the sciences—both the natural sciences, like physics and the human sciences, like psychology, as well as the deliverances of naive experience in human life as lived.

---

8. L. Bautain, *La morale de l'Evangile comparée à la morale des philosophes* (Strasbourg-Paris, 1827), p. 73–76, cited P. Poupard, *L'Abbé Louis Bautain*, op. cit., pp. 98–99.

9. "The twelfth-century distinction between philosophy and theology is not only non-Augustinian; it is more generally non-patristic . . . [A] Christian "theologian," most commonly at that time, is a type of metaphysician, except that through God's Revelation in Scripture and in the tradition of the Church he has more data": thus J. Rist, "Augustine of Hippo," art. cit., p. 7.

Not that such data and deliverances taken by themselves pointed to the truth of Christianity, any more than rational arguments originating outside of revelation did. But once Christianity was accepted, these data and deliverances could be more coherently understood, notably in their relation to each other, as all sectors of study and understanding now became more fully related to each other precisely through being related to the Creator of man and the cosmos, Redeemer of the former (man), Consummator of the latter (the cosmos).

SCIENTIFIC STUDIES AND ORDINATION

Naturally enough, Bautain's reports on the sciences presuppose the point various disciplines had reached in the early nineteenth century. By those standards, however, he was well informed. A member of the *Société des Sciences, Agriculture et Arts* of the *département* of the Lower Rhine, this was just as well, since in 1822 his academic philosophical work was suspended by the Bourbon government after complaints about its maverick nature, compounded with doubts as to his political reliability. This was a professional crisis which he survived financially by re-training as a physician. In 1826 he acquired a doctorate in medicine to complement his doctorate in philosophy, but in 1828, after making a pilgrimage to a Marian shrine, he determined to enter a seminary, and five days before Christmas that year, being dispensed—imprudently—from almost all clerical studies on account of his self-acquired ecclesiastical culture, he was priested in Strasbourg Cathedral.

AN EXPOSITION OF BAUTAIN'S THOUGHT

Bautain's thought is best expressed in three main sources: *La Philosophie du Christianizme*, published in 1835; the (unpublished) conferences he delivered to the *Cercle Catholique de Paris* between 1842 and 1846, and the posthumously published *Journal d'un Philosophe* of 1868. However, as with Günther, an essential aspect of Bautain's project consists in his distinctive way of narrating the history of philosophy in order to exhibit its failings, seeking by contrast to highlight the strength of the position he is commending.

In his critique of other schools, Bautain begins in effect from MacIntyre's contest of competing rationalities, all the more painful in an age like, he says, his own—roughly, that of Romanticism—when the young are generously ardent in their pursuit of *la science,* well-founded knowledge. Christianity, he predicts, will prove to be their "plank of salvation in the shipwreck of [conflicting] beliefs, in the midst of the sea of doubt."[10] But if they are to become Christian again this will first be by becoming philosophers. In this regard, the university milieu in France was dominated, he reported, by five schools: sensationalism; the Scottish "common sense" school; Eclecticism; Idealist rationalism, and pantheism. Sensationalism, for which sense perceptions are the only means of acquaintance with reality, Bautain dismisses for its inability to explain the transition from sense experience to general ideas. The Scottish school practice natural history applied to the mind of man. By induction from psychological facts they admit the existence of a soul, but their refusal to enter into questions of its nature, principle, law or goal convicts them of philosophical superficiality, and will not satisfy young people seeking, rightly, the resolution of fundamental metaphysical problems. Eclecticism deserves respect for its attentiveness to all systems of philosophy, ancient and modern, in an effort to disengage universal truth, but it lacks adequately defensible criteria for identifying the latter. Idealist rationalism attracts disillusioned Eclectics by its proposal to show that the human mind can raise itself to the level of a transcendental act which puts it in relation to the Absolute. In Idealist systems, the Absolute in man contemplates the Absolute outside man, since God, man and the world are distinct modes of the same monistic subject. If so, then Idealism is covert pantheism—that was also Günther's conviction—and the topic of Idealism brings Bautain to the last philosophical fashion, pantheism, better described, he thinks as a cultural fashion since its influence is equally apparent in literature, the arts, and morals. Bautain's critique of pantheism is ethical: to suppose one is, *au fond,* identical with the divine, cuts the nerve of ethical effort.

The upshot of this journey through the civil schools is or should be increased awareness of the human need to give adhesion to a universal doctrine which can furnish a well-grounded account of

---

10. L. Bautain, *La Philosophie du Christianizme* (Strasbourg-Paris, 1835), II, p. 20.

all the chief philosophical problems. The trouble is, for Bautain, that while the Church should be in a position to answer this need, the commitment of the ecclesiastical faculties to Scholasticism, often in a Cartesianised form, gets in the way. Teaching Aristotelian logic served up in Scholastic Latin is bad enough: as Bautain acidly remarks, "The immutability of the form perfectly suited the absence of thought."[11] But to combine this with the Cartesian insistence that philosophy, proceeding by methodical doubt, must be altogether disjoined from theology, since faith is irrelevant to its mode of inquiry: this is only one step away from declaring faith "contrary to the philosophical spirit."[12] Clerics brought up on such fare are incapable of showing how Christian doctrine enjoys a coherent overall unity, how it meets the needs of the human person, and finds illustration in the data provided by the universe. In sum, the Church faculties are no better than the State's. In both, the philosophies taught rest on human reason, which of itself is impotent to construct true philosophy.

The very word "philosophy" should have given the representatives of these schools pause. Does the word not mean "love of wisdom"? That requires, then, the presence of a subject who loves, and of an object existing in relation with that subject. Saint Paul, in preaching the wisdom of God, to be welcomed by faith working through love, met the needs of that definition in an ancient world where the competition of philosophical schools was driving people by reaction to either skepticism or superstition. In Christianizing philosophy, on the basis of the teaching of the Word of God, the Fathers raised intellectual speculation to the highest level of which it is capable, showing not only the tight mutual entailment of doctrines but also their harmony with human need and the condition of the cosmos. With the high medieval Schoolmen, up to Thomas, faith still remained the starting point of speculation. Modern philosophy, however, beginning in France with Descartes, who locates the foundation of knowledge in man, and in England with Francis Bacon, who locates it in exterior nature, renews what Bautain calls "the errors already exhausted by the pagans."[13] The systems that ensue—materialism, empiricism,

---

11. Cited P. Poupard, *L'Abbé Louis Bautain,* op. cit., p. 157.
12. Cited ibid., p. 158.
13. L. Bautain, *La Philosophie du Christianizme,* op. cit, II, p. 17.

rationalism, Eclecticism, Idealism—have abandoned the revealed source of true wisdom and inevitably a general skepticism results.

How, then, *should* a Christian philosophy be written? How can it present itself as the truth for which pagan or neo-pagan philosophical teaching aroused the desire, but without the power to satisfy it? As in the early centuries, Christianity has to present itself with the characteristics of universality and infallibility vainly sought in human doctrines since these qualities belong only to God. To replace the chimera of a philosophical religion with the truth of a Christian philosophy will not be innovation but a return to the genuine tradition of the Church. Once the historic revelation is given, there can be no question of an autonomous philosophy. As Bautain writes, "What is the sovereignty of reason in face of the sovereignty of faith? Can there be two sovereigns, or two masters in the kingdom of truth?"[14] As Bautain's chief modern interpreter, Paul Poupard, puts it:

> Now that eternal Truth has manifested itself to the world by its Word, the only wisdom henceforth possible for man is to listen to this incarnate divine Wisdom; it is from the Son, from whom the Father has no secrets, that, made docile by the movement of the Spirit, we shall receive in a sure fashion what the philosophers propose with no certitude: the knowledge of God, of man and of the universe.[15]

The role of philosophy is not to discover truths. Rather, it is to verify or justify the truths that issue from revelation, whether that be the primordial, if rudimentary, revelation, as communicated by tradition in human culture at large, or the historic and climactic revelation, as laid out in the sacred tradition of the Church.

By revelation God has made us participate in his own knowledge, than which there can be none more certain or more universal. The exploration of revelation's inexhaustibly rich intelligibility and its deployment by way of illuminating particular sectors of human or cosmic activity, will never be exhausted by the human mind. This participated knowledge of God's own unified understanding gathers together in a coherent fashion all valid elements in the cognitive disciplines practiced by mankind, and allows us, at least in an inchoate manner, to accede to a unitary science which will find its ultimate perfection

---

14. Cited P. Poupard, *L'Abbé Louis Bautain,* op. cit., p. 241.
15. P. Poupard, *L'Abbé Louis Bautain,* op. cit., p. 242.

beyond death in the vision of God. Theology and philosophy must be synthesized in the service of this goal, reversing the centuries-long process of separation which has rendered them moribund and sterile.

In effect, we can say, Bautain recreated a type of Christian Platonism in nineteenth-century Latin Catholicism. Most philosophers, he thought, have neglected the all-important distinction between reason and intellect, with the notable exception of Plato. Reason is a faculty situated midway between the sensuous and the intelligible orders. Phenomena are vital to its functioning, through the senses, memory, and imagination. But so also are higher principles which reason can only receive from intellect and without which it cannot apply itself to its proper work. As for intellect: as Plato divined, and the Word of God disclosed, it is the immortal soul made to contemplate eternal truth. Unfortunately, the essentially inferior capacity we call reason seeks to justify its procedures by kinds of argumentation that are in principle beyond its capacity to ground. Hence the continual oscillation between realism and Idealism to which the history of philosophy bears witness. Kant's attempt to determine by critical reason what theoretical reason can know is a typical example of what happens when reason exceeds its sphere. Famously, the Kantian critique ends in the false conclusion that ontology or metaphysics, a science of being, is impossible. In actuality, the divine idea which founds the existence of the world manifests itself to intellectual intuition as at once divine substance and the cause of phenomena, but to appreciate this requires a turning of the intellect towards the divine light. For that, humility of heart is needed, the quality which, as mentioned in the introduction to the present book, Saint Augustine had already identified as a moral precondition of the kind of understanding which leads, precisely, to faith. Though Bautain recognizes the existence of outstanding masters, geniuses who transmit spiritual life in the intellectual order and thus can count as spiritual fathers of humanity (he evidently regarded Plato as such, along with the Old Testament prophets and above all the prophetic mind of Jesus Christ which was personally united to the divine Word), nonetheless the statistically normal media of intellectual contact with God—normal for most people, then—are, rather, speech and tradition which, when they reflect revelation, fertilize human knowledge at the level of intellect, and so reorient the activity of reason in a proper way.

Bautain's Apologetics

Accordingly, Bautain's version of apologetics does not consist in attempting to prove the fact of revelation or the credibility of its contents by means of reason. That for him is a patent example of the wrong tool. Indeed, one important if negative task of apologetics is to show the debility of reason, reason's incapacity to answer the questions of our origin, our destiny and the meaning of our life in between. More positively, apologetics seeks in a first stage to show how the idea of God communicated in primordial revelation by "refraction" in the prism of human consciousness, gives rise to the key ideas of beauty, goodness and truth—the transcendental determinations of being—which are the lamps of all human existence, guiding our path to what is aesthetically, morally, and cognitively worthwhile. Then at a second stage, apologetics sets out to demonstrate that the obscurities of human culture—where this refracted idea has only a fragile hold on people's attention—are dispelled by the Judeo-Christian revelation, where from the patriarchs, through the history of Israel, to Jesus and the apostles the Word of God becomes ever more lucidly articulated. Then third and finally, Bautain hands to apologists the enormous task of showing that all sectors of human inquiry are illuminated by this Word, of which the example he gives most frequently is the maieutic role for human understanding of the revelation of the Trinity, which draws our attention to "the law of the ternary," *la loi du ternaire*. The simplest geometrical figure is composed from three lines, each body has three dimensions, three words constitute the proposition, three propositions (the syllogism, despite his attack on Aristotle's logic) constitute reasoning. That is an example of how the truth of dogma is demonstrated by the fecundity of its applications, and in no other way.

In the following century, "Christian philosophy," Bautain's key idea, would be separated from the connotations of fideism and traditionalism with which he had charged it. (Chapter 7 of this study, on the work of Etienne Gilson, will investigate why.) In the next chapter we shall see how the magisterium of the nineteenth-century Catholic Church sought to intervene rather more directly in regard to all three thinkers considered so far—Hermes, Günther, Bautain.

Chapter 5

Magisterial Interventions: Gregory XVI and Pius IX

Introduction

So far in this study we have looked at three thinkers, each with an original "take" on the relation of faith and reason. What we have not yet considered is the reaction to these theologies of church authority. And yet the work of all of these writers was the object of censure by the ecclesiastical magisterium, whether posthumously or in their lifetimes, whether sharply or more mildly. For those who consider that theology necessarily takes, among other things, an *ecclesial* form, which makes approbation—or at any rate nondisapprobation—by church office one crucial criterion of acceptability, the travails endured by *Hermesianismus, Güntherianismus* and *bautainisme* at the hands of bishops and popes will be of importance in principle.[1] For other students of these figures, the topic I shall be investigating in this chapter belongs rather to the "reception history" of the relevant texts and ideas—and, of course, to the wider dynamics of nineteenth-century church history.

Those "wider dynamics" certainly need to be borne in mind. The Church is not an academic seminar in permanent session: magisterial interventions cannot be completely separated from issues of Church governance. If a particular theology, or philosophy, is entwined with other issues in society, whether ecclesial society or civil society, this will not be irrelevant to how it is viewed by those who consider themselves guardians of the Church's common life.

---

1. For a concise account, see A. Dulles, SJ, *Magisterium. Teacher and Guardian of the Faith*, op. cit. A fuller study is F. A. Sullivan, SJ, *Magisterium. Teaching Authority in the Catholic Church* (New York, 1983).

That is so, not necessarily because episcopate and papacy in making doctrinal judgments are instrumentalizing questions of truth, but because pastoral considerations enter into responsible thinking when the question is, Should theology or philosophy X or Y be encouraged or discouraged—not least in some particular place or at some particular time?

Gregory XVI

Georg Hermes' death in 1831 coincided with the election to the papacy of a Camaldolese monk, Maurus Cappellari, whose fifteen-year pontificate saw the first—if not the most weighty—censure of Hermesian teaching. Cappellari was born in 1775 in a sub-Alpine region of northern Italy, to a family of minor gentry. In 1783 he entered the monastery of San Michele at Murano, in the lagoon of Venice. At this period the Camaldolese Order in Italy had bifurcated into distinct Congregations, which, contrary to the original Camaldolese inspiration, were either fully eremitical in character or totally coenobitic (rather than combining the two). The Congregation Cappellari joined was coenobitic, study-oriented, and noted for its humanistic culture. Despite a lack of the more expensive scientific equipment, such as state-of-the-art telescopes, Capellari taught natural science as well as philosophy at Murano until in 1795 he was called to Rome to assist the Procurator of the Congregation, an official appointed to mediate its relations with the Holy See. Except for a period when expelled by the French for opposing the doctrines of the Revolution, Cappellari spent the rest of his life in Rome, where he became a trusted counselor of Pope Pius VIII. Not irrelevant to his rise was his 1799 treatise *Il Trionfo della Santa Sede*, a spirited defense of the Roman primacy against those, notably in Germany, Holland and France who sought to reduce it to a form of subordinated service to the wider episcopate: Febronians in Germany, Jansenists in Holland, Gallicans in France.[2] Not much in this background equipped him to deal with Catholic Kantianism.

---

2. M. Cappellari, *Il trionfo della Santa Sede contro gli assalti dei Novatori, respinti e combattiti colle stesse loro armi* (Rome, 1799). It was reprinted at Venice in 1832, the year after Cappellari's election to the papacy.

Gregory and Hermes

Relevant to Cappellari's dealings with the Hermesians is his role in drafting Pius VIII's letter to the German bishops on marriages between Catholics and Protestants—than which, at first sight, any topic further removed from Hermes' "positive" and "philosophical" introductions to theology could scarcely be conceived. That a quarrel between the Catholic Church and the Prussian state over the issue of mixed marriages should be relevant to the fate of Hermesianism illustrates my claim about the interweaving of doctrine and pastoralia. Also worth noting more generally is the psychology of the papal court at the time of Hermes' death. The years 1830 to 1835 witnessed major civil upheavals in Europe, notably in France, Poland, Spain, Portugal and Italy itself, creating a climate of anxiety. Was the turmoil of the revolutionary period from 1789 to 1815 about to be reenacted, with a repetition of the accompanying destruction of church institutions and influence, not to say outright prescription of the faith? The pontificate was marred by five outbreaks of civil violence in the Papal States, in 1831 (put down by Austrian arms), and then again in 1833, 1837, 1843 and 1845. On four occasions, Gregory legislated for situations of emergency in the event of a pope's death, envisaging the holding of conclaves either outside Rome or, if in the city, then in conditions of enforced haste.[3]

Meanwhile in Germany, Hermesianism was by 1835 virtually the official philosophy and theology of the Church in the kingdom of Prussia—at any rate for the dioceses of the West, where the bishops, most of whose predecessors, before 1806, had been prince-bishops, were accustomed, partly under Febronian influence, to determine policy with little, if any, reference to the Holy See. (The advance of Hermesianism in the eastern dioceses, formed from the other strongly Catholic region of the country, Silesia, is, for want of evidence, harder to assess, though the theology faculty at Breslau was Hermesian. Hermesians could also be found in the kingdom of Hanover and the grand duchy of Nassau.[4]) The rapid dissemination of Hermesian influence in the theology faculties, seminaries and cathedral chapters of the Rhineland and Westphalia was undoubtedly due in part, however,

---

3. See G. Martina, sj, *Pio IX* [1846–1850] (Rome, 1974), p. 53.
4. H. W. Schwedt, "Georg Hermes," art. cit., pp. 222, 224–226.

to the support given it by civil authorities. The aim of the Prussian state at this period was to integrate the new population it had acquired in the 1815 European peace settlement at the Congress of Vienna by reducing and where possible eliminating the religious differences among them. The restructuring of established Protestantism as a combined Lutheran-Evangelical Church (that is, synthesizing the two distinct Reformation traditions of Lutheranism and Calvinism) was the—mostly—successful realization of a wider strategy which, in regard to Catholicism, had two prongs.

The first was to break down church resistance to mixed marriages between Catholics and Protestants, to the solemnization of such marriages before Catholic or Protestant ministers indifferently, and to the education of children as Protestants if that seemed appropriate. The second was wherever possible to secure the appointment of Hermesian professors and senior clerics. In the eyes of government strategists, Hermesianism, a combined form of philosophy and theology indebted to Kant, could only bring Catholicism closer to both civic reason and Protestantism. After all, Kant's contribution to religious thought was precisely that of a rationally enlightened albeit non-churchgoing Lutheran. And in any case, as a student of Hermes' Protestant contemporary F.D.E. Schleiermacher has remarked, in the eyes of Prussian officialdom, unused to the non-negotiable ecclesial commitments of Catholic theology, "[t]eaching at a public university" (such as the Friedrich Wilhelms Universität at Bonn) "was . . . the act of a civil servant."[5] The two prongs converged. Pope Pius VIII had already agreed that Catholic priests could attend passively and witness formally weddings where no appropriate marriage promises about the future religious practice of spouses and any offspring had been given. Prussia's determination to press the Church for further concessions in this matter gave extra impetus to the emerging controversy over Hermes' thought.

The first stirrings of German Catholic discontent with the steady advances of Hermesianism date from the years 1825 to 1829, when the vicar general of the diocese of Münster, Clemens August von Droste zu Vischering, later to be Archbishop of Cologne and to

---

5. R. Crouter, *Friedrich Schleiermacher. Between Enlightenment and Romanticism,* op cit., p. 16.

undergo arrest and imprisonment for impeding Prussian law, forbad his ordinands to attend Hermes' lectures at Bonn. But on Hermes' death in 1831 no one in the nunciatures or the Roman Congregations could be found who had even heard his name.[6] In 1832, however, a formal complaint was made by a parish priest to the nuncio in Munich (the Prussian government allowed no nuncio to operate in Berlin), alleging that in his *Philosophische Einleitung* Hermes had made reason the "principal norm and unique medium for knowledge of supernatural truths."[7] That was at any rate a partial misunderstanding: reason for Hermes was not a principle for knowing the content of supernatural revelation, only a principle for crediting its fundamental claim to be true (whatever its particular contents might turn out to be). The Roman Curia, laboring under the misapprehension that the name "Hermes" was a pseudonym taken from the Greek god of interpretation, knew even less of the matter than did the outraged parish priest.

The Roman authorities, preoccupied with the assault in the early 1830s on legitimist Catholic rulers, not least by the French secular priest and later apostate, Robert Félicité de Lamennais (the encyclical *Singulari nos*, on the errors of Lamennais, was promulgated in 1834),[8] and handicapped by a limited acquaintance with the German language, were slow to act. Words of caution emanated from the Vienna nuncio, alerted by visitors from north Germany. Hermes' teaching was complex. Modified, it might be capable of bearing a Catholic sense. Hermes' most substantial critic, Heinrich Klee (1800–1840), who would leave Hermesian Bonn in 1839 to take up the chair of theology at Munich, judged that Hermes had made human wisdom, wrongly, the foundation of faith and the foundation, more especially, of the certainty of faith, but he sought only an official Roman *monitum*, or warning, to be sent to the German bishops. A condemnation, by giving the appearance of hostility to reason, would only please the enemies of the Church.[9] To defend their master, Hermes' pupils set

---

6. H. W. Schwedt, *Das römische Urteil über Georg Hermes, 1775–1831. Ein Beitrag zur Geschichte der Inquisition im 19. Jahrhundert* (Rome, Freiburg, Vienna, 1980), p. 23.

7. Ibid., p. 33.

8. For this figure, see A. Vidler, *Prophecy and Papacy. A Study of Lamennais, the Church and the Revolution* (London, 1954).

9. H. W. Schwedt, *Das römische Urteil über Georg Hermes, 1775–1831*, op. cit., p. 104.

about publishing a posthumous work from his hand, *Christkatholisch Dogmatik* ("Christian and Catholic Dogmatics") in three volumes, of which the first two appeared in 1834, and the third, which was unfinished, the year after. Before the emergence of volume three of the dogmatics, a commission of Roman cardinals had met and—based on excerpts chosen and translated by two German-speaking consultors—delivered a negative verdict on the two Introductions and the first volume of the dogmatics. Gregory wrote the Brief against Hermesianism personally, which explains why its bibliography, probably given him by the consultors, could include works not submitted to the cardinalatial consultation.

This manner of proceeding caused considerable confusion, and rendered the interpretation of the Brief something of a task for a Solomon come to judgment.[10] Published in 1835 and known according to Curial style from its opening words *Dum acerbissimas,* it opens by connecting Hermes' writings to the wider ideological uproar in Europe. The link Gregory found was twofold. First: advocacy of the critical philosophy—"positive doubt"—as the basis of the theological enterprise. In the *Philosophische Einleitung* Hermes described how he had prescribed for himself strong medicine: "To doubt as long as possible, and then for the first time definitively to decide where I could show an absolute necessitation of reason in favor of such decision."[11] Positive doubt—the *dubium hermesianum*—was understood at Rome, correctly or not, as real, serious doubt. It was to be distinguished, then, from the (more acceptable) *dubium cartesianum,* a fictive or hypothetical doubt invoked only in order to generate arguments helpful to Catholic doctrine.[12]

The second possible linkage between Hermesianism and the contemporary assaults on traditional authority was an exaltation of reason as the only organ human beings have for recognizing some putatively supernatural truth. With the important nuance that it is *practical* reason we are speaking of, Hermes had held just that. What

---

10. There is a German language collection of the relevant documents: *Damnatio et prohibition operum Georgii Hermes in tribus tomis Germanica lingua editorum* (Rome, 1835).

11. G. Hermes, *Einleitung in die christkatholische Theologie, Erster Teil: Philosophische Einleitung,* op. cit., p. x.

12. K. Eschweiler, *Die zwei Wege der neueren Theologie,* op. cit., p. 126.

"expresses itself in the thinking and acting of the believer," he had written, is "surrender to the leading of reason."[13] If we ask how such "surrender" (*Hingebenheit*) can engender a Christian existence, Hermes' reply runs: "Doubt-addicted proof is the root and condition of devout faith, just as devout faith is the root and condition of all virtue."[14]

Conscious perhaps of the linguistic and conceptual gulf which separated author and critic, Gregory did not state explicitly that these positions are fully exemplified in Hermes' works. He contented himself with saying that they are, in the first place, false, and, in the second, have been denounced to the apostolic see as insinuated by Hermes' writings. Commenting on a number of themes in fundamental theology and soteriology which the cardinal consultors found, in Hermes' version, either dangerously ambiguous or frankly "alien to Catholic teaching," Gregory declares that the propositions identified lead to skepticism, indifferentism, and the subversion of divine faith. We are not surprised to find the theme of the act of faith singled out here — fundamental theology was at the heart of this dispute. The soteriological concern turned on Hermes' notion that only "actual" grace, providing a momentary assistance against willful temptation, is necessary for practical reason to proceed to the act of faith — and not the more radical sanctifying grace, taken as transforming the conditions of operation of mind and will, which is what traditional theologians would have argued. The minimalizing of any notion of the grace needed for faith will have suggested to the cardinals that Hermes had a thin doctrine of original sin, redemption — the antidote to original sin — and justification — the manner of laying hold of that antidote. Hermes' inclination is to treat original sin as the predominance of the senses over the intellect, and paradisal righteousness (original or regained) as purity of rational existence in perfect, albeit grace-assisted, self-mastery — rather than the loss or perdurance of intimate communion with God.[15] In terms of fundamental theology, the weakness of Hermesianism was spotted three-quarters of a century later by the innovative Jesuit theologian Pierre Rousselot, who will be appearing

---

13. G. Hermes, *Einleitung in die christkatholische Theologie, Erster Teil: Philosophische Einleitung*, op. cit., p. xviii.

14. Ibid., p. xvii.

15. K. Eschweiler, *Die zwei Wege der neueren Theologie*, op. cit., pp. 120–121.

in Chapter 9. For Hermes, grace justifies all right—but it *does not illuminate*.[16]

Back in Germany, the Hermesians reacted to the Brief by deeming the pope ill-informed, a "mere marionette of German intriguers."[17] Some of the pope's inferences were insecure. While it was the case that Hermesians opposed Ultramontanism as obscurantist (Ultramontane opponents dubbed them "rationalists in soutanes"[18]), in the matter of church reform the Hermesians kept at arms' length the really radical Liberal Catholicism which grew up in southwest Germany in the 1820s and '30s under pressure from the progressive bourgeoisie: its program was government by synods with lay involvement, abolition of clerical celibacy, and a vernacular Liturgy.[19] Hermesians sought a degree of reform of church life but under the leadership of bishops.[20] In a period of waxing self-confidence in Prussian Protestantism,[21] Hermes was sufficiently removed from crypto-Protestantism to complain of "intolerant" Protestant attacks on Catholicism, attacks which had redoubled in the wake of the fourth centenary of Luther's revolt and the union of the Lutheran and Reformed Churches in Prussia (both events in his adult lifetime).[22] Nonetheless the removal from teaching of Hermesian professors began at once at Bonn, by the hands of Droste zu Vischering, now Archbishop of Cologne.[23] In 1836 a leading Hermesian published *Acta Hermesiana*, a work designed to show Rome had condemned a "pseudo-Hermes" and was received in audience by the pope who heard him out. The General of the Jesuits told its author the sublimely obvious. It was Hermes' theological method which had offended the pope.

---

16. P. Rousselot, *The Eyes of Faith and Answer to Two Attacks* (English translation, New York, 1990), p. 22.
17. H. W. Schwedt, *Das römische Urteil über Georg Hermes*, 1775–1831, op. cit., p. 199.
18. Idem., "Georg Hermes," art. cit., p. 222.
19. K. Schatz, *Zwischen Säkularisation und Zweitem Vatikanum*, op. cit., pp. 73–75.
20. C. Weber, *Aufklärung und Orthodoxie am Mittelrhein*, 1820–1850 (Paderborn, 1973).
21. R. Bigler, *The Politics of German Protestantism. The Rise of the Protestant Church Elite in Prussia, 1815–1848* (Berkeley, CA, 1972).
22. See his *Einleitung in die christkatholische Theologie, Erster Teil: Philosophische Einleitung*, op. cit., p. xii.
23. R. Lill, "Cologne, Mixed Marriage Dispute," in *New Catholic Encyclopaedia* 3 (New York, 1967), p. 1018. This article condenses a major study by the same author: *Die Beilegung der Kölner Wirren, 1840–1842* (Dusseldorf, 1962).

Gregory and Bautain

We have not yet finished with Gregory, in whose pontificate the case of Bautain opens as well, running parallel with that of Hermes. In contrast with Hermes, Bautain's doctrinal case took place fundamentally in the local church with objections lodged by his bishop, Jean-François Le Pappe de Trévern, the metropolitan of Strasbourg, Legitimist, Gallican, *grand seigneur*. Le Pappe de Trévern had welcomed Bautain's ordination with enthusiasm, making him a canon of his cathedral immediately after he was priested. This was that *rara avis*, a scholarly, intellectual ordination candidate with a high culture, in sharp contrast to the Alsatian clergy whose *patois* the bishop often failed to understand. Not till 1833–1834, so between four and five years later, did the bishop indicate anxiety about Bautain's teaching, and in interviews seek to convince him that his was not the mind of the Fathers of the first six centuries, to whom Bautain had appealed. The controversy became public. Bautain was attacked by many clerical writers, notably Sulpicians and Jesuits; he was defended by the local Prefect and various Government ministers in the July Monarchy of King Louis-Philippe.[24]

Why? These were culture wars. The Strasbourg bishop was holding up the ideal of seventeenth-century France, the golden age of the *ancien régime*, whose Scholastic philosophy and theology had been one of its glories. In contrast, the constitutional liberals of the bourgeois monarchy associated Bautain's desire for a "new philosophy," to replace Scholasticism, with the liberal progress proper to the dynamic nineteenth century—not, then, with returning to the patristic sources which was more the spirit in which Bautain himself conceived it.

Aside from culture wars, a serious doctrinal point was also in view. Rightly, in the light of scripture and tradition, Bautain refused to make faith the *inevitable* conclusion to a process of rational argument. But in the course of making this refusal, he also, wrongly (by the same lights) sought to deprive faith of its character as *reasonable* adherence to the Word of God. Though ignorant of Hermes, the Strasbourg prelate showed a marked tendency to make faith, like the Hermesians, the "necessary conclusion of a rational demonstration"—albeit a

---

24. P. Poupard, *L'Abbé Louis Bautain*, op. cit., pp. 191–194.

demonstration by pure reason, not practical.[25] In questions put formally to Bautain in April 1834, his bishop asked whether reasoning can prove the existence of God and the divine perfections and how; whether the truth of the Mosaic revelation can be proved by reasoning; and how Bautain would convince of the truth of Christian revelation a Jew, a Deist, and, as he put it "all those who reject it, and those too who without admitting it desire it." Bautain was further interrogated as to whether faith, or adherence to Christian revelation, did not rest on the miracles of Christ, above all his Resurrection, and how these could be proved other than by reference to the authenticity of the writings left by eyewitnesses; and, more widely, as to whether in various matters reason did not precede faith and lead to it. In sum, as the seventh and last question phrased it,

> However enfeebled reason is by original sin, does it not retain sufficient force and clarity to guide us with certainty to the existence of God, to the revelation made to the Jews by Moses and to Christians by the adorable God-man?[26]

To the bishop's questions, Bautain returned nuanced replies, which can be summed up in turn in the last sentence of his response:

> Demonstration by reasoning of the truth of Revelation [wrote Bautain to the bishop] implies the prior existence of Revelation and belief in its truth; thus reason, before proving Revelation, has already been enlightened and vivified by its power.[27]

At the end of September, the bishop issued a formal *Avertissement*, declaring Bautain's teaching unsound; at the start of November he withdrew from him all ministerial faculties. Bautain retorted that the bishop had acted *ultra vires*. The Church allows free discussion of all three key questions: the nature of certainty and the manner in which it is acquired; the relations between faith and reason; the proofs of the existence of God. Moreover, Le Pappe de Trévern's own doctrine that the force of philosophical or other arguments suffices by itself to engender faith was itself impossible to reconcile with the Second Council of Orange, and thus with the conciliar tradition of the

---

25. Ibid., p. 196.
26. Cited ibid., p. 202.
27. Cited ibid., p. 202.

Church since for that council it is divine grace, not human reasoning, which is the *initium fidei*, the "beginning of faith." The bishop was a Semi-Pelagian. In Germany, his *Avertissement* certainly encouraged the Hermesians.[28]

Meanwhile Le Pappe de Trévern had sent the *Avertissement* to Rome and from the Curia there proceeded in December 1834 a response which congratulated the bishop on his zeal for orthodoxy but made no attempt to resolve the disputed question. Bautain, whom this arrow had pricked rather than wounded, appealed to what was increasingly the most prestigious Catholic theological faculty of the period, Tübingen, from where its leading light, Johann Adam Möhler, whom Bautain could suppose supportive,[29] composed in March 1835 a lengthy reply which gave Bautain some second thoughts.[30] Though sympathetic, it was, through its nuanced adjudication of the faith-reason relation, by no means as wholehearted in his support as he expected.

Möhler praised Bautain for abandoning a theological method which merely sought to "demonstrate from without."

> You fight against a theology which furnishes a quantity of proofs, but does not teach knowledge of the very object which has to be proved; against

---

28. J. B. Braun, *Die Lehren des sogenannten Hermesianismus über das Verhältnis der Vernunft zur Offenbarung gutgeheissen, und die entgegenstehenden Ansichten als falsch und gefährlich verworfen von dem Bischofe von Strassburg, Herrn Le Pappe de Trévern* (Bonn, 1835).

29. On the grounds of an 1834 review: J. A. Möhler, "Recension über 'De l'enseignement de la philosophie en France au dix-neuvième siècle,' par l'Abbé Bautain, professeur de philosophie à la Faculté des letters de Strassbourg, docteur en Médecine, etc., à Strassbourg, 1833," *Theologische Quartalschrift* 16 (1834), pp. 138–152. The Tübingen school was rightly reputed to be anti-Hermesian—though Möhler himself would leave the University for Munich the following year.

30. Ibid., p. 211. For Möhler's German text, see "Sendschriben an Herrns Bautain, Professor der Philosophischen Fakultät zu Strassburg," in ibid. 17 (1835), pp. 421–453; a modern French translation, with explanatory notes, is found in P. Poupard, "Lettre de Möhler à Bautain sur les rapports de la raison et de la foi," *Revue des Sciences Philosophiques et Théologiques XLII*. 3 (1958), pp. 455–482. Möhler's Tübingen colleague Johannes Evangelist von Kuhn would later seek to identify the errors in the positions (at opposite "extremes") of Bautain and Hermes in "Über Glauben und Wissen, mit Rücksicht auf extremen Ansichten und Richtungen der Gegenwart," *Theologische Quartalschrift* 21 (1839), pp. 382–503. Kuhn's critique mirrors, on premises all his own, the papal and episcopal critiques; cf. also his "Princip und Methode der speculative theologie," ibid., 23 (1841), pp. 1–80, where Kuhn combines patristic texts and Idealist vocabulary to argue for the mutual immanence of faith and reason. Though faith may have a priority, it enjoys compatibility with speculative thought. On Kuhn's response to Hermes and Bautain, see G. Kaplan, *Answering the Enlightenment. The Catholic Recovery of Historical Revelation* (New York, 2002), pp. 112–122.

a theology which by force of arguments does not attain the heart of the matter, and which has a better idea about bringing men the garments of Christianity than of transforming them into Christians.[31]

But this was not to say that Möhler approved all of Bautain's formulations. Far from it. "Certain rectifications seem to me highly desirable."[32] Bautain had not distinguished sufficiently between, on the one hand, the saving faith which welcomes with joy the divinely sent Redeemer and makes possible the sanctification of the redeemed, and, on the other, the rational faith which recognizes God in creation, at any rate in those of the divine attributes which the revelation of nature can disclose. By a close analysis of the texts of the Second Council of Orange, Möhler explained how, in its attempt to isolate for special inspection the first sort of faith (certainly the more crucial in the perspective of man's ultimate goal), the synod showed its understanding that there was *another* sort of faith, by no means worthless though not of itself salvific, outside the Church. Humanity fallen and not yet set on the way of redemption retains, after all, experience of the cosmic creation. Moreover it moves in a cultural environment where the naming of God still goes on, even if the quality of the knowledge of God is now far different from the immediacy it enjoyed in Eden.

> *Having* to demonstrate [the existence of God] is the sign that the image of God is unspeakably obscured in us; but *being able* to demonstrate it is the sign that this image is not entirely suppressed, much less effaced.[33]

Möhler thought Bautain had confused the intrinsic truth of a demonstration with the recognition of that demonstration as valid. A refractory will often mean people do not want to recognize evidence or argument for what they are. When the practical consequences mean a change of lifestyle the badly disposed will soon make their excuses. Doubtless investigating possible miracles by itself does not *convince* anyone of the claims of the Gospel and the Church. But if the miracles were not intended at least to provoke consideration of those claims, why on earth were they enacted? The role of grace, on Möhler's

---

31. P. Poupard, "Lettre de Möhler à Bautain sur les rapports de la raison et de la foi," *Revue des Sciences Philosophiques et Théologiques*, art. cit., p. 464.
32. Ibid., p. 465.
33. Ibid., p. 472.

view, was to dispose the will to receive a duly attested fact (the question of the Resurrection was central here) in all its far-reaching implications. If the fact was *not* duly attested by reliable witnesses, "the sinner would evidently be excused when he does not believe."[34] The act of faith precedes the state of faith which alone allows "the deeper and scientific penetration of the content of faith," yet "this act of faith is itself also the work of reason with the will mysteriously sustained by grace."[35] By accepting one half, only, of this dialectic Bautain had, quite unnecessarily, ranged Anselm and Nazianzen against Aquinas and "in general all the theologians of the School."[36]

With clear support forthcoming neither for the bishop from Rome nor for Bautain from Tübingen, the interested parties agreed on a modified version of the *Avertissement* which Bautain and his collaborators signed in November 1835. But whereas Bautain saw a significant change of meaning in the modifications made, the bishop saw only unimportant rewordings designed to minimize humiliation for the signatories.

The condemnation of Hermes' writings in late 1835 emboldened Bautain, but did not prevent the bishop from sending Bautain's works to Rome in the hope of eliciting a condemnation from the Congregation of the Index. Bautain followed the parcel, in spring 1836, with an opposite end in view. He explained to the Curia that, in the wake of Hermesianism and what he termed "philosophisme" (rationalism more widely), he was taking the Church's side in refusing to affirm with his bishop that reason is the foundation of faith. But discussions with the leading theologian at the Collegio Romano, Giovanni Perrone—who would later play a major part in John Henry Newman's dealings with the Holy See over the question of the development of doctrine—convinced Bautain he had not made adequate concession to the element of truth in his bishop's view. One could give a place to reason in the process of coming to faith without being a rationalist or evacuating the role of grace.[37]

---

34. Ibid., p. 477.
35. Ibid., p. 479.
36. Ibid.
37. See A. Brent, "The Hermesian Dimension to the Newman-Perrone Dialogue," *Ephemerides Theologicae Lovanienses* 61 (1985), pp. 73–99.

The subsequent Roman letter to De Trévern asking him to receive Bautain back into the active ministry had nil effect. Bautain remained suspended from the priesthood until 1840 when a new bishop of Strasbourg reconciled him with the local church, inviting him to sign a slightly qualified version of the modified *Avertissement* which he found himself able to do.

Bautain returned to France convinced he had exaggerated the expression of what he called his "sentiment fidéiste," and minded to correct his system while, however, maintaining its distinctive tendency. He sought to express a doctrinally acceptable semi-fideism. The reason which can prove God's existence is what he now termed "developed" reason. By that he meant, as he explained, using the characteristic idiom of "mitigated traditionalism": "with reason, all the means and all the conditions of its exercise, and in the first place, language without which it cannot develop and whose primitive formation presupposes a higher aid given to man at the time of his origin."[38]

Thus while reason can indeed, in Bautain's revised position, prove God's existence (to limit oneself to that), "human reason," as he put it, "does not suffice for its own development," and this point he declared to "have a great importance against rationalism."[39] Only the primordial revelation made to Adam, and expressed in the linguistic expressions of religiosity found in all succeeding human culture, can enable reason to function adequately in divine matters. He remained, in other words, a mitigated traditionalist. In a wildly different context, his confidence in the referential value of religious "language games" might remind one of the later Wittgenstein.

Despite these reservations, the censures *bautainisme* suffered were not lost on Hermesians who appealed to the judgment on Bautain as an argument for the exoneration of Hermes, to which Gregory replied in audience:

> You are wrong: it is just as much an error to give everything to faith and nothing to reason as it is to give everything to reason and nothing to faith . . . But in any event you have not come to Rome to teach but to learn.[40]

---

38. Cited P. Poupard, *L'Abbé Louis Bautain,* op. cit., p. 221.

39. Ibid.

40. Cited in M. Cordovani. OP, "Gregorio XVI difensore della fede," in Miscellanea Historiae Pontificiae XIII. Gregorio XVI. *Miscellanea commemorativa. Prima Parte* (Rome, 1948), pp. 123–134, and here at p. 132.

Pius IX

Gregory XVI died on June 1, 1846. Just over two weeks later his successor, Giovanni Maria Mastai-Ferretti, was elected pope, taking the name of Pius IX. He was born at Ancona in 1792, like his predecessor to a family of the lower nobility. At school the onset of what appears to have been epilepsy saved him from conscription in the Napoleonic army, though continuing ill-health seemed to rule out finishing his subsequent studies for the priesthood. Nonetheless, after the intervention of Pius VII he was duly ordained, and in 1827 when only thirty-five named Archbishop of Spoleto. An enlightened conservative rather than, as rumored, a political liberal, the general amnesty he gave to political prisoners at the start of his pontificate was misinterpreted. The consequences were disproportionate. Giacomo Martina, author of a magisterial three-volume history of the pontificate, calls it "the beginning of a collective delirium on the part of public opinion."[41] It was the "spark which, falling on long accumulated powder, lit a fire that spread to the whole of Italy and a large part of Europe," and had its conclusion in the various European revolutions of 1848.[42]

Some account of the extreme political turbulence of the pontificate's beginning will serve as a foil for the contrasting equilibrium of Pius's *aperçus* on the faith-reason relation in the opening encyclical of his reign. In the days following the amnesty, a positive mania of festivity overtook Rome and other cities of the pontifical state, somewhat disorienting the pope who now enjoyed celebrity status. Pius initiated some moderate reforms, notably a degree of freedom for the press, and a council of lay notables to oversee administrative improvements. Wavering between moderates and conservatives, he soon found himself in the position of the sorcerer's apprentice—a comparison made by the Austrian chancellor, Metternich—unable to control the spirits he had summoned up.[43] Pius was (in this period) an Italian patriot, but radicals committed to a unitary national republic used the explosion of sentiment to raise popular expectations in the pontifical state, exacerbating feeling against Austria, hitherto the most solid of the Catholic powers. Such radicals, hostile in principle to the pope's temporal

---

41. G. Martina, sj, *Pio Nono [1846–1850]*, op. cit., p. 101.
42. Ibid.
43. Ibid., p. 127.

claims, were in any case little preoccupied by the good of the Church. Under pressure, Pius permitted the formation of a Civil Guard, and in March 1848, introduced representative government (though with a limited franchise, juridical incapacity to consider questions touching directly the life of the Church, and a papal power of veto over its decisions) under a constitutional charter allowing for all liberties except those of worship and propaganda. Naturally, liberals found it insufficient. By the end of the month, the pope had decided he could no longer guarantee the safety of the Roman Jesuits, known for their conservatism, and they left the city. With Habsburg-governed Milan in uproar, Pius came under pressure to support a war of liberation in Lombardy. His refusal to countenance resort to arms unleashed a crisis. Neither liberal nationalists nor radical democrats could tolerate the fidelity to the Charter of Pius's prime minister, Pellegrino Rossi. Rossi's assassination in November 1848 and an orchestrated demand that the pope accept a government reflecting the mind of his critics precipitated his flight, incognito, to the territory of the Kingdom of Naples. There followed the declaration of a Roman Republic with leaders who, though by no means altogether homogeneous in outlook, were determined to eliminate from public life the influence of the Church.[44]

Pius's subsequent appeal to the powers bore fruit. France, concerned to offset Austrian influence in Italy and, if possible, retain at Rome some elements of constitutionalism, enabled the pope to return on its bayonets. Pius came back convinced that his spiritual independence was incompatible with democratic forms. To repeat the constitutionalist experiment meant risking a replay of events so far. So far as central government was concerned, the Law of September 12, 1849 foresaw only consultative organs, not deliberative ones. This was fateful for the rest of his pontificate.[45] Henceforth "liberalism" no longer meant for Pius the amelioration of structures of governance. Rather, it meant *ideology*. It was the spirit of the Great Revolution of the West, inevitably antithetical to a Christian civilizational order. Such an order

---

44. Actually, the last contributing factor seems to have been the arrival on November 17 of a gift from the Bishop of Valence: the pyx (a kind of locket to carry the Eucharistic Host) Pius VI had carried on his chest in his enforced journey of exile to France. Pius IX took this to be a sign from heaven as to how he should tread. Ibid., p. 298.

45. Ibid., pp. 355, 366–369.

issued from natural law, supernatural revelation, and the recognition of historically founded legitimate rule, as affirmed by the Church. That uncompromising (but also coherent) attitude would guide his policy for the following twenty and more years. It did not prevent him, as temporal ruler, from making considerable advances in various domains: notably health care, free primary education, the prison service—though the cost of the first two to the treasury was small, given the gratuitous services offered by Religious, both women and men, in these domains.[46]

Pius and Hermes

Back in 1846, rumors were reaching Germany that the new pope was not a political liberal—the fear of the civil authorities in Austria—so much as he was a Hermesian. *Qui pluribus*, his first encyclical letter, published in November amid the tumultuous political uncertainties at Rome that year, took the form of a kind of "state of the Union" address to the universal Church.[47] It had certainly touched on the issue of faith and reason, but in deliberately balanced terms. At any rate for this topic, it is difficult to identify in it the negative qualities Martina alleges: its supposedly "harsh tone, pessimistic, without a gleam of light."[48] *Pace* accusations of crypto-Hermesianism, the letter *was* anti-fideist. But it was *also* anti-rationalist. The true position, the pope explains, is that faith and reason are reciprocally supportive. As he puts it:

> [T]hough faith is above reason, no real disagreement or opposition can ever be found between them; this is because both of them come from the same greatest source of unchanging and eternal truth, God. They give such reciprocal help to each other that true reason shows, maintains and protects the truth of the faith, while faith frees reason from all errors and wondrously enlightens, strengthens and perfects reason with the knowledge of divine matters.[49]

---

46. Idem., *Pio IX* [1851–1866] (Rome, 1986), pp. 9–12.

47. *Acta Pii IX*, I., pp. 6–24.

48. Ibid., p. 121. But in order to present this pope as self-conflicted, *un intimo dissidio nell'animo*, Martina needs to portray the encyclical in this light as a foil to the "moderation and personal warmth which Pius IX evidenced in his personal contacts," ibid.

49. *Qui pluribus*, 6.

Granted the tumultuous political circumstances in which the letter was written (and the politics were hardly nonideological), these comments on the faith-reason relation are remarkably serene.

For students of magisterial documents, the most troublesome passage will be the seventh section of *Qui pluribus*. There the pope attempts an exegesis of Saint Paul's phrase, *logikê latreia*, "reasonable worship," in the Letter to the Romans, chapter twelve.[50] Pius IX declared it to be "in the fullest agreement with reason itself to accept and strongly support doctrines which it has determined to have been revealed by God who can neither deceive nor be deceived."[51] Admittedly, the "proofs" of Christianity Pius proceeds to list do not include proofs from Kantian practical reason as interpreted by Hermes. The faith which "teaches for life and points towards salvation" has been established, we read, by the "birth, life, death and resurrection, wisdom, wonders and prophecies of Christ Jesus," along with, in apostolic and post-apostolic times, "the steadfastness of so many martyrs, and the glory of so many saints."[52] Still, Pius had clearly taught that reason can recognize that God is the institutor of faith, even though it must subsequently follow faith in relation to what God has revealed.[53] The cry went up, then, "Hermes has spoken through Pius."

To appease the Archbishop of Cologne, who had complained to nuncios and Roman cardinals that Hermesians were making shameless use of the encyclical, Pius issued a renewal of the relevant acts of his predecessor. That may be considered a preamble to the solemn confirmation of the condemnation of Hermes at the First Vatican Council, over which Pius presided.

Pius and Günther

In the 1850s, Pius was actually far more concerned with the Güntherians. The way the wind was blowing was already apparent from his 1856 encyclical, *Singulari quidem,* on the concordat agreed between Rome and the Austrian Empire of Franz Joseph, "our dear

---

50. Romans 12: 1.
51. *Qui pluribus*, 7.
52. Ibid., 8.
53. Ibid., 9.

son in Jesus Christ, emperor of Austria and apostolic king."[54] The concordat was preceded by an 1850 set of ordinances reflecting a conscientious as well as a political decision on Franz Joseph's part. He now recognized the full liberty of the bishops and faithful in communications with Rome "about spiritual matters," while at the same time assuring the bishops of the support of the civil authority in their legislative and judicial decisions. This was music to papal ears. "The ideal Pius IX wanted to realize was: freedom *and* the support of the state."[55] The concordat signed in 1855 with the Habsburg government—now in its "neo-absolutist" phase—did not make of Austria in all regards a formally Catholic polity, not least because the emperors saw themselves as protectors of the other confessions. Nonetheless, despite what Rome regarded as incoherences (the mixed marriages issue proved irresoluble, and the Episcopal right to a "preventive censure" of religious literature remained a dead letter), Josephinism had passed into history.[56] Of course Günther, the disciple of Clemens Maria Hofbauer, was personally no Josephinist. But in the new situation, what the pope, and indeed bishops in the empire, made of Güntherianism suddenly began to count for a great deal more—at any rate for the crucial period when Günther's case was raised and settled. In 1870 (when, for him, it was too late), liberal constitutionalists would secure the unilateral repudiation of the concordat from a monarchy weakened both by its 1866 defeat in the Austro-Prussian war and the need to accommodate the Hungarians, whose ruling class was chiefly Calvinist, in the 1867 *Ausgleich* ("compromise") which turned the empire into the last of its succeeding incarnations: Austria-Hungary. Only the very farsighted could have foreseen that outcome fifteen years before.

In *Singulari quidem*, then, after various ceremonious remarks, Pius IX went on to identify as the two chief intellectual evils of the day, indifferentism and rationalism. On the latter Pius comments:

> This tender mother [i.e., the Church] recognizes and justly maintains that reason is the most notable of the heavenly gifts since it is through reason

---

54. Idem., *Singulari quidem*, 1.
55. G. Martina, sj, *Pio IX* [1851–1866], op. cit., p. 64.
56. For an evaluation, see ibid., pp. 203–209.

that we raise ourselves above the senses and display a certain image of God in ourselves.[57]

Seeking until we find we then accept with faith what is proposed to us to be believed. But, adds the pope:

> [W]e must also believe, in addition, that there is nothing else to believe and to seek once we have found and believed what was taught by Christ who does not command us to seek anything other than what he taught.[58]

It seems not implausible to suppose that Günther is in mind in this last sentence not least because by the spring of 1856 there was already a question mark against his name at Rome.[59] In the German lands, church circles were aware of his personal apostolic fervor, and the success with which his writings had deflected people from philosophical pantheism. But by the mid 1850s the voice of the Hegelian siren was largely stilled, and what came uppermost in the minds of the senior clergy was the disquieting boldness of Günther's ideas and ambitions —to render the truths of revelation truths of reason for the first time. Above all was this the case in milieu unsympathetic to post-Cartesian philosophy.

Moreover, during the attempted revolution of 1848 in Austria, the Güntherians came to be regarded as unsound on the question of political Liberalism, which left them in bad odor afterwards. Given their hostility to Western medieval thought-ways, what debts would they acknowledge to a form of political legitimacy inherited from the same period of Christendom? Their confidence in the eventual victory of Günther's system made them regard with equanimity the liberal freedoms—of the press, of religion, and the public expression of conscience.[60] After the passing of the crisis of the year of revolutions, a new archbishop of Vienna, Joseph Othmar von Rauscher, erstwhile tutor of Franz Joseph, studied to frustrate them.

---

57. *Singulari quidem*, 6.
58. Ibid.
59. The Archives of the Congregation of the Index include *Acta* pertinent to Günther's case from 1855 to 1857: G. Martina, sj, *Pio IX* [1851–1866], op. cit., p. 612, note 23. But Martina ascribes the beginning of the process against him to April 1853: paradoxically it took the form of a decision not, for the moment, to proceed, ibid., p. 614.
60. A. Bunnell, *Before Infallibility. Liberal Catholicism in Biedermeier Vienna*, op. cit., p. 124.

Further north, in the German Confederation, a number of former Hermesians had rallied to Güntherianism, above all at Bonn but also at Breslau, and now the old anti-Hermesian front began to reform, especially in the Rhineland.⁶¹ When a Güntherian was proposed as professor of dogma at Trier the consequence was German delation of Günther's writings to the Congregation of the Index.

All was not yet lost. Günther retained powerful Church allies: notably his former pupil Cardinal Friedrich Schwarzenberg, Archbishop of Prague, the Archbishop of Breslau, Heinrich Förster, and at Rome itself the abbot of the papal basilica of Saint Paul's without the Walls, Simplicio Papalettere (later, abbot of Monte Cassino, where he fell foul of the pope for inviting the despoiler of the Papal States, Victor Emmanuel II, to Benedict's abbey, and was obliged to resign⁶²). Most tellingly of all, Günther was supported by the chamberlain of the papal court, Clemens August von Hohenlohe-Schillingsfürst, a German prince.⁶³ In Adam Bunnell's words: "Although fought on Roman soil, the battle was a peculiarly German battle; fought by German academics, ecclesiastics and diplomats on the turf of Italian bureaucrats."⁶⁴

The Congregation of the Index proposed that either Günther or his representatives should come to Rome for talks. In the end, the "representatives" came. Their barely concealed contempt for the condition of Roman philosophy did not commend them.⁶⁵

Caught between conflicting pressures, Pius IX had no desire to crush Günther.⁶⁶ Perhaps Günther erred on the side of theological rationalism; but there were others whose sins were at least equally serious in the contrary direction. In exactly the same period, more precisely in 1855, the Congregation of the Index required of the French

---

61. R. Aubert, "Les sciences ecclésiastiques jusqu'au Concile du Vatican" in idem., *Le pontificat de Pie IX* [1846–1878] (Paris 1952), p. 201.

62. T. Leccisotti, "Pio IX e il 'caso' dell' abate Papalettere (1860–1863)," *Pio IX* 4 (1975), pp. 204–279.

63. Other supporters were the Wolter brothers, the founders of the archabbey of Beuron, and bishops in Trier, Münster and Laibach. Some members of the Catholic Tübingen school, notably Möhler and Staudenmaier, were influenced by him. For a full catalogue of names, see J. Reikerstorfer, "Anton Günther," art. cit., pp. 269–270.

64. A. Bunnell, *Before Infallibility,* op. cit., p. 154.

65. G. Martina, sj, *Pio IX* [1851–1866], op. cit., p. 614.

66. For Pius's personal attitude, see ibid.

layman, Antoine Bonnetty, editor of *Annales de Philosophie chrétienne*, subscription to four propositions, amounting to an affirmation of reason's inherent theological capacity.[67] At the beginning of 1857, accordingly, Pius contented himself with choosing from his arsenal a middling sort of canonical penalty. Günther's works were placed on the Index of Prohibited Books (excepting those still to be published, two of which were in the press). An index of forbidden books was not as such an index of forbidden authors. Günther replied to the news with a graceful submission.[68]

In fact, the Güntherians were by no means totally downcast. The Roman decree, they said, was merely disciplinary: young clerics should not (for now) read Günther's works. As we saw at the end of Chapter 3, they assured the master that his rehabilitation was only a matter of time. This was false prophecy. The complacent resistance angered Archbishop Johannes von Geissel of Cologne who succeeded in extracting from Pius IX in June 1857 a Brief condemning Güntherianism, *Eximiam tuam*. Its sharpest censure was reserved for the way Günther had given "human reason and philosophy," which should be auxiliary to revelation, a right of judgment vis-à-vis revelation—meaning, vis-à-vis revelation's contents. This led, wrote Pius, to the suppression of any distinction between knowledge and faith. That was indeed arguable. Günther had equated knowledge, *Wissenschaft*, with speculative reason in its constructive mode, *Vernunft*, and treated as the "Tabor" or transfiguration of theology the transposition into terms of *Wissenschaft-Vernunft* of any element in the revealed content hitherto taken to be supra-rational. But to look at the same matter through Günther's eyes: his fear was that, unless it assumes in a rationally legitimated guise the doctrine of God as Trinity, at once different from the world (as subject) and yet its pattern (as substance), Christian philosophy in the modern age will fall into pantheism. Yet,

---

67. Ibid., p. 617. Controversy over "moderate [or 'mitigated'] traditionalism," as represented by the Louvain theologian Gérard Casimir Ubaghs, would continue till 1866. Was Ubaghs' doctrine compatible with the four propositions of 1855? The final decision, after much tergiversation, was negative: ibid., p. 621.

68. H. H. Schwedt, "Die Verurteilung der Werke Anton Günthers (1857) und seiner Schüler," *Zeitschrift für Kirchengeschichte* 101 (1990), pp. 301–343. Schwedt concludes that Pius IX, on the advice of Italian curialists, first supported moderates then changed over to supporting intransigents, pressed thereto by German churchmen.

as the highly original German Scholastic theologian Matthias Joseph Scheeben would write in 1865:

> Have we not seen how in Günther's system a transition is effected from the inner productions in the Godhead to the outer, and how an attempt is made to represent the latter as the necessary development and complement of the former? Even if this is not formally pantheism, in the last analysis it leads to pantheism, just as every doctrine does which represents the universe as the necessary complement of the Infinite.[69]

Passages from *Eximiam tuam* were soon incorporated into the classic anthology of magisterial utterances, the *Enchiridion* of Heinrich Denzinger, professor of dogma at Würzburg, the early editions of which were produced in just this period—four between 1854 and 1865—so as to remind theologians (and to a lesser extent philosophers) of the need to bear in mind credal, conciliar, papal and synodal pronouncements when doing their work. That collection would shortly after include, in its fifth edition, the decree *Dei Filius* of the First Vatican Council.

Pius' Council

Why, then, did these cases—Hermes, Günther, Bautain—recur at Vatican I? The answer lies in the methodology adopted by the curialists who prepared the Council. As his pontificate developed, Pius IX had a policy of drawing together the themes of his earlier encyclicals and other documents and acts. The first public sign of this penchant for synthesis was the 1864 *Syllabus of Errors* which, as its name might suggest, is basically an anthology reprobating this or that error of the age. A decade earlier, it had been in the mind of the pope—as in that of the Jesuit editors of the Roman journal *Civiltà Cattolica* and the founder of Solesmes, Dom Guéranger, to link to the proclamation of the dogma of the Immaculate Conception a condemnation of modern errors, notably secularism. The proposal was abandoned,[70] but the

---

69. M. J. Scheeben, *The Mysteries of Christianity* (English translation, St. Louis, MO, 1946), p. 125. Scheeben argued that a conception of God as infinitely active in the knowledge and love of himself and in that way sufficient to himself for his own beatitude can—even without reference to God's hypostatic fruitfulness as the Trinity, known only through faith—safeguard Christian thought against pantheism, which was Günther's principal concern.

70. G. Martina, SJ, *Pio IX* [1851–1866], pp. 266–269.

conflict between the Church and the liberal state which led in 1859 to the seizure by the House of Savoy of part of the States of the Church reawakened enthusiasm for a compendious refutation of contemporary ideologies, whether socio-political or philosophical. (For Pius himself, it was essentially a defense of the supernatural order.[71]) Martina's research in the Vatican Archives has uncovered the complex process of elaboration of the *Syllabus*, which lasted for five years.[72] Preparation of the Vatican Council followed broadly the same pattern as the drafting of the *Syllabus*. It is not surprising, then, that a document on the relation of faith and reason, placing in a clear doctrinal framework the censures inherited from the recent past, and solemnly reaffirming them, was envisaged from the start.[73]

At Vatican I

Composition of a draft was entrusted before the Council opened to a highly competent theologian, the Austrian Jesuit Johann Baptist Franzelin, the distinctive trait of whose work was the integration of positive theology (biblical and patristic) with speculative, a synthetic approach which reflected the historical preoccupations of German university theology but expressed its conclusions in Scholastic style.[74]

The lengthy text placed before the Council "on Catholic doctrine against the multiple errors derived from rationalism" fell into three parts. The first condemned materialism, various forms of pantheism, absolute rationalism, semi-rationalism, and the error, opposite in character to the last two, of traditionalism, which denied to reason any capacity to know something of God independently of revelation. A second section dealt with Scripture and Tradition as sources of revelation; the necessity of a supernatural revelation; the nature of the

---

71. Idem., *Pio IX* [1867–1878] (Rome, 1990), p. 179.

72. Idem., *Pio IX* [1851–1866], op. cit., pp. 287–348. Martina stresses the role (by no means entirely felicitous) in the finalizing of the *Syllabus* and also of the encyclical which accompanied it, *Quanta cura*, of the Barnabite Luigi Bilio, who later played a significant part at Vatican I, as well as the contribution at an earlier stage of Philip Gerbet, Bishop of Perpignan, a formal disciple of Lamennais and so a figure of some historical interest: see C. de Ladoue, *Mons. Gerbet, sa vie et ses oeuvres et l'Ecole menaisienne* (Paris, 1872).

73. R. Aubert, *Vatican I* (Paris, 1964), p. 60.

74. Idem., "Les sciences ecclésiastiques," in idem., *Le pontificat de Pie IX (1846–1878)*, op. cit., pp. 187–188. See also, G. Bonavenia, *Raccolto di memorie intorno alla vita dell'Em. Cardinale Franzelin* (Rome, 1877).

revealed mysteries; the distinction between the knowledge brought by faith and science; the necessity of the motives of credibility; the supernatural virtue of faith and the free character of the assent to the divine Word given by the believer; the necessity and supernatural solidity of faith; the relation between science and faith; the immutable character of dogma. The third and concluding section dealt with dogmas whose treatment by semi-rationalists was notably deformed: here the Trinity, creation, the Incarnation, redemption, as well as anthropology, the supernatural order, sin and grace were particularly in view. Güntherian theses lay behind much of this material, albeit in a simplified and, consequently, to a degree distorted form.[75] Apart from its prolixity the chief criticism leveled against the schema on the Council floor was its redolence of midnight oil in scholars' garrets. The technicality of the language, especially in the anti-Güntherian paragraphs, astonished bishops whose own studies, more modest in nature, lay in the past. They drew the not illegitimate conclusion that the text was, first, too little concerned with the crisis of faith among the masses which was essentially materialist/atheist, and second, too much concerned with idiosyncratic academics.

The rejection of the schema, at least as it stood, led Franzelin's Roman students to joke that his obscurity was already for them a certain truth, but never previously had it been recognized by an ecumenical Council.[76] A new schema, completely rewritten in form—it was both shorter and less technical—but maintaining many of the issues earlier identified, was distributed to the Council Fathers in March 1870. The principal theological consultor involved was another Germanophone Jesuit, Joseph Kleutgen, a leading light of the Thomist revival. The authors insisted that, if the main errors condemned in the schema originated among University teachers, what was in the academy today could be in the public square tomorrow. With amendments it was passed with only one abstention.

The pertinent aspects of the constitution *Dei Filius* may briefly be summarized. In chapter I the text added to the statements of the Creeds on the Creator God, and of Lateran IV (1215) on the non-eternity of the creative act, that God created the world not only with

---

75. For detailed exegesis, see L. Orban, *Theologia Güntheriana et Concilium Vaticanum* (two volumes, Rome 1949–1950).

76. R. Aubert, *Vatican I*, op. cit., p. 131.

full liberty but *for his glory*: this against Hermes whose Kantian commitment to human persons as ends-in-themselves excluded any such suggestion (Günther may also be in view though that is somewhat more problematic[77]). Over against traditionalist fideism, as well as atheism, Chapter II affirmed the human possibility of knowing by the natural light of reason some metaphysical truths such as the existence of God, but left open the question, Is the natural knowledge of God independently of all revelation a fact, or merely such a possibility?[78] Divine revelation is of great utility for helping people to know in a sufficiently exact fashion what it is in theory possible to know of the true God by dint of reason alone. The question whether human reason requires in this respect an education of a certain type for its own full development was left deliberately to one side. Over against deism, the Council defined the unconditional necessity of revelation so as to gain knowledge of the supernatural order. So far all these points concern truths a preliminary knowledge of which is presupposed by the act of faith.

In Chapter III the constitution turned to the act of faith for itself. After an initial description of faith in anti-rationalist terms, *Dei Filius* went on to define the reasonable character of the act of faith, against an illuminism, whether Protestant or *bautainien*, which would make exclusive appeal to inner evidence, and against also a rationalism which denies the probative force of the classical motives of credibility, notably miracle.[79] Against Hermesianism, it underlined that faith is in its entirety a free adhesion of the person made possible by an act of divine grace. Lastly, in this chapter, after affirming the obligation to embrace faith and persevere in it, the constitution explained how God helps us to fulfill this duty: in part through the Church which, as well as presenting to us the truths to be believed, is by her own life, notably as the mother of saints, a guarantee of her divine origin, but also by the help of interior grace which encourages unbelievers to believe and confirms believers in their faith. This was asserted over against those Hermesians for whom the faithful have the right to put their faith in

---

77. J. Reikerstorfer, "Anton Günther," art. cit., p. 271.

78. See R. Aubert, "Le Concile du Vatican et la connaissance naturelle de Dieu," *Lumière et Vie* 14 (1954), pp. 21–52.

79. G. Paraids, "Foi et raison au Ie Concile du Vatican," *Bulletin de literature ecclésiastique* 63 (1962), pp. 200–226; 268–292; 64 (1963), pp. 9–25.

doubt, suspending their assent until they have formed a conviction of a philosophical type of the truth of their belief.[80]

Chapter IV offered a synthesis of the different aspects of the faith-reason relationship. It recalled the existence of a twofold order of knowledge, natural and supernatural: to the latter belong those mysteries inaccessible to man outside of revelation. While condemning the Güntherian thesis according to which reason can attain an understanding of supernatural truths on the same basis as natural truths once the former, communicated by revelation, have achieved their own rational mediation, *Dei Filius* accepted the role of reason in exploring the revealed data, and indicated some fundamental elements of theological method in this regard, among which is the principle of analogy. Reason and faith help each other mutually; any appearance of contradiction between them can only rest on misunderstanding of one or the other. The sciences have a legitimate liberty but they can also abuse it: an attached canon reserves to the Church the right to proscribe any scientific opinion that conflicts with revelation.[81] Finally, and this is a last anti-Güntherian note, the Council condemned any so-called "transcendental philosophy" which would seek to give the dogmas new meanings, held to be more perfect than those entertained by the Church.

From a theologian's standpoint Avery Dulles made two perfectly fair comments on the contribution of this Council. In the first place: since its focus of concern was the faith-reason relation, it approached the question of faith in primarily intellectual, not moral terms—without, however, denying that faith could be "treated from other perspectives," including disobedience (compare Saint Paul), worldliness (compare Saint John), and pride (compare Saint

---

80. That the Archbishop of Westminster, Henry Edward Manning, took a large part in the drafting of the anti-Hermesian canon seems prima facie barely explicable: Hermes' writings were virtually unknown in England, though Lord Acton possessed a copy of the documents relevant to the doctrinal inquiry: *Damnatio et prohibitio operum Georgii Hermes in tribus tomis Germanica lingua editorum*, op. cit., now in the Acton Collection of Cambridge University Library. But this canon "was also, in Manning's eyes, an explicit rejection of the claims advanced by those who, on the basis of the new scientific theories or the findings of the so-called school of historical criticism, felt justified in questioning the faith of the Church and the recent pronouncements of the magisterium": J. Pereiro, *Cardinal Manning. An Intellectual Biography* (Oxford, 1998), p. 282.

81. A. Alsteens, "Science et foi dans le chapitre IV de la Constitution 'Dei Filius'," *Ephemerides Theologicae Lovanienses* 38 (1962), pp. 461–503.

Augustine).⁸² Second, the Council sought to trace a "narrow path between the errors of fideism and rationalism," and in so doing it "particularly emphasized the reasonableness of the decision to submit to the authority of God as witness." It is partly owing to historical accuracy and partly owing to a predilection for something a touch more Bautain-like that this same Jesuit author, who is rather in reaction against his Baroque and nineteenth-century forebears, adds that "in assessing the arguments of credibility the Council was concerned with their de jure value rather than with the de facto question of what moves a given individual to believe."⁸³ From a historian's standpoint, Giacomo Martina considered that *Dei Filius* "preserved, despite its complexity, a good equilibrium between opposed tendencies." Distinctly "positive," and genuinely "foundational," it can bear comparison, he thought, with "the best documents from before and after Trent."⁸⁴ It did not, however, address the historical dimension of revelation: that would be left to *Dei Verbum*, the dogmatic constitution on revelation of Vatican II (1962–1965). The other issue whose omission Martina records, namely the possibility of internal revelation (for example, at the moment of death), still awaits some public judgment of the Church.⁸⁵

The years after Vatican I saw the passage to Old Catholicism of several leading Güntherian writers—Peter Knoodt, author of what is still the standard life; Johannes Baptista Baltzer; Josef Peter Elvenich, composer of the *Acta Hermesiana* under Gregory XVI; Ernst Melzer; and the historian of the medieval papacy Johannes Watterich, who, however, returned to the Catholic Church and died as a monk of the Beuronese abbey of Maredsous, in Belgium. Günther himself had died in 1863, aged seventy-nine. As for Bautain, his subsequent ecclesiastical career was spotless. In the year of Günther's death, he was made *grand vicaire* of the Archbishop of Paris and honorary dean of the faculty of letters of Strasbourg University. He died four years later, at the age of seventy-one, leaving no dissident disciples.

---

82. A. Dulles, sj, *The Assurance of Things Hoped For*, op. cit., p. 89.
83. Ibid.
84. G. Martina, sj, *Pio IX* [1867–1878], op. cit., p. 189.
85. For further comments on the theological problematic of the document, see R. Latourelle, sj, *Théologie de la Révélation* (Montreal 1969, 3rd edition), pp. 277–292.

The second occupation of Rome in 1870, this time by the House of Savoy engaged on its successful strategy of the unification of Italy, left Pius a voluntary "prisoner of the Vatican" once he had rejected the so-called Law of Guarantees in May 1871.[86] Those events brought to a premature end the general council of the Church he had called in 1869–1870. Pius IX, who erected over two hundred bishoprics and approved literally hundreds of new Religious Congregations, many of them for missionary work, died in February 1878. His centralizing policies were ordered to overcoming the interference of national governments—whether absolutist or, as increasingly, liberal—in Church life. His "Ultramontanism" (as recent historiography shows, the term should be differentiated and used carefully[87]) belongs in a context of "mutual support between the Holy See and local churches,"[88] exemplified in the assistance Pius gave the episcopate in their efforts to evolve clear plans of pastoral action. He stated general principles. With the help of his advisers he also could be found "drawing up a detailed picture of the situation of the Church in different countries" for their benefit.[89] His impulsive, emotional nature made him at times a somewhat imprudent supreme pastor. But as his late twentieth-century beatification indicates, he was also a courageous one.

Blessed Pius IX died on February 7, 1878. A fortnight later there was elected a very different figure, Gioacchino Pecci, who adopted the style "Leo XIII." His was a less analytic or negative and more constructive or positive project.

---

86. G. Martina, SJ, *Pio IX* [1867–1878], op. cit., pp. 254–260.
87. G. Fleckenstein—J. Schmiedl (ed.), *Ultramontanismus. Tendenzen der Forschung* (Paderborn, 2005).
88. G. Martina, SJ, *Pio IX* [1851–1866], op. cit., p. xi.
89. Ibid.

Chapter 6

Return to the Schoolmen: Joseph Kleutgen and Leo XIII

Introduction to Leo

In the case of Pius IX's successor Leo XIII, early experience brought closer contact with the intellectual question in the Church.[1] Leo was born Vincenzo Gioacchino Pecci in the central Italian town of Frosinone, then under Napoleonic rule, in 1810. Leo's academic formation was more serious than that of his two predecessors. After the Collegio Romano and the so-called "Academy for Noble Ecclesiastics," dedicated chiefly to those destined for a career in the papal diplomatic service, he had studied at La Sapienza, the civil (though not secular) University of the States of the Church. Moreover, as papal nuncio to Belgium in the 1840s, he had witnessed sympathetically the revival under church auspices of the medieval university at Louvain where the faculties of theology and philosophy were paramount. Lastly, as Bishop of Perugia, from 1846 until the year preceding his election as pope in 1878, he had taken a close interest in the teaching provided in his diocesan seminary, reforming its content according to a definite plan. As a voting participant at the First Vatican Council he had necessarily been made aware of the vicissitudes of Hermes, Günther, Bautain, and of the importance of a sane view of the faith-reason relationship for thought and teaching in a Church committed at one and the same time *both* to the truth-claims of a special revelation in history *and* to the view that human intelligence is of itself at all times and in all places a vehicle for metaphysical truth. The Conciliar constitution

---

1. Leo has not yet found his Giacomo Martina. Meanwhile, see L. P. Wallace, *Leo XII*, but like most students of his pontificate, her interest centers on the social question. Wider aspects are included in a collection from the Ecole française de Rome: P. Levillain, J.-M. Ticchi, et al., *Le pontificat de Léon XIII. Renaissances du Saint-Siège?*

Dei Filius laid down some basic principles, and in its canons it cleared away negatively the inadequate solutions offered by some nineteenth-century thinkers. But *Dei Filius* was short on positive proposals. Less than eighteen months into his pontificate, Leo produced the single most influential encyclical of the nineteenth century, *Aeterni Patris*, a proposal for the restoration of Christian philosophy. Its aim was nothing less than the restructuring, in the light of nineteenth-century experience so far, of the intellectual culture of the Church.

The Encyclical Aeterni Patris

In the preamble to *Aeterni Patris*, Leo recalled the duty of the supreme pastors to "provide with special care that all studies should accord with the Catholic faith, especially philosophy, on which a right interpretation of the other sciences in great part depends."[2] The subject he would address is the mode of taking up the study of philosophy which shall respond most fully to the excellence of faith, and at the same time be consonant with the dignity of human science.[3]

Erroneous philosophical ideas, he complained, now infect, with varying degrees of sophistication, all levels of civil society. While the chief antidote for these must be the intellectual medicine furnished by supernatural revelation, divine wisdom had also provided some natural aids to the human race, among which should be counted the "right use of philosophy."[4]

Leo offered three reasons for this high place accorded philosophy. The first—the role of philosophy in the *preambula fidei*—will detain us longer than the remaining two. First, then, philosophy, as used by *sapientes*, "the wise," tends to a degree to smooth the path to faith and prepare people to receive revelation, which is why in the writings of Clement of Alexandria and Origen it can be called a "Stepping-stone" to the Christian faith, or its "prelude and help," or even "the Gospel teacher."[5] While not appealing to *Dei Filius*, Leo's text was certainly consonant with the Constitution when it explained that revelation covers not only "those truths which human intelligence

---

2. *Aeterni Patris*, 1.
3. Ibid.
4. Ibid., 2.
5. Ibid., 4.

could not attain of itself" but also other truths, "which reason can attain," included in revelation's purview to the end that "by the help of divine authority [these rationally knowable truths] may be made known to all at once and without any admixture of error."[6] Pagan thinkers had already discovered and demonstrated with appropriate argument a number of truths which *either* coincide with some of these rationally attainable truths thus divinely proposed for human assent *or* are closely bound up with the truths uniquely found in revelation. To turn these two sets of rationally well-grounded truths "to the service of revealed doctrine" is not to follow a practice that is, as Leo put it, "of recent introduction" (we shall see in a moment what may be at stake in those defensive words). Rather it is to follow the example of many of the Fathers of the Church. Names and references to Fathers both Greek and Latin are then given to show the antiquity and ubiquity of this practice of "despoiling the Egyptians."

What the pope was chiefly concerned with here, as the next section of *Aeterni Patris* indicates, is the existence of God and the divine perfections—and notably God's wisdom and justice, since on these two latter attributes there rests for Leo, the claim that God is, as he wrote, "not only true but truth itself, which can neither deceive nor be deceived." Human reason—having established to its own satisfaction that God is the measure of truth—will ascribe maximal credibility and authority to the Word of God in special revelation.

This brought Leo to the other key area in a philosophical preamble to faith: the signs of the facticity of revelation found in the gospel tradition and the subsequent life of the Church. There are back references to *Dei Filius* and, though not actually cited, the encyclicals of Pius IX. If we bracket these two sets of areas together—divine existence and perfection, on the one hand, and, on the other, the signs of a *de facto* revelation both apostolic and post-apostolic—we have the raft of issues with which Bautain's bishop confronted him, minus (whether significantly or not) the question of Old Testament revelation seen as, above all, disclosure made to Moses.

The preamble of faith, then, is the first area where philosophy can help. The second, for Leo, is the way philosophy by integration with the body of theology can confer on theology what he termed "the

---

6. Ibid.

nature, form, and genius of a true science."⁷ What is meant by calling theology "scientific"? Hermes' answer would have been: theology is scientific when its fundamental claim is fully legitimized by philosophy, which is the *Grundwissenschaft* or foundational science for every discipline. Günther's answer would have been: theology is scientific when its content is completely rethought in terms of the philosophy of spirit, *Geist*. Bautain's answer would have been: theology is never scientific, it is sapiential; the question is badly posed. Leo's answer already implied in effect a return to Scholasticism. It ran: a theology is scientific when it has the ability to organize revealed doctrines; when it can show how they exhibit common principles, and when it serves an enhanced or more lucid understanding of these doctrines in and of themselves. Here Leo could draw attention to the remarks of the First Vatican Council about theological method, highlighting the Council's appeal to analogy (that is, the understanding of dogma by analogy with things naturally known, a point queried by Günther) but also the suggestive value of the connection of the revealed mysteries with each other and their further connection to human destiny, man's final end (this last was something of whose importance Hermes was conscious, but, through a humanistic horizontalism, misconstrued). In these various ways, then, philosophy can help theology become *scientia*.

Leo's third and last reason for not neglecting philosophy was its value in fighting off attacks on Christian doctrine as false or irrational. "It is the glory of philosophy," he wrote, "to be esteemed as the bulwark of faith and the strong defense of religion."⁸ Leo recalled that the last of the pre-Reformation general councils, Lateran V (1512–1517), had exhorted philosophers to "pay close attention to the exposition of fallacious arguments."⁹

So much for the services philosophy should perform. But how is an appropriate philosophical culture to be constructed? Here we come to what would be in the future something of a *crux interpretum*, a disputed point in the encyclical's interpretation. The pope had two proposals. First, "human reason," *ratio humana*, aware of its own infirmity, will account it "the highest honor to wait upon heavenly

---

7. Ibid., 6.
8. Ibid., 7.
9. Ibid.

doctrines like a handmaid and attendant, and by God's goodness attain to them in any way whatsoever." But second, "in the case of such doctrines as human intelligence may receive," it is also true that "philosophy," *philosophia,* should use what Leo termed "its own method, principles, and arguments," albeit, he remarked in a qualifying clause, not in such a way as "to seem rashly to withdraw from the divine authority."[10] Notice the contrast or at any rate the distinction between human reason and philosophy here: human reason is to serve the Word of God as its handmaid, yet philosophy is to retain quasi-completely its own methodology. What, then, was Leo seeking? Did he want a philosophy informed by revelation and integrated with theology (Bautain would strongly have approved), or rather was he calling for a separate philosophy for which revelation or its interpreter, the Church's teaching authority, functions as a purely negative index for any erroneous conclusions reached? In the later nineteenth and twentieth centuries that would be the common position of the school of Louvain.

From the 1920s through to the 1950s and even 1960s there would be a long-running dispute over the meaning or even the legitimacy of the phrase "Christian philosophy."[11] Was such a term, which, in their different ways, Günther, Bautain and Leo had all treated as axiomatic, in actuality a contradiction in terms? Gilson, to whom I shall be turning in the next chapter, was under no illusion that those Catholic thinkers who said so had failed to read on to the succeeding ninth section of *Aeterni Patris* where Leo states specifically:

> Those . . . who to the study of philosophy unite obedience to the Christian faith, are philosophizing in the best possible way, for the splendor of the divine truths, received into the mind, helps the understanding, and not only detracts nowise from its dignity, but adds greatly to its nobility, keenness, and stability.[12]

In sections 10 to 14 Leo provided a rundown of the history of Christian philosophy. The rundown, however, was really a run-up

---

10. Ibid., 8.

11. L. Bogliolo, *Il problema della filosofia cristiana* (Brescia, 1959); M. Nédoncelle, *Existe-t-il une philosophie chrétienne?* (Paris, 1956); A. Renard, *La querelle sur la possibilité de la philosophie chrétienne* (Paris, 1941).

12. *Aeterni Patris,* 9.

because the history in question shows cumulative advance, reaching a provisional apogee with John Damascene in the East, Anselm in the West. It achieved climax, however, in the Scholastics of the thirteenth century on whom Leo cited words of praise for Thomas Aquinas and Bonaventure from the Franciscan pope Sixtus V whose pontificate ran from 1585 to 1590, though by section 17 of *Aeterni Patris* Thomas will stand alone.

But actually Sixtus's praise had been for Scholastic theology, not Scholastic philosophy. Leo had a reply to this: "Since it is the proper and special office of the Scholastic theologians to bind together by the fastest chain human and divine science, surely the theology in which they excelled would not have gained such honor and commendation among men if they had made use of a lame and imperfect or vain philosophy."[13] Leo's eventual singling out of Thomas was, accordingly, on grounds both theological and philosophical. The ground for theological acclaim he took from the sixteenth-century commentator on Thomas, his namesake Thomas de Vio, better known from his birthplace as "Cajetan." Thomas Aquinas was a supreme interpreter of the Fathers, collecting together their insights, re-ordering them in an improved fashion and enhancing them with fresh insights. But the chief reason for drawing readers' attention to Thomas was his philosophical work, on which, Leo claimed, "philosophy has no part which he did not touch finely at once and thoroughly."[14] Furthermore,

> Clearly distinguishing, as is fitting, reason from faith, while happily associating the one with the other, he both preserved the rights and had regard for the dignity of each; so much so, indeed, that reason, borne on the wings of Thomas to its human height, can scarcely expect more or stronger aids from faith than those which she has already obtained through Thomas.[15]

Leo's Anxiety

I hinted that *Aeterni Patris* betrays a certain anxiety that people will respond to its central message—if you want to mediate the relations of faith and reason well, and achieve a genuinely "Christian philosophy,"

---

13. Ibid., 16.
14. Ibid., 17.
15. Ibid., 18.

then look to Thomas—by deploring this piece of strongly worded counsel as recent innovation. The next five sections of the encyclical are devoted, accordingly, to the rebuttal of this claim. Why was the word "innovation" used by Leo's expected opponents? It reflected awareness of how recent and patchy had been the revival of Thomism in, chiefly, Italy, and to a lesser degree Germany (there had also been some mild interest by the historically-minded in France). Moreover, as we shall see, one key person to whom Leo looked for support, the outstanding figure in the call for a return to the philosophy and theology of *die Vorzeit*, the pre-modern period, he had just discovered to be a serious embarrassment.

Pre-Leonine Scholasticism

With the benefit of hindsight, many accounts of the Leonine revival of Thomism, especially those that favor the Leonine project, give the impression that a rash of Neo-Thomism was bursting out all over Europe. To appreciate Leo's letter, it seems important to get a just historical perspective.

"Scholasticism" had endured till the end of the European *ancien régime*, but merely to mention that it took Protestant as well as Catholic forms alerts us to the fact that Scholasticism is a far wider concept than Thomism. Much Catholic Scholasticism in the early modern period continued the differing trends of the medieval schools or underwent transformation through alliances with rationalist philosophies, notably those of Descartes and Wolff. Though by 1789 Thomist institutions could still be found—notably Dominican studyhouses but also, for example, the Benedictine university at Salzburg, the sweeping away of the church academies in the avalanche of the Great Revolution of the West (1789–1815) created a *tabula rasa* in nominally Catholic Europe after the Congress of Vienna.[16]

Most standard histories give a predominant role in the reawakening of Thomism to Italy. But Italian Thomism was an

---

16. See U. G. Leinsle, "Die Scholastik der Neuzeit bis zur Aufklärung," in E. Coreth, sj, W. M. Neidl, G. Pfligersdorffer (eds.), *Christliche Philosophie im katholischen Denken des 19. und 20. Jahrhunderts. Band 2. Rückgriff auf scholastisches Erbe* (Graz, 1988), pp. 54–69. Leinsle finds the most interest in Thomas in study-houses in the care of Dominicans, Benedictines and Discalced Carmelites (the Calced preferred John Baconthorpe, d. 1348).

extremely fragile plant. Under the influence of the Renaissance philosophies and literary humanism Scholasticism had largely withered away in Italy, and where it survived it was, thanks to the strength of Italian Franciscanism, chiefly Scotist in form.[17] At Rome, the Collegio Romano, like all Jesuit institutions, was officially Suarezian: that is, faithful to the Scholastic eclectic Francisco Suárez who had died in 1617. Judging by the most recent scholarship, the return to Thomas began in Naples, where Thomas himself had not only studied and taught but died, and where he had been declared a patron of the city, with two chairs of University philosophy named for him. One name bandied about is the Dominican, Salvatore Roselli whose *Summa philosophica ad mentem Angelici doctoris Sancti Thomae Aquinatis* had a wide dissemination, serving as the model for numerous philosophical Summas in later nineteenth-century Italy, Spain and France (Thomas, by contrast, had never written a *Summa philosophiae,* and, we may be fairly sure, would never have dreamed of it). But Roselli had died before the Revolution, in 1784. The only major figure to favor Thomism publicly in post-Revolutionary Italy was the secular canon, Gaetano Sanseverino, whose own dates are 1811 to 1865, professor at the University of Naples, philosopher lecturer at the *Liceo arcivescovile,* the archiepiscopal school, and founder of the first Thomist learned society in Italy, the Accademia di Filosofia Tomista, which still exists under the title Accademia di San Tommaso d'Aquino. Sanseverino would have considerable impact on various key players among the Jesuits in Rome but, owing to the official requirement in the Society to follow Suárez, Jesuit Thomism was kept in the closet until after *Aeterni Patris.* There were also modest attempts at reviving Thomism by academic clergy in two Italian dioceses: Piacenza, where the journal *Divus Thomas* was founded, but not, significantly, till 1879, the year of Leo's encyclical, and Perugia, whose Thomas academy had as its chairman Giuseppe Pecci, the brother of the pope. Leo, qua bishop of Perugia, had brought him to the Umbrian city in order to teach philosophy at the seminary there. It cannot be said that this adds up to a very great deal.

---

17. A report of an English visitor to Italian Dominicans is eloquent of the neglect of Thomasian study among them and in the wider Italian scene: *The Letters and Diaries of John Henry Newman XI* (London, 1961), pp. 263, 279.

In Germany the situation was no different. Any revival of Thomism was highly localized, the concern of a handful of individuals. At the Philosophical-Theological Academy of Münster the married layman Franz Jakob Clemens (1815–1862), trained at Bonn after its cleansing of Hermesianism, argued for a renewal of Christian philosophy through a return to Thomas, who had been its summit, though Thomasian philosophy, Clemens concluded, required, and was capable of, extension and completion. Key to Thomas's success was his discrimination between the natural and supernatural levels of analysis of reality, revelation and knowledge.[18] In a lengthy essay, "Our Standpoint in Philosophy," published in a Rhenish journal *Der Katholik* whose editor shared his outlook, Clemens claimed that human reason is specified by a variety of conditions, of which Christianity is one. *Christlich gebildete Vernunft*, "reason cultivated in a Christian way," is still *Vernunft*, i.e., reason. Christian philosophy is a legitimate transformation of a common human patrimony stemming from ancient Greece and rightly taken up in the formation of dogmatic concepts —for example in Christology and Triadology, the doctrine of the Holy Trinity—at the Ecumenical Councils of the Church.

Hermann Ernst Plassmann (1817–1864), who studied for a while with the Roman Dominicans at the College of the Minerva, was for part of the 1850s professor of philosophy at the Paderborn Philosophisch-Theologischer Lehranstalt, but he found the combination of teaching and writing too onerous and resigned to write his five-volume study of the "school of Saint Thomas."[19] Plassmann saw Thomas's philosophy as a necessary healing instrument for modern thought, whose development since Descartes was ever more manifestly a cul-de-sac. *Pace* Günther, once we reject the spontaneous realism of the mind's natural knowledge of being as presented through the senses, to seek instead a grounding within the subject for certainty of knowledge, we enter, as the example of Idealism should warn us, a maze that has no exit. Moreover, *pace* Hermes, human reason is socially formed; it cannot be reconstructed on the basis of methodical

---

18. C. J. Klemens, "Unser Standpunkt in der Philosophie," *Der Katholik* 39. 1 (1859), p. 9, cited in E. Coreth, sj, W. M. Neidl, G. Pfligersdorffer (eds.), *Christliche Philosophie im katholischen Denken des 19. und 20. Jahrhunderts. Band 2. Rückgriff auf scholastisches Erbe*, op. cit.

19. H. E. Plassmann, *Die Schule der heiligen Thomas von Aquin. Zur genaueren Kenntnisnahme und weiteren Fortführung für Deutschland neu eröffnet* (Paderborn, 1859–1862).

doubt; in a Christian context it will learn from reflective faith, that is, from theology. Plassmann's Thomas is more Aristotelian, less Platonist than the historical Thomas, but he anticipated later discussion of Leo's encyclical in insisting that Thomist philosophy simply *was* Catholic philosophy, period.

In the way they presented the service Thomism could do to modern intellectual culture, Clemens and Plassmann can certainly count as harbingers of the Leonine project. But a layman who wrote a manifesto and a priest who retired to become a private scholar—after a massive early work on Giordano Bruno and Nicholas of Cusa (Renaissance philosophy, then), Clemens' only other books were broadsides against Günther:[20] these were not especially weighty authorities to invoke. In any case, Clemens and Plassmann, like Sanseverino, had died in the early 1860s. They were no longer around.

Enter Kleutgen

Hence the importance of a third German figure who, however, worked for much of his adult life in Italy, Joseph Kleutgen. Kleutgen, born in Dortmund in 1811, had two advantages. He was a prolific and philosophically incisive author. And he was still alive. An almost exact contemporary of the pope's (they were born within a few months of each other), he would not die until 1883, and so saw the publication of *Aeterni Patris* which he hailed as the confirmation of his life's work.[21] A solitary child, attracted to nature-rambles and poetry, he became a philosophy student at Munich while Schelling was teaching there (Plato and Schleiermacher especially interested him), but abandoned his course during the political troubles of 1830–1831. In 1833, he had a profound experience of Christ as Savior. This seems to have given a strongly devotional and mystical caste to his piety which, as we shall discover, unfortunately contributed to his downfall. He resumed his studies, this time in theology at Münster; enrolled at the diocesan seminary of Paderborn, but before receiving the diaconate applied to

---

20. Notably *Die spekulative Anthropologie A. Günthers und die katholische Kirchenlehre* (Cologne, 1853), one of a number of critiques of Günther's thought from the early 1850s.

21. K. Deufel, *Kirche und Tradition. Ein Beitrag zur Geschichte der theologischen Wende im 19. Jahrhundert am Beispiel des kirchlichtheologischen Programms P. Joseph Kleutgens sj* (Munich-Paderborn, 1976), pp. 383ff.

enter the Society of Jesus—only legally possible in German-speaking Europe at this period in some of the Swiss Catholic cantons.

In 1837 Kleutgen was priested at Fribourg, which lies on the linguistic border between German-speaking Switzerland and *la Suisse romande*. In 1843 his superiors called him to Rome, to work in the Jesuit Generalate and act as father confessor to ordinands in the Jesuit-run Collegium Germanicum-Hungaricum. In 1851, he became a consultor to the Congregation of the Index: the cases of Hermes and Günther had made the Roman Curia aware they needed German-speakers, and preferably ones familiar with the complex and exigent German philosophical tradition. (Kleutgen had already crossed swords with Günther.[22]) In 1858 Kleutgen was appointed Secretary of the Jesuit Society, a prestigious post. Straightaway he set to work on a possible Thomistic scheme of studies with the "closet Thomists" among the Jesuits at the Gregorian University.

Kleutgen's Thought

What were Kleutgen's ideas relevant to the issue of faith and reason? Kleutgen's fundamental intuition is that, with the rejection of the approach to philosophy found in the Fathers and high medievals, certain questions—above all the nature of consciousness and the theory of knowledge—had proved in post-Cartesian philosophy essentially intractable and incapable of solution. In the disturbed years following the Roman Revolution of 1848, Kleutgen embarked on his massive defense of Scholastic thought, originally in six volumes. As their names suggest, *Die Theologie der Vorzeit verteidigt* and *Die Philosophie der Vorzeit verteidigt* are in no way a history of Scholasticism. They are, rather, an apologia for its methods and presuppositions in the light of its content. In its philosophical guise, the rejection of Scholastic thinking in the early modern period meant skepticism in England, critical Idealism in Germany, and sensationalism in France. The efforts of Catholic philosophers after the Revolution (Hermes, Günther, Bautain are mentioned, *inter alia*), were led astray by the defects of the very speculation against which they were fighting.

---

22. T. Schäfer, *Die erkenntnistheoretische Kontroverse Kleutgen-Günther* (Paderborn, 1961).

Kleutgen considers the objection, made most fully by Günther, that Scholasticism has no theory of knowledge. It failed to reflect on the subjective conditions of knowledge, satisfying itself with an account of universal concepts gained through abstraction, when what it should have asked after were the principles of what is given in experience. Kleutgen convicts the critics of ignorance. They have confused Thomas with John Locke, for whom generalities are arrived at by analysis and synthesis of particulars. But on Thomas's account of knowledge, the concept, though it begins from the abstractive work of the active intellect on sensuous particulars, enjoys metaphysical depth. It gives access to the form whereby substance has its determinate being.[23]

Nor, *pace* Günther, was Thomas unaware of the importance of subjectivity, self-consciousness. For Thomas, notably in the *De veritate,* the spirit, through reflection on its operations, can come to a grasp of itself. Kleutgen stresses against Günther—and going beyond Thomas's text—that spirit has to be moved to self-reflection by the experience of one like itself, or what he called "another already self-conscious essence."[24]

Against the traditionalists (and we have seen that Bautain counts as a mitigated example thereof), Kleutgen explains how for Thomas the norm of certainty in human knowledge is not a primordial revelation coming down to us in historically patterned human discourse. Rather it is the light of reason itself, which light is a participation in divine light. The Scholastics, with Thomas at their head, furnish a thoroughly satisfying account of *Erkenntnisprinzipien,* basic principles of knowledge, defined by Kleutgen as "those universal truths which lie at the foundations of our thinking:"[25] the law of non-contradiction, the principle of identity and, not stated explicitly until Leibniz but clearly at work in their writing, the principle of sufficient reason. Kleutgen adds that what, according to the laws of logic, is unthinkable cannot be: in other words, these laws of thought have metaphysical validity. It is also true that not all that is thinkable is realized, or real, at least now or as yet: and this is a presupposition

---

23. J. Kleutgen, *Die Philosophie der Vorzeit verteidigt,* I. (Münster, 1860–1863), p. 150.
24. Ibid., I., p. 180.
25. Ibid., I., p. 455.

of divine freedom. *Ens reale* includes potential being as well as actual being. This was a lesson Hermesians needed seriously to learn. (That "the real may be possible as well as existence" would be regarded by Etienne Gilson, whose attempt to fulfill Leo XIII's dream will occupy the next chapter, as symptomatic of Kleutgen's imperfect hold on Thomas's doctrine of *esse*.[26])

In his conclusion to the first volume of *Die Philosophie der Vorzeit*, Kleutgen considers the question, does philosophy have a material principle such that the ground of all other—subordinated and proximate—causes can be deduced from it. In other words, is there such a thing as "the Absolute" as radical Idealists conceive it? Every attempt to show as much—including Günther's who, unlike ontologists for whom the grasp of being is *ipso facto* the grasp of God, at least begins from the conditioned and works back to the Absolute—entails in the description of this relation (i.e., the relation of the conditioned to the Absolute) ascribing a necessary character to all causal activity. Such an ascription denies the contingency of the world and therewith the freedom of God.

This brings Kleutgen, finally, to the second volume of *Die Philosophie der Vorzeit*, which deals with metaphysics: specifically, general ontology, and then nature, man, and God. For Kleutgen any attempt to explain the term "to be" is pointless: all explanations presume this first and simplest of all ideas. What can be done is to show the further determinations the concept of being can sustain. Kleutgen opposes the modern habit of replacing the terminology of "uncreated" and "created" being by the language of "absolute" and "relative" being. That opens the way to pantheism by treating created being as a relation to the Absolute rather than highlighting its *Eigenständigkeit* or independent consistency. Scholastics did not make this mistake. For them a thing has its formal cause in its own essence, which does not prevent it from having an archetypal cause in the divine ideas, and thus in God. Using the tools of participation thinking and the analogy of being, Thomas was well able to bring this out.

Kleutgen defends the "traditional" proofs of God's existence (including Thomas's "five ways") against Kant and others; he is inclined to say that Günther's objections to the cosmological proofs

---

26. E. Gilson, *Being and Some Philosophers* (Toronto, 1952), p. 106.

are only verbal—Günther himself pursues a rational approach to God from the conditioned to the Unconditioned (the Absolute). It is, for Kleutgen, through the human mind's capacity for abstraction that it can find what he calls the "uncreated archetype in the created image,"[27] and this culminates in an account not simply of a primordial Cause of the world but of the divine properties of infinitude, unity, subjecthood and difference from the world as its Creator. Kleutgen defends Thomas against the Güntherian accusation of quasi-pantheism, explaining the correct understanding of Thomas's use of the term *emanatio*.

Still on those same accusations, divine being is not for Thomas the *esse commune*, "common being," which all creatures share. Moreover, it was precisely Thomas's emphasis on the freedom of God to create or not create, drawn by him from Scripture, which enabled him to go beyond Aristotle in affirming that the world exists not eternally but in time.

It is easy to see that at Kleutgen's hands Neo-Scholastic philosophy is chiefly conceived as a critique and purification of other philosophies in the Church, philosophies judged to serve less well the creation metaphysic which in different senses is both taught and presupposed in Scripture. Only in this very limited sense is it true to say that in philosophy (as distinct from theology) whereas "traditional Scholastic teaching began with disputed questions, . . . modern Scholastics began with theses about church teaching."[28]

Kleutgen's companion work, *Die Theologie der Vorzeit*, shares the ethos and aim of its philosophical companion. Drawing especially but by no means exclusively on Thomas, for Kleutgen invokes other medieval theologians, notably Bonaventure, and often appeals to the Fathers directly, it is chiefly a statement of thoroughly classical

---

27. J. Kleutgen, *Die Philosophie der Vorzeit verteidigt*, II., p. 728.

28. F. S. Fiorenza, "Systematic Theology: Task and Methods," in idem. Also J. S. Galvin (ed.), *Systematic Theology: Roman Catholic Perspectives* (Dublin, 1992), p. 31. On the theological side Fiorenza's comment is very apt: "Medieval Scholasticism had given a priority to the Scriptures and much of the instruction was basically a commentary on Scripture. Disputed questions were resolved by an appeal to authority, the most proper and intrinsic being Scripture, for, as Thomas had maintained, an argument based on the authority of the Scriptures bore intrinsic and necessary probity. For Neo-Scholasticism the situation was radically different. In reaction to the Reformation's appeal to the Scriptures, Neo-Scholastic theologians began to argue that the Scriptures are often misinterpreted. Therefore they argued that the Church's official teaching is the primary and proximate rule of faith," ibid.

(and not especially magisterium-centered) theological doctrine.[29] Beginning from a preamble on the "norm of faith" in the Word of God written, traditioned, and interpreted by the ecclesiastical magisterium, the work moves through an account of God (one and three, very Thomasian, notably on the processions of the Persons, in sharp contrast to Günther's version), the creation (a free divine act whose end goal is the glorification of God attained through his securing the greatest good for rational creatures), the regimes of grace and sin (with particular reference to the supernaturality of man's original righteousness and the elevating, and not simply healing, character of sanctifying grace—Hermes is in view here), to the Savior (a good deal, prompted by Nestorianizing language in Günther, on Christ's self-identity through the hypostatic union), and his redeeming work (an emphasis on salvation or deification as the especial aim of the Incarnation). The four-volume work ends with an extended *Prinzipienlehre* setting out the relation of speculative theology to the act of faith, and of the act of faith to its own grounds. In this context Kleutgen takes the opportunity to defend the Fathers for their prudent use of pagan philosophy,[30] and the Scholastics for their openness to a Christian mysticism which is far from *Schwärmerei*, "fanatical enthusiasm."[31]

The distinguishing feature of the work—apart, that is, from its conceptual thoroughness and elegance—is the way that, throughout, Kleutgen has in mind, both explicitly and implicitly, the heads of the chief non-classical schools of the Catholic nineteenth century, notably, of course, Hermes and Günther,[32] but also the Württemberger Johann Baptist Hirscher (1788–1865), professor of moral theology and catechetics at Freiburg, whose work, which evidently aroused in Kleutgen fears of its naturalistic thrust, is probably best regarded as a forerunner

---

29. F. Lakner, SJ, "Kleutgen und die kirchliche Wissenschaft Deutschlands im 19. Jahrhundert," *Zeitschrift für katholische Theologie* 57 (1933), pp. 161–214.

30. J. Kleutgen, SJ, *Die Theologie der Vorzeit verteidigt*, IV, (Münster, 1860, 1st edition), pp. 151–196.

31. Ibid., pp. 55–57.

32. This defensive aim, already indicated in the titles of Kleutgen's principal writings, is set forth explicitly at the outset of volume I of his "ancient theology": thus *Die Theologie der Vorzeit verteidigt* I., (Münster, 1867, 2nd edition), pp. 8–24. N.b.: the only copy of this work held in a public library in the United Kingdom (at the Bodleian) consists in two volumes of the first edition and two of the second: hence the alternation of editions in the references that follow.

of twentieth-century "political theology."³³ Kleutgen is especially exercised to make plain the sense in which theology can or can not "make progress," vis-à-vis demands for its radical restructuring in the name of the progress of *Wissenschaft* (Hermes), the progress of speculation (Günther), and progress in terms of social and political practice (Hirscher).³⁴ The message is plain: the theological tradition inherited from Fathers and Schoolmen remains intellectually coherent and spiritually serviceable, and in both regards scores higher than its rivals.

Should Kleutgen be termed an intransigent (the customary word in the Roman Curia was *zelante*)? To what extent did he feel the need to modify or extend that inherited tradition on the basis of the work of his contemporaries? His discussion of, for example, original sin, attests his awareness that the tradition did not always speak in monotone.³⁵ Changing the metaphor from aural to visual, Catholic divines belonged together on a spectrum. The problem with his particular interlocutors (at any rate Hermes and Günther) was their own strict adherence to principles they themselves had formulated.

Kleutgen exemplifies the confidence in the classical theological inheritance which was increasingly the mark of the papacy of the nineteenth century. It is the more striking that his relations with the papal office soon suffered shipwreck.

THE KLEUTGEN FIASCO

1858, when Kleutgen became the Jesuit Secretary, was a crucial year for him on more than one count. In the same year he agreed to become confessor to the enclosed Franciscan nuns of the monastery of Sant' Ambrogio.³⁶ It must have seemed an innocuous enough extra duty but

---

33. In *Die kirchlichen Zustände der Gegenwart* (Tübingen, 1849), Hirscher envisaged a reform of the Church, aimed at conscientizing its members about their full responsibility for the incoming of the divine Kingdom, as a precondition of radical reform of the political order. There is a good account of Hirscher's work in D. J. Dietrich, *The Goethezeit and the Metamorphosis of Catholic Theology in the Age of Idealism*, op. cit., pp. 198–214.

34. J. Kleutgen, SJ, *Die Theologie der Vorzeit verteidigt* IV. (Münster, 1860, 1st edition), pp. 999–1021 (Hermes), 1022–1034 (Hirscher), 1035–1043 (Günther).

35. Ibid., III. (Münster, 1870, 1st edition), pp. 663–675.

36. This sad saga is set out in K. Deufel, *Kirche und Tradition*, op. cit., pp. 56–63. Though this study is cited by Martina in this context, all reference to the (alleged) attempted murder is

this connection would embroil him in a scandal which later rendered him useless to Leo XIII, despite the impressive character of his intellectual work. That year, 1858, there entered the convent a devout widow, Princess Katharina von Hohenzollern, born Princess von Hohenlohe, and the cousin of the Archbishop von Hohenlohe who was the pro-Güntherian chamberlain of Pius IX's court. Following the Poor Clare tradition, Sant'Ambrogio had an abbess, but the community was in practice ruled by a vicaress, Maria Luigia, an unstable and indeed, as it (apparently) proved, malign personality. Katharina soon complained to Kleutgen about disturbing features of conventual practice. The vicaress had set up altars to the foundress and first superior of the monastery, Agnese Firrao, who in 1816 had been removed for questionable spiritual doctrine and dispatched to a convent at Gubbio. Among other irregularities one was notable. When the princess was asked for her help with translating letters from English into Italian, it emerged that the vicaress was engaged in an amorous correspondence with an American. The upshot of the princess's complaint to Kleutgen was (she believed) an attempt on her life by the administration of poison. The vicaress sought to detain the highly connected novice-nun within the enclosure, fearful she would make contact with her influential cousin, the papal chamberlain. She *did* make contact, whereupon an investigation by the Holy Office led to the closure of the monastery and the imposition of censures on Kleutgen. Kleutgen had not only refused to hear any criticisms of the vicaress, whom he regarded as a model of piety and devotion, but (it seems) sought to defend the ideas of the disgraced foundress whom the vicaress had effectively canonized. Hohenlohe (viscerally anti-Jesuit, and, according to Martina, increasingly eccentric[37]) convinced himself that the Jesuit was complicit in a conspiracy to murder, though the evidence was not forthcoming. Initially, Kleutgen was condemned to five years' imprisonment in the cells of the Inquisition (this was still the period of the States of the Church when ecclesiastics could get such things done), but Pius IX commuted the sentence. Instead, Kleutgen was stripped of all his posts and suspended from the priesthood. He did not regain

---

omitted in his account; thus G. Martina, sj, *Pio IX* [1851–1866], op. cit., p. 243. Possibly Martina considers the entire story a farrago.

37. Ibid., pp. 235–236, note 49 (hostility to the Society); pp. 635, 670 (growing eccentricity).

the right to hear the confessions of women in particular until 1870 (or possibly even 1879).

Having lost his Prussian citizenship through the circumstances of his entry into the Jesuit Society he was unable to return home to Germany, and lived a peripatetic life at various Italian locations, mostly in the German-speaking areas in the sub-Alpine north. Despite the use Pius IX made of him at the First Vatican Council and his subsequent appointment as a consultor to the Holy Office, Kleutgen never fully recovered from this episode. When in 1879 Leo approached him with a view to enlisting his aid for a campaign of Thomistic persuasion of Güntherians, Kleutgen felt obliged to tell him of the penalties that had been imposed, to which the pope replied, "*Ci penseremo et ci informeremo.*" "We shall think about it and take advice." Not surprisingly, nothing happened. It was some consolation to Kleutgen that when in the same year, 1879, a Güntherian who had become an Old Catholic published an article in the German press denouncing him as a proven accessory to murder, Katharina von Hohenzollern, by now foundress of the German Benedictine monastery of Beuron, sent Kleutgen a warm letter expressing her personal belief in his total innocence.

Kleutgen would not become the lodestar of a new Thomist, "Neo-Thomist," philosophy. Fulfilling that role was postponed. As we shall see in Chapters 7 and 9, it was taken up by members of the immediately subsequent generations.

Leo's Case for Thomas

It was precisely Leo's awareness of the limited extent of the Thomas revival even in Church institutions which fuelled the inclusion of sections 19 to 23 of *Aeterni Patris* whose aim was to show how differently things once stood. Leo summoned to the witness stand: the constitutions of various Orders, not just the Dominicans, the practice of many of the pre-Revolutionary Universities of Europe, statements of the Popes from Clement VI, an Avignon pope of the mid-fourteenth century, to Benedict XIV in the 1750s, the honor paid to Thomas at the General Councils of Lyons II, Vienne, Florence and Vatican I, even the grudging testimony of heresiarchs like the Strasbourg Reformer Martin Bucer. Fortified by these supporting voices, Leo echoed

Kleutgen when he remarked: "To the old teaching a novel system of philosophy has succeeded here and there, in which we fail to perceive those desirable and wholesome fruits which the Church and civil society itself would prefer."[38]

In the post-medieval period, "struggling innovators" began to philosophize without reference to faith; systems of philosophy "multiplied beyond measure"; doubt and skepticism resulted. And as men are "apt to follow the lead given them," the pope went on: "This new pursuit seems to have caught the souls of certain Catholic philosophers, who, throwing aside the patrimony of ancient wisdom, chose rather to build up a new edifice than to strengthen and complete the old by aid of the new—ill-advisedly, in sooth, and not without detriment to the sciences."[39]

And so, and here we come to the crunch: "With wise forethought, therefore, not a few of the advocates of philosophic studies, when turning their minds recently to the practical reform of philosophy, aimed and aim at restoring the renowned teaching of Thomas Aquinas and winning it back to its ancient beauty."[40]

Leo assured the bishops, to whom the encyclical was in the first place directed, that civil society itself, as well as the liberal arts and the natural sciences will benefit from this revival which, however, must be nuanced. As the pope explained, it is a question of revivifying Thomas's wisdom, not every dot and iota of his writings. "The wisdom of Saint Thomas, We say; for if anything is taken up with too great subtlety by the Scholastic doctors, or too carelessly stated—if there be anything that ill agrees with the discoveries of a later age, or, is, in a word, improbable in whatever way—it does not enter Our mind to propose that for imitation to Our age."[41]

How his project fared at the hands of a classic twentieth-century embodier—Etienne Gilson—the next chapter will seek to show.

---

38. *Aeterni Patris*, 24.
39. Ibid.
40. Ibid., 25.
41. Ibid., 31.

Chapter 7

Embodying the Leonine Project: Etienne Gilson

It remains to be seen how the Leonine project was embodied in mature form in a fully twentieth-century figure. While Jacques Maritain would have been a highly plausible candidate, my chosen exemplification is Etienne Gilson whose work bears a certain affinity with Kleutgen's—above all, in its combination of thorough knowledge of the sources with what has been called an "eschatological" view of Thomas. For the proponents of the latter, Thomas's thought furnishes the most powerful version of Christian philosophy, towards which all others before his lead up, and from which those after him, insofar as they depart from his principles, are declensions.

GILSON AS EMBODIER OF LEO'S PROJECT

Etienne Gilson was born, the son of a Parisian draper, in 1884, one year after Kleutgen's death and five after the promulgation of *Aeterni Patris*.[1] He was educated in the so-called "free" or Church schools but in 1902 transferred to the prestigious Lycée Henri Quatre, and in 1904 enrolled at the Sorbonne, the premier French University, stripped of its theology faculty with the fall of the Second Empire in 1870 but with a (secular) philosophy faculty still intact. Gilson expressed pleasure that, as a consequence of this educational history, he had never been obliged to study Neo-Scholastic textbooks. As a result he was able to come to Thomas with new eyes.[2] (He was particularly annoyed by the way the authors of Neo-Scholastic handbooks often

---

1. For the narrative of Gilson's life, see L. K. Shook, *Etienne Gilson* (Toronto, 1984).
2. E. Gilson, *Le philosophe et la Théologie,* op. cit., p. 42.

contented themselves with deriding as "absurd" the positions of other philosophers, rather than engaging with them on their own terms: a bad habit contracted, he thought, from the humanists of the sixteenth century.³) When working on his Sorbonne doctoral thesis on the medieval sources of Descartes's ideas, he discovered that Cartesianism had not necessarily improved things by the way it transformed key concepts Descartes found not among the ancients but in the much maligned Scholastics.⁴ "From Scholasticism to Descartes, the loss of metaphysical substance seemed to me immense."⁵ Like Maritain, Gilson was indebted to the Jewish agnostic philosopher Henri Bergson, whose metaphysical explorations he compared in their range and finesse to Aristotle's. It was Bergson who saved him, while at the Sorbonne, from any temptation to yield to materialism in ontology, associationism in psychology, and determinism in morals, and thus enabled a young man hitherto formed exclusively in the Catholic school system to proceed confidently to the lifelong professional study of philosophies open to the divine.⁶

Gilson's first major excursion into Thomasian studies came in 1919, when he was professor of philosophy at Strasbourg. This was the first edition of his *Le Thomisme*, subsequent versions of which chart shifts in his estimate of what was most fundamental in Aquinas.⁷ All his life Gilson would work within the official civil educational system in France, something which, given the coolness towards the Church of the Third French Republic, was rather unusual for a protagonist of the Christian philosophical tradition, and he would pick up that system's greatest prizes, teaching posts at the Sorbonne and the Ecole Pratique des Hautes Etudes in 1921, membership of the Collège de France in 1932, and then after the Second World War and the foundation of the Fourth Republic, a seat in the Senate and election to the Académie Française. His enthusiastic Republicanism would have helped.⁸ Yet

---

3. Ibid., p. 44.

4. These studies saw the light of day in 1913 as *La liberté chez Descartes et la théologie* and *Index scolastico-cartésien*.

5. Idem., *Le philosophe et la Théologie*, op. cit., p. 81.

6. The reader of Gilson's intellectual autobiography, *Le philosophe et la Théologie*, cannot but be struck by the inordinate amount of space given to "le cas Bergson."

7. Idem., *Le Thomisme. Introduction au système de saint Thomas d'Aquin* (Strasbourg, 1919).

8. L. K. Shook, *Etienne Gilson,* op. cit., p. 6.

in the early days of his career he had to cross the occasional sword with representatives of the secular establishment nonetheless.[9] Less as an insurance policy, more out of a desire to be directly useful to the Church, he also lived a second, alternative life in Canada, where the Institute of Medieval Studies he had co-founded in Toronto acquired in 1939 a Pontifical Charter, enabling it to grant not just ecclesiastical but pontifical degrees.

In 1919, when *Le Thomisme* appeared, Gilson could not perhaps be called a Thomist, only a historian of medieval philosophy interested in Thomas.[10] So much was shown by his publication in 1922 of a very general study, *La philosophie au moyen âge, des origines patristiques à la fin du XIVe siècle,* while in 1924 he brought out *La philosophie de Saint Bonaventure,* a lengthy and admiring study of Thomas's Franciscan contemporary, the Bonaventure whose name Leo had briefly recalled but subsequently forgot.[11] Gilson could not follow those scholars (such as Maurice de Wulf) who saw Bonaventure as an incipient Thomas, nor those (like Pierre Mandonnet) for whom Bonaventure was not a philosopher at all. For Gilson, Bonaventure had decided quite legitimately to philosophize within the theological order—and to use to that end some Aristotelian theses, and rather more Neo-Platonic ones, purely as helpful adjuncts to his own theological doctrine.[12] Gilson treated Bonaventure as very much Francis's spiritual son. Bonaventure's work gave "abstract expression" to the concrete spirituality of the Poor Man of Assisi, who found God in Christ in the cosmic friary of the world.[13] Subsequently, much struck by a review of a new edition of *Le Thomisme* by the Dominican Gabriel Théry, Gilson realized that *all* the medieval divines should be regarded as primarily theologians. Philosophical theses could be

---

9. E. Gilson, *Le philosophe et la Théologie,* op. cit., p. 32.

10. Though Gilson later decried the first edition of *Le Thomisme* as "wretched," his future battles with some Neo-Thomist circles were foreshadowed in the layout of the work: "Gilson did not believe that a philosophy that extrapolates ideas from the *Summa* and lays them out in an order judged appropriate on Aristotelian grounds is authentic Thomism," F. A. Murphy, *Art and Intellect in the Philosophy of Etienne Gilson* (Columbia, MO, 2004), p. 58.

11. E. Gilson, *La philosophie de saint Bonaventure* (Paris, 1924; Paris, 1943, 2nd edition).

12. See on this, J. F. Quinn, *The Historical Constitution of Saint Bonaventure's Philosophy* (Toronto, 1973).

13. F. van Steenberghen, "Etienne Gilson, historien de la pensée médiévale," *Revue philosophique de Louvain* 77 (1979), pp. 487–508, and here at p. 500.

extracted from their work just as once they had been, of set purpose, integrated there. Thomas was by no means an exception to this general rule.[14] The sheer quantity and quality of such theses was what made one particular group of such theologians (Thomas at their head) those we call *Scholastics*.

In 1925, Gilson came out of the Thomasian closet. Not only did he devote another work to Aquinas which, as one of a series entitled *Les moralistes chrétiens,* inevitably gave priority to moral philosophy, though, as Gilson insisted, in Thomas's case ethics could hardly be considered in isolation from metaphysics.[15] More importantly, perhaps, Gilson accepted an invitation to address a congress in Naples called somewhat belatedly to celebrate the sixth centenary of Thomas's canonization, which had fallen in 1923, two years earlier then, and had been marked by an encyclical *Studiorum Ducem* from the reigning pope, Pius XI, warmly endorsing and even extending the appeal made in *Aeterni Patris*.

In between *Aeterni Patris* and *Studiorum ducem* had come three things. First, in an apostolic letter of 1880 Leo had given *Aeterni Patris* the weighty interpretative title "On Christian philosophy according to the mind of Saint Thomas Aquinas, the angelic doctor, to be restored in our Catholic schools."[16] *To be restored*—so *Aeterni Patris* was to be the charter of an institutional program. Second, there had been and gone, more or less, Catholic Modernism, which appeared to show far more graphically than had the cases of Hermes, Günther and Bautain, the disastrous consequences of abandoning Christian Scholasticism. ("More or less": I mean to imply how adjudication by Church authority can be said to settle doctrinal issues but hardly scholarly questions put by the academy.) And then third, in 1917–1918 the Code of Canon Law of the Latin Church, the first such codification of the huge unwieldy *Corpus Juris Canonici* which preceded it, had turned Leo's theoretical desideratum and the lesson learned from the Modernist crisis into at any rate juridical reality. For the new Code required the study of Thomas's philosophy in all teaching institutions within the Church, from Catholic faculties in universities to

---

14. E. Gilson, *Le philosophe et la Théologie,* op. cit., pp. 85–86.

15. Idem., *Saint Thomas d'Aquin* (Paris, 1925).

16. See G. van Riet, "Le titre de l'encyclique *Aeterni Patris*: Note historique," *Revue philosophique de Louvain* 80 (1982), pp. 35–63.

seminaries and even to high schools if philosophy were studied there. Gilson appears to have been impressed by Pius XI's strong if warm language: "It is not without reason [wrote Pius XI in *Studiorum ducem*] that [Thomas] has been given the sun for a device; for he both brings the light of learning into the minds of men and fires their hearts and wills with the virtues."[17]

When Pius lauded Thomas's combination of two wisdoms, an acquired natural wisdom based on study and an infused supernatural wisdom based on grace, he was unconsciously stating Gilson's personal life-aim, as we know of it from Gilson's letters and many other testimonials: to combine rigorous scholarship with a serious, indeed fervent, spiritual life.

In 1926, Gilson's potential influence was greatly expanded when he was named a professor at the Sorbonne and simultaneously established a major Francophone journal for medieval philosophy, the *Archives d'histoire doctrinale et littéraire du Moyen-Age*. In 1929 he published his *Introduction à l'etude de Saint Augustin*, mainly an account of those elements of Augustine's corpus which throw light on the soul's journey to God.[18] That did not imply an abandonment of Thomas for the world of the Fathers. Augustine was, after all, the author whom Thomas had cited most frequently. Gilson called Augustine a real metaphysician, albeit with a strongly psychological bent. Augustinianism was a "metaphysics of conversion," or a "metaphysics of interior experience." Augustine sought to reconstruct the relation of man, the world and God by re-centering philosophical concepts in the order of grace and charity. And why not? But Catholic philosophers at Louvain, also Neo-Thomists of a kind, strongly criticized Gilson here. This, they said, was at best theology, not philosophy at all, and at worst an illicit mixing of the two, a bastardization of both reason and faith. Gilson responded by repeated attempts to propound and clarify a concept of "Christian philosophy" based ultimately on Leo's letter (which now, in 1930, he read for the first time). He was not above propounding for his opponents a disreputable genealogy. Their (Christian) "rationalism" was, he thought, nothing more than an excessive reaction against the traditionalism and fideism of the early nineteenth century

---

17. *Studiorum ducem*, 2.
18. E. Gilson, *Introduction à l'étude de saint Augustin* (Paris, 1929; Paris 1943, 2nd edition).

(compare Bautain), which in turn was nothing more than a similarly excessive reaction against the (non-Christian) rationalism of the Enlightenment *philosophes*.[19]

Supported by the other principal exemplifier of the Leonine project, his fellow layman Jacques Maritain, Gilson took various opportunities to defend the "Christian philosophy" concept, most fully in his 1931–1932 Gifford Lectures at Aberdeen, published in English as The Spirit of Mediaeval Philosophy.[20] For Gilson, any system of philosophy or way of philosophizing could de facto be made richer and more fruitful if it were pursued in the context of religious doctrines that expanded or deepened a view of reality. As he put it in *The Spirit of Mediaeval Philosophy*: Christian philosophy is "every philosophy which, although keeping the two orders [i.e., of philosophy and supernatural revelation] formally distinct, nevertheless considers the Christian revelation as an indispensable auxiliary to reason."[21]

By the 1930s Gilson had come to think of not only Bonaventure and Augustine but Thomas too for that matter as theologians who also philosophized—a view which is the dominant one today. But, he continued to insist, the philosophical elements in Thomas's corpus, so far from being invalidated by this fact, could be enhanced by it: philosophical speculation might be the healthier for beginning where faith left off.[22] That explains his apostrophizing, in *Le philosophe et la Théologie*, those "fortunate pagan philosophies" which had achieved not only an afterlife but, of greater importance

---

19. Idem., *Le philosophe et la Théologie*, op. cit., p. 69. For how things looked from the other side, see F. van Steenberghen, "Etienne Gilson et l'université de Louvain," *Revue philosophique de Louvain* 85 (1987), pp. 5–21.

20. E. Gilson, *L'esprit de la Philosophie médiévale* (1932; 2nd edition Paris 1948; English translation, *The Spirit of Mediaeval Philosophy*, London 1936; Notre Dame, IN, and London, 1991). Not that Maritain's approach was in all respects the same as Gilson's: at a celebrated 1931 public debate on this topic organized by the Société Française de Philosophie, it became apparent that: "[f]or Maritain, the philosopher's 'nature' operates in a new ethical or psychological context, if he is a Christian, whereas for Gilson the philosopher's 'nature' is set on new, supernatural ground, if he accepts revelation," thus F. A. Murphy, *Art and Intellect in the Philosophy of Etienne Gilson*, op. cit., p. 117.

21. E. Gilson, *The Spirit of Mediaeval Philosophy*, op. cit., p. 37. For a nuanced account of the "Christian philosophy" debate and Gilson's role therein, see the chapter in Francesca Murphy's study, *Art and Intellect in the Philosophy of Etienne Gilson*, op. cit., pp. 102–129.

22. See from this period his *Christianisme et philosophie* (Paris, 1936; English translation, *Christianity and Philosophy* (New York and London, 1939), originally lectures to the Parisian theology faculty of the (Calvinist) Reformed Church.

still, a more penetrating prosecution of their key theses in Christian Scholasticism. These philosophies are "happy" because a "tutelary theology has led them beyond the term of their course," not merely in temporal terms but in sapiential ones as well.[23]

More specifically, Gilson sought to interrelate the ontology, or philosophy of being, of the great Hellenic and Hellenistic philosophers to its subsequent fate in the creation thinking of the chief Scholastics. It was now that he began to develop his notion of the "metaphysics of Exodus," drawing attention to the way the divine Name revealed in Exodus 3:14, put into Latin as *Ego sum qui sum*, "I am who am," and of vast importance for Aquinas in the early questions of his *Summa theologiae*, furnishes a key for a creation metaphysic that marks a huge step forward compared with ancient Greek ontology.[24] All that is receives sustenance from an act of existence (Gilson's translation of the Latin verb for to be, *esse*, though the version *actus essendi* also occurs in his medieval sources) of which beings (in Latin *entes*, from the present participle of *esse*, *ens*) are the consequence. Beings are the consequence when the act of existence finds its terminus in an essence which stands to the original act of existence as potency to act. In other words, the abundance of the creative gift, which reflects the divine being as "He who Is," the great "I Am," is limited only by the finite capacity—the potentiality—of creatures who are always of this or that sort, of this or that determinate essence. Thus report the fourth and fifth editions of Gilson's *Le Thomisme*, from 1942 and 1944 respectively.[25] This was a doctrine of creation which showed how philosophy issuing from Catholic orthodoxy could meet all the demands of contemporary secular Existentialism for thinkers to go beyond a so-called "static" account of the human essence in particular (these years, the 1930s and 1940s, were dominated in much Continental philosophy by the early Heidegger, the early Sartre), and yet not lose hold of the general importance of essence, with which is bound up the

---

23. Idem., *Le philosophe et la Théologie*, op. cit., p. 97.

24. Fergus Kerr's *After Aquinas. Versions of Thomism* (Oxford, 2002), pp. 73–96, sets Gilson's "Existential Thomism" in the context of some competing ontologies (and rival interpretations of the Exodus text).

25. E. Gilson, *Le Thomisme. Introduction à la philosophie de saint Thomas d'Aquin* (Paris, 1942; Paris, 1944). The change of sub-title from the first three editions was significant. The standard English version, the work of Gilson's biographer, the Basilian father L. K. Shook, is based on the fifth edition of *Le Thomisme*.

idea of the intelligibility of things, in their different kinds.[26] Gilson's discovery of the "existentiality" of Thomas's conception of God—God as sheer, unconfined, ever-energetic, act-of-being—leads him to find the resemblance of creatures to God in *their* (limited) act-of-being, too. As Francesca Murphy points out, henceforth it will not suffice Gilson to commend medieval thought at large for its invigoration by the revealed doctrine of creation. From now on, "Christian philosophy only holds water as Thomistic existentialism."[27]

The discovery of the metaphysics of Exodus probably stiffened Gilson's resolve not to abandon under pressure—indeed, rather to reinforce—his interpretation of Leo's phrase *philosophia Christiana*. In 1938 in his Richards Lectures at the University of Virginia, *Reason and Revelation in the Middle Ages* he had suggested that Thomas had sought to exclude from theology all demonstrations of a purely rational nature (on the ground that theological conclusions can only follow from principles that are articles of faith). But by 1960, when he published his autobiographical *Le philosophe et la Théologie* (and probably well before), he had come to think this an illusion, if a common one.[28] A conclusion demonstrated from two rational premises can perfectly well be used theologically if it helps to understand the faith. By analogy with the divine knowledge, of which sacred doctrine is an imprint in the human mind, theology contains in principle, he wrote, "all human science . . . to the extent at least to which it deems it advisable to incorporate it within itself and make it serve its own ends."[29] Philosophy is present within theology preserv-

---

26. In effect Gilson explained this strategy in his article "Le thomisme et les philosophies existentielles," *La Vie intellectuelle* 13 (1945), pp. 144–155. From the vantage point of 1960, however, he was inclined to find in the desire to integrate Bergson's emphasis on the dynamism of being the real catalyst of the rediscovery of the metaphysics of Exodus. Thus *Le philosophe et la Théologie*, op. cit., p. 154.

27. F. A. Murphy, *Art and Intellect in the Philosophy of Etienne Gilson*, op. cit., p. 205. She takes Gilson's *L'Etre et l'essence* (Paris, 1948; 1962, 2nd edition; partial English translation as *Being and Some Philosophers*, Toronto, 1949; 2nd edition 1952) to be the proof.

28. E. Gilson, *Le philosophe et la Théologie*, pp. 86–97.

29. Ibid., p. 100. On *sacra doctrina*, see Gilson's excellent explanation of Thomas's usage in the essay of that name in *Elements of Christian Philosophy* (New York, 1960; 1963), pp. 23–45 and notably on p. 23: "By these words Thomas means any body of instruction (doctrine) made holy by its divine origin (sacred); in short, any body of instruction whose teacher is God. Sacred Scripture preeminently deserves this title, because it contains the very word of God. Still, as will be seen, the title extends to all that which, under any form, derives its truth from the divine revelation or cooperates with it in view of its divinely appointed end."

ing its own rationality precisely so as to be of service to theology, and yet, as incorporated within theology and used by it, philosophy is part of theology.

Thus, when philosophy is incorporated into theology, it can be viewed from two angles. In the perspective of philosophy itself: as philosophy, it retains its essential rationality, deepened and enlightened by the higher wisdom within which it dwells; so, for example, metaphysics can make progress thereby in understanding the notion of being (compare Exodus 3:14). But in the perspective of theology, when philosophy enters theology's service, philosophy then belongs to theology's household, and with its aid theology achieves the structure of a science, gaining at the same time a deeper understanding of the contents of faith. As with the two natures of the Word incarnate according to the Christology of Chalcedon, two wisdoms—sacred doctrine and the philosophy of being—collaborate intimately but without confusion.[30] (I shall return to this "Chalcedonian" concept of the philosophy-theology—and hence reason-faith—relationship in my Conclusion.)

The philosophies of the medieval Schoolmen, Aquinas at their head, so Gilson concluded, owed not their shortcomings but their excellence to their presence within theology. With Descartes, the link between religion and metaphysics is broken, and at first metaphysics prides itself on cutting loose from theology. But soon it turns out that metaphysics is losing its sense of identity (there is an anticipation here of the late twentieth-century movement Radical Orthodoxy), and philosophy in critical or positivistic mood takes up arms against it. As Gilson put it in his William James lectures at Harvard in 1936, published as *The Unity of Philosophical Experience*:

> Hume had destroyed both metaphysics and science; in order to save science, Kant decided to sacrifice metaphysics. Now, it is the upshot of the Kantian experiment that, if metaphysics is arbitrary knowledge, science also is arbitrary knowledge; hence it follows that our belief in the objective validity of science stands or falls with our belief in the objective validity of metaphysics. The new question, then, is no longer, why is metaphysics a

---

30. A. Maurer, "Introduction," in E. Gilson, *Christian Philosophy: An Introduction* (English translation, Toronto, 1993), pp. xvii–xix. This introduction was written especially for the Anglophone translation. See also, E. Gilson, "What is Christian Philosophy?" in A. C. Pegis (ed.), *A Gilson Reader* (Garden City, NY, 1957), pp. 177–191.

necessary illusion, but rather: Why is metaphysics necessary, and how is it that it has given rise to so many illusions?[31]

Gilson replies: metaphysicians have erred by not realizing that the true principle of unity present in the human mind is being, which alone answers the question, What is it which the mind is bound to conceive both as belonging to all things and as not belonging to any two things in the same way? In the 1949 *Being and Some Philosophers* he marveled how, in the descent from Parmenides to Sartre, being, which rightly indicates the totality of reality, has been treated as so indeterminate—contentless—that it is virtually exchangeable with nothing. (A famous passage of Hegel's *Logic* says as much.) In the modern age, at the hands in England of skepticism, in Germany of the Kantian critiques and in France of positivism, metaphysics has withered. The condition of its revival is its return to theology. And notably to a theology which, in these matters, has learned from Thomas, whose thought

> assigns . . . to metaphysics the most profound interpretation of the notion of being that any philosophy has ever proposed. I say that this interpretation of the first principle is the deepest of all because, in its light, I can continue to hold as true whatever is true in each of the other philosophies, *without any exception* and because I owe to it truths about God, nature and man, which I can hold in no other way.[32]

The other major inner-Scholastic debate in which Gilson was engaged, aside from the philosophy/theology relation, concerned the issue of epistemology. For Gilson, it was imperative to make no concessions whatsoever to the epistemological doubt and skepticism of Descartes or Kant. As he wrote in *The Spirit of Mediaeval Philosophy*

> [T]hrough the dogmatism that Kant attacked it was medieval realism that he aimed at . . . But what he never seems to have suspected is that medieval realism can never be uprooted from the mind save along with the Christian spirit that ruled its evolution and assured its growth. The medieval thinkers learned from Genesis that the world is God's work and not man's; and from the Gospel that man's end does not lie in this world but in God. Turning the whole problem the other way about, critical idealism made it forever insoluble. If my thought is the condition of being, never by

---

31. Idem., *The Unity of Philosophical Experience* (London, 1938), pp. 312–313.
32. Idem., *Le philosophe et la Théologie*, op. cit., pp. 209–210. Italics original.

thought shall I be able to transcend the limits of my being, and my capacity for the infinite will never be satisfied.[33]

Even Maritain's preferred term "critical realism" elicited from Gilson allergic reactions. He found the adjective simply unacceptable. And as for the Louvain Neo-Scholastics, they deceived themselves when they wished to make epistemology a preamble to Thomist philosophy, fundamental though that was to their project. For Gilson, Thomism is lost as soon as it abandons what he termed "methodic realism."[34] "Realism" means that the human grasp on reality is immediate, direct and spontaneously certain, and the common sense of the man on the Clapham omnibus agrees with Thomas that it is so. Realism does not stand in need of critical reflection. As one student has put it, reflecting on this rather rare disagreement between Maritain and Gilson:

> For Gilson, "realism" and "critical" refer to mutually exclusive concepts: once you start talking about realism's inability to gain intellectual respectability without a critical approach, you are reaching beyond realism's crucial premise, to wit, that our knowledge of extra-mental reality is spontaneous, self-evident, and thus indemonstrable. That means attempting to justify extra-mental reality by knowledge itself: the very starting-point of idealism.[35]

It is a reasonable surmise that Gilson's extraordinarily high praise of G. K. Chesterton as a (self-taught) interpreter of Thomas turns significantly on this issue. By his own confession, Chesterton's 1933 intuitively brilliant study *Saint Thomas Aquinas,* where a realism based on the doctrine of creation receives center place, momentarily discouraged Gilson from writing any more on Thomas or Thomism.[36]

---

33. Idem., *The Spirit of Mediaeval Philosophy,* op. cit., p. 246.

34. The phrase gave its title to Gilson's *Le Réalisme méthodique* (Paris, 1936), which is not purely, however, a study in epistemology. Its four constituent essays offer grounds for metaphysical realism at large. He reverted to the topic in *Réalisme thomiste et critique de la connaissance* in 1939 (English translation, *Thomist Realism and the Critique of Knowledge,* San Francisco, 1986), which takes to task the Louvain Neo-Thomists (too Cartesian), the Roman Thomists such as Réginald Garrigou-Lagrange (too influenced by the Scottish "Common Sense" school), and the Transcendental Thomism of the Louvain Jesuit Joseph Maréchal (too Kantian).

35. R. Dennehy, "Maritain's Reply to Gilson's Rejection of Critical Realism," in P. A. Redpath, *A Thomistic Tapestry: Essays in Memory of Etienne Gilson* (Amsterdam, 2003), p. 61.

36. As he wrote in a memorial volume produced some three years after Chesterton's death in 1936. "He [Chesterton] has guessed all that which we had tried to demonstrate, and he has all that which they were more or less clumsily attempting to express in academic formulas."

Lastly, Gilson sought to show the explanatory power of a Christian philosophy of a basically Thomasian kind in a number of areas: notably, at book length, in linguistics,[37] aesthetics[38] and the philosophy of science,[39] and, in shorter format, politics[40] and education.[41] This was also Leonine: Thomas as the guide to the reconstruction not only of Christian thought but of Christian culture as well. On Gilson's view, which is supported by the thematic rather than chronological arrangement of his encyclicals Leo himself recommended, *Aeterni Patris* is the foundational document for all the subsequent texts promulgated by the pope in his reign: what Gilson termed the *Corpus Leoninum*, a phrase redolent of respect.[42]

Still, no matter how ramifying the life of a Christian culture can be—and must be, if it is to aim at the baptism of culture at large—its heart will have to be, if it is also to remain recognizably Christian, *assent to revelation*. Gilson called *Aeterni Patris* an appeal to human knowledge (*au savoir humain*), "in a time of social disorders, themselves resulting from an intellectual disorder, to put peoples back on the road of faith and salvation."[43] That is why our next major topic must be apologetics, from Blondel to Balthasar. A necessary preliminary is to come to terms with the "philosophy of action" of Blondel.

Chesterton was one of the deepest thinkers who ever existed; he was deep because he was right; and he could not help being right; but he could not either help being modest and charitable, so he left it to those who could understand him to know that he was right, and deep; to others, he apologized for being right, and he made up for being deep by being witty": a testimony printed in C. Clemens, *Chesterton, as Seen by his Contemporaries*, with an introduction by E. C. Bentley (Webster Grove, MO, 1939), pp. 150–151.

37. E. Gilson, *Linguistique et philosophie. Essai sur les constants philosophiques du langage* (Paris, 1969).

38. Idem., *Painting and Reality* (New York, 1957); *Introduction aux arts du beau* (Paris, 1963); *Matières et formes. Poiétiques particulières des arts majeurs* (Paris, 1964).

39. Idem., *D'Aristote à Darwin et retour* (Paris, 1971).

40. Idem., (ed.), *The Church speaks to the Modern World. The Social Teaching of Pope Leo XIII* (New York, 1954).

41. Idem., *Pour un Ordre catholique* (Paris, 1934).

42. *Le philosophe et la Théologie*, op. cit., pp. 194–196.

43. Ibid., p. 167.

Chapter 8

The Philosophy of Action: Maurice Blondel

Introduction

In the last chapter we saw how Etienne Gilson, working from within a civil rather than ecclesiastical context, at any rate in the French as distinct from Canadian settings of his life and teaching, answered positively Leo XIII's call for a return to the "wisdom of Saint Thomas." That wisdom—this was the message of Leo's 1879 encyclical *Aeterni Patris,* at least as Gilson understood it—was the main historical embodiment of a philosophy both genuinely rational in its criteria of judgment and yet at the same time accepting of goals and resources derived from revelation. In the phrase proposed by the 1880 letter in which Leo gave the encyclical a new explanatory title, Thomas's was a "Christian philosophy," and here noun and adjective were meant to carry equal weight. While Gilson recognized the historic pluralism of Christian philosophy (Augustine and Bonaventure, after all, could stand comparison with Thomas, and other names might be suggested), he was also concerned to *rank* the various versions of such philosophy, placing Thomas in lonely preeminence on the topmost row. Gilson's "eschatological" view of Thomism—Thomasian wisdom is the definitively best—could also be regarded, more modestly, as a prudential judgment about the different versions of Christian philosophy on offer. Thus, for instance, in recent years in Britain, Professor John Haldane of the University of St. Andrews treats "analytic Thomism"—namely, the marriage of Anglo-American analytical philosophy with the philosophical elements in Thomas's corpus, notably those found in the two great Summas—very much *non*-eschatologically as only *provisionally* the best: the "best," that is, until something "better" comes on the market.[1]

One reason for taking a more detached stand from Thomas and the commentatorial tradition of the Thomist school could already be found in the late nineteenth century, for it derived from another aspect of Leo XIII's pontificate. And that was Leo's call on Western Catholics to "rally" to the post-Revolutionary settlements in Europe, and the intellectual and cultural life which accompanied them, wherever this could be done without sacrifice of essential features of Catholic truth. This appeal for "rallying," *ralliement*,[2] was particularly directed to France where after 1870 the rupture between civil society and Church seemed particularly acute.[3] A quite different version of "Christian philosophy," little indebted to medieval thought forms and much more consciously in dialogue with a secular philosophical outlook, is found, accordingly, in the writing (at any rate, the early and most influential writing) of Maurice Blondel whose dates are 1861 to 1949. As we shall see, Blondel sought to work out, in a *civil* context in France, a "philosophy of action," as he called it, which while being thoroughly rational in character, and indeed constituting what he himself termed an "autonomous philosophy" (autonomous, that is, vis-à-vis faith) would nonetheless furnish *both* an apologia for Christianity *and* the basis for a fundamental theology—a sector of theology whose aim it is to exhibit the intellectual preconditions of specifically theological reason and to show how theological reason meets those pre-conditions and satisfies them. Whereas Gilson in effect wore two hats—the hat of a constructive metaphysician within the Church and the hat of a historian of ideas outside it, Blondel only had one hat to wear. It was

---

1. From a conversation with Professor Haldane at Blackfriars Oxford on the occasion of his 1998 Aquinas lecture, subsequently published as J. Haldane, "Thomism and the Future of Catholic Philosophy," *New Blackfriars* 80 (1999), pp. 158–171. That is, for a philosopher, the proper responsible attitude. But see J.F.X. Knasas, "Haldane's Analytic Thomism and Aquinas's *Actus Essendi*," in C. Paterson and M. S. Pugh, *Analytical Thomism. Traditions in Dialogue* (Aldershot, 2006), pp. 233–252, for the view that "Analytic Thomism" is not well placed to transmit certain aspects of Aquinas, notably his deep ontology.

2. Apparently Leo took the term from the French press, where in 1886 a cleric had used it for his willingness to consider active support of the Republic in the wake of the death of the (childless) Bourbon pretender, the Comte de Chambord, otherwise "Henri V." Thus M. Burleigh, *Earthly Powers. Religion and Politics in Europe from the Enlightenment to the Great War* (London, 2005), p. 347.

3. A. Dansette, *Histoire religieuse de la France contemporaine* (Paris, 1965), pp. 431–512.

the hat of a philosopher for whom the supernatural order was philosophically inescapable, and as a consequence found himself far less acceptable than Gilson to colleagues in the secular Universities—as well as, later on and for very different reasons, to theologians in the Church. Evidently, *ralliement* was not without its difficulties.

THE MAKING OF BLONDEL'S *L'ACTION*

Blondel was born in Dijon on All Souls' Day 1861, a child in a well-to-do family of lawyers. He began life with the inestimable advantage of knowing he would never be obliged to earn his own living, which helps to explain his *insouciance* towards other French academics in his field. Despite a parental preference that he should follow a legal career, in 1881 he applied and was accepted to study philosophy at the Parisian Ecole Normale Supérieure where he was given a good initiation into the history of Western philosophy and the two systems most in vogue in the 1880s in France. These systems were, first, the idealism of Kant with its three critiques—corresponding respectively to pure reason, practical reason and aesthetic judgment, and second, Herbert Spencer's evolutionism which found in Darwin's theory of evolutionary adaptation to environment by means of natural selection a key to understanding all areas of human activity. Kant's identification of three distinct and unrelated rationalities, and Spencer's implausible attempt to find a key to all reality in an extrapolation from Darwin's work on *The Origin of Species*, probably encouraged Blondel, by reaction, to formulate his own project: namely, a comprehensive theory of human action and its further implications. His account would be more unitary than Kant's, more differentiated than Spencer's.

At this time, the Ecole required of future philosophical teachers two theses, of which the shorter had to be in Latin; it is worth noting—in a subsidiary kind of way—that Blondel's choice for the latter fell on what might have seemed a historical curiosity.[4] The late seventeenth-century German Lutheran rationalist philosopher Gottfried Wilhelm Leibniz had proposed—initially in correspondence with French Jesuits about the ecumenically disputed

---

4. M. Blondel, *De vinculo substantiali et de substantia composita apud Leibnitium* (Paris, 1893). There is a modern French translation: *Le Lien substantial et la substance compose d'après Leibniz* (Louvain, 1972).

doctrine of Eucharistic transubstantiation—that a divinely provided "substantial bond," *vinculum substantiale*, (the phrase seems to derive from Suárez) makes of bodies and souls substantial selves, by analogy with the union of divinity and humanity in the single person of Christ. That could have application to the Holy Eucharist, where "the effect of transubstantiation—that is, the substantial presence of the body of Christ as a bond [for the de-substantiated bread and wine, q. v.]—expresses . . . the fact that God is the true cause of all substances."[5] The Leibnizian "bond" suggested to Blondel a philosophically animated Christology with far-reaching ramifications. As he wrote to a contemporary Jesuit, Pierre Teilhard de Chardin, with reference to Leibniz's own Jesuit correspondent, Bartholomé des Bosses: "The question raised by Leibniz and des Bosses concerning transubstantiation during the Eucharist leads us to conceive of Christ, without detriment to the constituent monads, as the bond which makes substantiation possible, the vivifying agent for all creation: *vinculum perfectionis*."[6]

We shall return to this topic later, in the context of the possibility (or otherwise) of philosophical adumbrations of dogmatic truths. Meanwhile, we can note that, in a way Blondel apparently found hard to conceptualize, Leibniz's work also suggested to him the key idea that *action is the link between thought and being*.[7]

Blondel had great difficulty getting the thesis topic of his *principal* dissertation accepted since, as he was told, the theme of action had never been, in and of itself, a *topos* of the philosophical tradition. His thesis, he was warned, would have to be virtually without bibliography or indeed footnotes. The struggle with the Ecole over the choice of topic was, however, nothing compared with the difficulties he faced over his eventual manner of treating the topic whose aim was to show

---

5. D. Grummett, "Blondel, Modern Catholic Theology and the Leibnizian Eucharistic Bond," *Modern Theology* 23. 4 (2007), p. 565.

6. *Pierre Teilhard de Chardin—Maurice Blondel: Correspondance* (English translation, New York, 1976), p. 23, cited in ibid., p. 568.

7. M. Blondel, *The "Letter on Apologetics" and "History and Dogma."* Texts presented and translated by A. Dru and I. Trethowan (London, 1964; Edinburgh, 1995), p. 46. See idem., *Une enigme historique: le "vinculum substantiale" d'après Leibniz et l'ébauche d'un réalisme supérieur* (Paris, 1930), which is Blondel's fullest attempt to indicate how he saw Leibniz's hypothesis (itself in its origin a way around the difficulties of the German thinker's monadology for the Catholic doctrine of transubstantiation) as the clue to a new concept of philosophy where the central place would go to *agency*.

that the internal logic of human action (the use of the word "logic" in that context was enough by itself to raise philosophical eyebrows) issued in a need to postulate the existence of the supernatural order. The work which, after revision, was published in 1893 under the title *L'Action* gained its examiners' support owing to its closely argued character and the strictly philosophical manner in which it proposed the hypothesis of the supernatural or as Blondel called it, citing the French version of words of Jesus to Martha of Bethany in Saint Luke's Gospel (10:42), "l'Unique nécessaire." In French, these words are usefully ambiguous: they can mean "the one thing necessary" (impersonal), or, alternatively, "the One [who is] necessary" (personal). That also works in the Greek, incidentally, though not in Latin, any more than in English. The completed whole (revamped, some think not happily, in 1936) corresponded to the ambition he had set himself, as that is laid out in his diaries, the *Cahiers intimes*.

> Like every man, I have a role, a mission to fulfill, a vocation. And I feel more and more drawn to the project of showing in thought as in my life, the natural necessity of the supernatural and the supernatural reality of the natural . . . I must show the actual paths of reason towards God incarnate and crucified; I must conciliate the claims of modern thought; I must move science and philosophy by the methods which are dear to them and which they are right to love; I must remain natural as long as anyone and longer than anyone in order to show more singly, more peremptorily, more pacifically, more broadly, more impersonally, the inevitable need for the supernatural.[8]

The Content of *L'Action*

How, then, does *L'Action* proceed? Some preliminary grasp of the shape and content of this work can be gleaned from its subtitle, which reads, "An essay in the criticism of life and in a science of practice." As the phrase "the criticism of life" might indicate, its method is phenomenological (we can say this even though Blondel only uses that word in later retrospects on *L'Action*), for phenomenology characteristically approaches objects in their *Lebenswelt*, their "life-world." And as the phrase "science of practice" might indicate, this is a philosophy which

---

8. Cited in ibid., pp. 44–45.

will find rationality to be inherent in human praxis before, often, it is conceptually or speculatively laid out in theory. The chief object of the book is to explore the nature of action considered as what constructs the destiny of man. As Blondel wrote in the preface to *L'Action*:

> Yes or no, has human life a meaning, has man a destiny? ... The problem is inevitable and inevitably man solves it; and this solution, right or wrong, but voluntary even when it is necessary, is carried in each one's actions. This is the reason why action must be studied: the very meaning of the word and the wealth of its content will be unfolded little by little.[9]

Blondel traced a whole series of endeavors in which human beings typically invest their energies, showing that one kind of enterprise tends to generate another to which, then, it leads, despite the differences between distinct fields of human action. These kinds of endeavor are, as Blondel put it, "heteronogeneous [different from each other in kind] but [nonetheless] solidary [profoundly inter-connected]."[10] In the course of exhibiting this dialectic of human action, Blondel simultaneously sought to show that at all levels, or in all the chief sectors of human activity, there is an "inadequation"—we might paraphrase that as a *disproportion* or, possibly, a *lack of equilibrium*—between the willed object in each case (what we are directly willing) and the spontaneous movement of willing (what we have the capacity to will). Between the will consciously invested in our particular choices (Blondel called this *la volonté voulante*) and the wider dynamism that animates the entire person (this he called *la volonté voulue*), there is a gap, the character and implications of which Blondel seeks to lay bare.

Though hundreds of pages in *L'Action* are devoted to this dialectical phenomenology of human action, we can look at it, however briefly, a little more concretely. By adding the word "dialectical" to qualify "phenomenology," I mean to underline a feature which distinguishes Blondel's work from phenomenology as normally understood. All the time he is concerned for "necessary" in the sense of "unavoidable" transitions. Blondel first clears away two possible life-structures: those of dilettantism and nihilism. (The Blondel scholar Bishop

---

9. M. Blondel, *L'Action: Essai d'une critique de la vie et d'une science de la pratique* (Paris, 1893; reproduced in photo-offset, Paris, 1950), pp. vii–viii.

10. Ibid., p. 435.

Peter Henrici has called the opening sections of *L'Action* "a gallery of possible—and mistaken—attitudes to life."[11]

In dilettantism, the topic of Part One of *L'Action*, life is treated as an amusing but meaningless game. But dilettantism requires a sustained act of suppression of the question of human destiny, thereby at a deeper level of analysis bearing witness to the unavoidability of exactly that question.

The dilettante may then react to this unfortunate discovery by embracing nihilism, which occupies Blondel in Part Two. The nihilist admits that the question of a final meaning to life cannot be bypassed, but finds that its answer is precisely nothing. (Blondel may have had Arthur Schopenhauer, the great philosopher of pessimism, in mind.) Blondel shows, however, that nothing can only be striven for by negation of something, and that the issue of such striving can only be in one of two manners. Either the person adopts a philosophy of mortification, a metaphysical experiment in which the world of the senses is sacrificed through entering upon a spiritual journey, but this is a project quite contradictory of nihilism. Or, alternatively, the nihilist must concede that he cannot break away from the factual "something"—whatever this may turn out to be—of the world of experience.

So far, then, Blondel has claimed that the problem of destiny cannot be avoided, nor can it have in any outright way a nihilist solution. That discovery induces the primitive assertion, "There is . . ."—in Blondel's language, *C'est*—which is also, we can add parenthetically, the starting point of Gilson's Thomist realism. Blondel's interest in this anti-nihilist assertion is not, however, that of a constructive metaphysician like Gilson. It is, rather, the interest of a philosopher of action. His question is, accordingly: what turns out to be the scope of the statement, "There is . . ." when considered as an affirmation, at one and the same time, necessary and yet consented to, which expresses the engagement with reality of human willing at its deep source?

To answer this question takes Blondel through diverse interrelated sectors of activity, evoked in the lengthy Part Three, the extended

---

11. P. Henrici, "Maurice Blondel (1861–1949) und die 'Philosophie der Aktion'," in E. Coreth, SJ, W. M. Neidl, G. Pfligersdorffer (ed.), *Christliche Philosophie im katholischen Denken des 19 und 20. Jahrhunderts 1. Neue Ansätze im 19. Jahrhundert*, op. cit., p. 549.

centerpiece of the whole work. The activity of sensation, sensing things, is the most elementary expression of the initial dynamism of "There is . . ." (This may be considered a transposition to the level of intellectual appetite of the Thomist maxim, "nothing is in the mind that is not first in the senses.") But sensation carries within it a lack of consistency—think, for instance, of the famous illusion (or is it an illusion?) of seeing a straight stick which looks bent when placed in water. Such inconsistencies lead people to create some version, however rudimentary, of scientific reflection. Science in turn supposes a synthetic activity, the constitutive action of the subject, imposing intelligible order on data. Awareness of such action by the subject, what we call self-consciousness (this was the stage of unfolding action when Günther had begun to get interested), then gives rise to an exploration of freedom. To be developed, freedom becomes incarnate in its own prosecution. Meeting elements of resistance, in the human body and the world, it proceeds to construct individuality: this is how personal distinctiveness emerges. Individuals, however, seek complementarity, whether to exert an influence or to elicit cooperation. Hence we find action directed to family, nation, and indeed humanity at large through the need to shape such action appropriately. Human intentionality now gives rise to ethics, and through ethics—and this for Blondel is quite decisive—to the attempt to seek a plenary kind of self-fulfillment by ascribing infinite value to one or other or more of the finite stages traversed so far.

Blondel emphasizes that at each stage, or level, an object is willed for itself. At each stage or level some kind of action has its own consistency. But he also seeks to show that, at each stage or level, the motive that prompts us to cleave to each stage or level, to cling firmly to it, is also in the end the motive that prompts us to go beyond it even if we also, simultaneously, retain it. The very amplitude of the human dynamism (the human will seen as inclusive of intellectuality) invites us to embrace each stage. But the same amplitude, in seeking to adequate or equal itself in the phenomena it encounters in this total series, also moves us to situate the infinite within it, and this generates a contradiction called by Blondel "superstition."

It is superstitious to equate the infinite with intentional objects on any of these levels or at any of these stages, since this is to make limited phenomena infinitely more than they are. Yet the dynamism of the will to express its own amplitude is inescapable. Part Four of *L'Action*, in describing the "necessary being of action," furnishes in effect Blondel's full response to the life-attitude of nihilism set forth in Part Two. The flowering or expanding of human action, thus analyzed, leads Blondel to the following conclusion: "It is impossible not to recognize the insufficiency of every natural order and not to experience a further need; it is [also] impossible to find within oneself the wherewithal to satisfy this religious need. It is necessary, and it is impracticable."[12]

As a magisterial study of Blondel's philosophy has put it in an important comment on this analysis: "Blondel does not measure the various steps of action against the antecedently known amplitude of the will; on the contrary, it is the inexorable development of action which progressively reveals the amplitude of the spiritual dynamism by which it is secretly animated from the beginning."[13]

But Blondel's aim is not just to write an anthropology, even a philosophical anthropology which points towards its own theological counterpart. His aim is, rather, to show the inescapability of an option for the supernaturally transcendent. To cite the same commentator, Henri Bouillard:

> The human will has gone through the entire order of phenomena without exhausting its own *élan* [the thrust of its own onward and upward movement]. It must now will and ratify itself [in its amplitude, i.e.]. But it cannot attain itself [in that amplitude, i.e.] directly, even though it necessarily wills itself. Out of this conflict arises the idea of [*l'Unique nécessaire*] . . .[14]

which, be it noted, is not yet determined as the God of Christian revelation. Rather, the "one thing necessary," or "One [who is] necessary" is "the supernatural," understood simply as that which transcends the order immanent in the human world and in that sense "goes beyond nature" which is what the word "supernatural" means. In this context, not to open oneself to the supernatural entails the enduring frustration of action (Blondel will consider this a philosophical analogue to the theological idea of damnation), whereas, to open oneself to it—by

---

12. M. Blondel, *L'Action*, op. cit., p. 319.
13. H. Bouillard, *Blondel and Christianity* (English translation, Washington and Cleveland, 1969), p. 10.
14. Ibid., p. 8.

what means we must consider in a moment—is to reach our true end. (That will be, then, the philosophical analogue of the theological idea of salvation.)

In *L'Action*, so we have seen, the role of philosophy is to make manifest the relations between phenomena encountered in the inevitable expansion of human acting. But the necessary development of these relations, openness to the supernatural, once fully consented to, generates an ontological affirmation which goes beyond phenomenology. That is the message of the last section of Blondel's work, Part Five of *L'Action*, which, by underlining the need for decisive action expressed in serious religious practice, constitutes Blondel's full response to the life attitude of dilettantism as expressed in Part One. The emphasis on ontology, now more and more clearly emerging, cannot be called unsuspected since, as we recall, a first affirmation of being, albeit one that is primitive in kind, namely, "There is . . . ," was made virtually at the outset. That is already, evidently, a philosophy of being *in nuce*, in embryo. It was not simply from considerations of ecclesiastical prudence that in later years Blondel integrated a good deal of Thomist thinking into his work.[15]

The late Trilogy—*La Pensée, L'Etre et les êtres*, and the two volumes of the re-worked *L'Action*—belongs to the period when Blondel was seeking to introduce elements from Thomas into his thought, as do likewise *La Philosophie et l'esprit chrétien* and *Les exigences philosophiques du Christianisme*.[16] Blondel became convinced that another Thomas than the one presented by strongly Aristotelianizing Neo-Thomists was possible, and could be summoned to the service of a "concrete, integral realism." But for the Blondel of the "first" *L'Action* no philosophy of being worth the name is accessible to us until we have worked through the developing logic of human action to its issue in confrontation with the supernatural and made for ourselves the

---

15. M. Blondel, *La Pensée* (Paris, 1934); idem., *L'Etre et les êtres* (Paris, 1935); idem., *L'Action* (2 vols., Paris, 1936–1937).

16. Idem., *La Philosophie et l'esprit chrétien* (two vols., Paris, 1944–1946); idem., *Les exigences philosophiques du Christianisme* (Paris, 1950). Blondel's discovery of Thomas was facilitated by Pierre Rousselot's *L'intellectualisme de saint Thomas* (Paris, 1912): Rousselot's contribution to the debate about apologetics opened by Blondel is considered below, in Chapter 9. For the whole issue of Blondel and Thomas, see A. Fabriziani, *Blondel interprete di Tommaso. Tra rinascità del tomismo e condanna del pensiero modernista* (Padua, 1984). Blondel describes his own intellectual journey in the pseudonymous *L'itinéraire philosophique de Maurice Blondel* (Paris, 1928).

religious option. And the reason is that only then do we retroactively appropriate the entire succession of phenomena encountered in their real relation to the Absolute. Only then, in Blondel's language, is our relation to being possessive rather than privative. It *would* be privative were our response to the option for *L'Unique nécessaire* a refusal, for such a refusal would be equivalent to a rejection of the one reality that confers coherence on the entire chain of finite objects that leads up to it. And being able to make one's own reality as humanly inhabited in its relation to the Absolute and in no other way is the true possession of it: this *is* the philosophical idea that corresponds to the notion of salvation.

IMPLICATIONS OF BLONDEL'S WORK FOR THE REASON/FAITH RELATIONSHIP

Blondel's work has implications for the reason/faith relationship—as, of course, he realized. Its locus was novel: a new way of situating the relation of thought and practice. In a letter explaining his theme he wrote: "Between Aristotelianism, which depreciates and subordinates practice to thought, and Kantianism, which separates them and exalts the practical order to the detriment of the other, there is something to define, and it is in a very concrete manner, through the analysis of action, that I propose to define it."[17]

To do so would be, he considered, nothing less than to "disengage" the "philosophy" inherent in "the Catholic form of thought."[18]

At the Ecole Normale Blondel had discovered a great disdain for Christianity and a refusal even to consider its truth claims. Nevertheless, right from the beginning of *L'Action* Blondel admits that Christian faith has furnished him with what he calls the "directing hypothesis" of the work. There is reason to think that the spiritual theology and not least the theological anthropology of Saint Bernard

---

17. *Lettres philosophiques de Maurice Blondel* (Paris, 1961), p. 10. In the early twenty-first century, when Aristotle's ethics have enjoyed a widespread revival, and the importance of *praxis* in his outlook is generally acknowledged, this may seem a more maverick judgment than a century ago. But we note that in his *Metaphysics* (1072B28) "thinking," *noêsis,* is equated with life itself. It is in the *Nicomachean Ethics* (1103A) that Aristotle explains how the faculty of reason has two aspects: the "power of assenting to reason and the power to initiate rational actions." Thus J. M. Rist, *Human Value. A Study in Ancient Philosophical Ethics* (Leiden, 1982), p. 44.

18. *Lettres philosophiques de Maurice Blondel,* op. cit., p. 34.

was in his mind.[19] In this sense, Blondelianism is not a "separated philosophy" such as was desired by the Neo-Scholastics of Louvain. But at the same time Blondel insists strongly that the philosophical effort *L'Action* represents proceeds according to its own autonomous law. Once the directing hypothesis is formulated, at no further point in the move to affirmation of the supernatural are assumptions made or arguments proposed which depend even materially on revelation. I mean by "materially" assumptions or arguments which, while they may in principle be rationally defensible, derive as a matter of historical fact from the biblical patrimony. Thus, Blondel's attitude to philosophy as practiced by Christians amounts to saying, it should be autonomous but not separated. His is a halfway house between Gilson and the school of Louvain.

The particular manner in which Blondel's directing hypothesis was conceived challenged the secularism of the Ecole Normale in the most direct possible way. The objection of the Ecole philosophers was to a doctrine—namely, Christian doctrine—which claimed to impose on the human mind and human conduct supernatural requirements that came from without, coming from outside the human being. These requirements on which access to human destiny turned—both a just idea of human destiny and the actual realization of that destiny—were *heteronomous*. And this for humanists was and is the supreme stumbling block. It goes against human autonomy, and thus not only human rationality but human moral dignity, to require men to submit to a law, a *nomos*, which is other, *heteros*, to their own reason and thus to their own being. *A fortiori* is this the case if insult is added to injury by the claim that rejection of this supernatural invitation from without produces as its malign fruit eternal damnation. Blondel sought to confront this fundamental secularist objection by showing—using, as I say, purely autonomous philosophical methods—that the

---

19. C. Maharné, "Les auteurs spirituels dans l'élaboration de la philosophie blondelienne (1883–1893)," *Recherches de Science religieuse* 56. 2 (1968), pp. 231–234. The following account of Bernard's theology of man under grace is pertinent to the program of *L'Action*: "To be distinguished from redemptive grace (gratia salvans) . . . is the grace received in creation itself (gratia creans), the divine love that constitutes us what we are, images of God. By nature we love, but only by grace (gratia salvans) do we love the good. Bernard reflects, not upon the hypothetical possibility of God's declining to elevate humanity by withholding grace, but upon the actuality of God's presence in grace to the human person. A 'merely human' level of humanity, then, has never existed." Thus E. Stiegman, "Bernard of Clairvaux, William of Saint Thierry, the Victorines," in G. R. Evans (ed.), *The Medieval Theologians*, op. cit., p. 136.

supernatural, *L'Unique nécessaire,* the "Unique Necessary," answers the most profound desire of the human will, in such a way that rejection of the supernatural entails for that will permanent frustration. In other words, he sought to show that autonomy *requires* heteronomy, not only in reality—in lived existence—but also in thought. In thought, free investigation in the philosophy of action necessarily brings about an encounter with the kind of demand that the Christian concept of supernatural grace embodies.

From the outset Blondel's text provoked controversy, and this is not surprising given the nature of its claims, though it must be admitted that the waters were sometimes muddied owing to the more than occasional literary obscurity of this huge and seemingly unwieldy but in fact very carefully structured work. From the rationalist side, the objection was lodged that, since *L'Action* terminated in an account of the supernatural it inevitably transgressed the due limits of philosophy. As one such reviewer—anonymous but in fact the leading light of the Ecole Normale, Léon Brunschvig, put it in the year of publication, 1893, "modern rationalism has been led by the analysis of thought to regard the notion of immanence as the basis and very condition of all philosophical doctrine."[20] Blondel would find, Brunschvig warned, "among the defenders of the rights of Reason, courteous but staunch adversaries."[21] Blondel replied that the method he had followed reflected precisely a notion of immanence.

> Simply by following the continuous evolution of our rational exigences [requirements], I make emerge from consciousness, from within, what appeared at the start of this movement to be imposed on consciousness from without . . . Turning to action, reason discovers there more than when it is applied to reason itself, but without ceasing to be rational. And if I speak of the supernatural, what I am giving expression to is a cry of nature, an appeal of moral conscience.[22]

This clarification, which should hardly have been needed by an attentive reader anyway, is probably what enabled Blondel to receive an appointment in a state University, at Aix-en-Provence, where he

---

20. [L. Brunschvig] in "Supplément," *Revue de Métaphysique et Morale* (1893), cited in H. Bouillard, *Blondel and Christianity,* op. cit., p. 16.

21. Ibid.

22. In "supplément," *Revue de Métaphysique et Morale* (1894), p. 7.

became *chargé de cours* in 1896 and a full professor in 1897, remaining in that post for the rest of his life.

But just at the time that Blondel was winning the support of philosophers he was losing that of theologians, who, to judge by the initial reviews, had at first welcomed his work. Alarmed by the way that a well-disposed clerical reviewer in the *Annales de philosophie chrétienne* had congratulated him on taking apologetics into the realm of psychology, he wrote in the course of 1896 a series of six articles in that journal explaining what he really considered to be his aims. These were published under the impossibly lengthy title *Lettre sur les exigences de la pensée contemporaine en matière d'apologétique et sur la méthode de la philosophie dans l'étude du problème religieux*—generally known to Anglophone readers as Blondel's *Letter on Apologetics*. Blondel admitted that *L'Action* had an apologetic intent, but he strenuously denied that its approach was psychological. He was not, that is, simply appealing from conscious to unconscious aspirations. Its approach was, to the contrary, strictly philosophical. Its author was convinced that modern philosophy, since Kant that is, had greater resources than medieval Aristotelianism possessed for resolving the conflict between reason and faith. The way to resolve that conflict was to borrow the methods of contemporary rationalism but to develop those methods to their limits, showing in that fashion how reason could be brought to the threshold of faith. The immanent dialectic of reason—Blondel means, in the philosophy of action—leads necessarily to the option of faith which, while genuinely an option—i.e., a choice—alone enables such reason to appropriate fully the lessons it has learned in following the development of its own dialectic. In Blondel's own phraseology in the *Letter on Apologetics*: the problem of the supernatural is the very condition of philosophy; the notion of immanence is realized in our consciousness only by the effective presence of the notion of the transcendent; the supernatural is indispensable to man, as well as inaccessible to him—inaccessible, that is, without a divine gift. This, Blondel opined, is the only kind of Catholic apologetics self-consciously modern people are likely to consider worth thinking about anyhow.

The *Letter on Apologetics*, like the reply to Brunschvig, helped to clarify the aims of *L'Action* but it also unleashed two theological controversies, both of which extended far beyond Blondel's person and work—though up until his death in 1949 he was involved, often unwillingly, in each. One, which we shall consider more fully in the next chapter, centered on the question of the adequacy or otherwise, in the light of Blondel's comments, of classical apologetics, with their themes of miracle, prophecy, the moral perfection of the divine Messenger, Jesus of Nazareth, and the congruence with human nature of the revealed Message. Writers who considered that Blondel's method was Kantian, his metaphysics phenomenalist, his epistemology pragmatist, were, reasonably enough, especially harsh on his seeming departure from the apologetic program laid out in *Dei Filius*.

The other debate focused on the legitimacy or otherwise of Blondel's statement that the supernatural can be shown by philosophical methods to be "necessary" to man. This second controversy was often described in the first half of the twentieth century as the debate between "intrinsicists" and "extrinsicists": those, that is, who considered the concept and the reality of a supernatural vocation to be intrinsic to a full description of the human condition, and those who, by contrast, took that concept and reality to be extrinsic to such a description, on the ground that any other view would eliminate the gratuity of grace, the sovereignly free act whereby the spiritual creature, man, is divinely elevated into a new condition where, from that moment on (and whenever one considers that moment to be: Adamic creation, the Incarnation, personal justification?), the human goal is, for the first time, participation in the divine life. On that second controversy a word is in place here.

The Controversy over the "Necessity" of the Supernatural

Whatever the merits of, respectively, intrinsicism and extrinsicism, the link of this debate to Blondel's work, though historically firm, is conceptually tenuous. Blondel was not a theologian, and had no intention of declaring an opinion on the interrelation of nature and grace, a topic discussed in Catholic theology since, in particular, the sixteenth century. His was not a theological concept of nature at all, but a common-sense one. For the Blondel of *L'Action* "human nature" means simply the human world. Only in the 1930s, when he brought out his trilogy on being, thought and action, and the 1940s when he published the series "Philosophy and the Christian Spirit," incomplete at his death, did he attempt to factor in the theological issues concerned, at a certain price in terms of literary coherence and as part and parcel of satisfying Thomists. So when in *L'Action* from an analysis of the meaning of human action in its totality Blondel arrives at the conclusion that confrontation with the idea of the supernatural is inevitable, he prescinds from the question, does human life as we know it in the world proceed on an exclusively natural basis, in the theological sense of the word "nature," or does it already include an *orientation* which is, theologically speaking, more than natural, i.e., the supernatural, grace, a direction towards glory.

Furthermore, the idea of the supernatural as such in *L'Action* is insufficiently determined to be identifiable as Christianity's God of grace and glory. Any occasion when Blondel invokes the divine under that description is always a matter of suggesting how a *further determination* of the meaning of the supernatural along these lines is congruent with the philosophical concept of the supernatural at which he has arrived. The same tentative quality also attaches to his suggestion that, were this proposal to be accepted, congruity could likewise be discerned in the identification of the Leibnizian "substantial bond" of all phenomena as not God *simpliciter* but the Word incarnate, who is precisely, on the Chalcedonian definition of his being, the union of finite with infinite reality in a single person.

The Philosophical Anticipation of Theological Reason

That said, there is clearly a sense in which Blondel claims to find in Christian dogma theological meanings for which he can produce a philosophical if not equivalent then at least analogue. The doctrine just mentioned, the *vinculum substantiale* of all beings and the status of the Word incarnate, is as good an example as any.[23] And as this example

---

23. D. Grummett, "Blondel, Modern Catholic Theology and the Leibnizian Eucharistic Bond," art. cit., p. 574, suggests the dialectical relation of theology and philosophy: "Leibniz develops the concept of the *vinculum substantiale* because he perceives the aporia inherent in any non-theological metaphysics, urging a theological cosmology against metaphysical metanarrative. The contrary notion that material reality is entirely separable from divine action—or in other words, is really distinct from it—provides the basis for modern scientific and philosophical paradigms divorced from theological reality. Leibniz through Blondel urges a theological turn to

shows, by "Christian dogma" here is meant those revealed mysteries which the Church considers to be supernatural in their essential content and not simply supernatural in their mode—as would be, for instance, the revealed moral law in the Ten Commandments, or the existence and natural perfections of God. Arguably, Blondel was in this regard what could be called a "Neo-Anselmian." Both Blondel and Saint Anselm sought on the basis of faith a rational argument for dogma which, while not implying any premise of faith, would be *in some fashion* valid in principle for every mind. But how, then, we may ask in conclusion, would the cases not only of Blondel but of Anselm himself—a doctor of the Church, no less—differ from that of Günther who was condemned, we recall, precisely for teaching that in his thought the revealed mysteries had achieved their own rational mediation for the first time?

The case of Anselm (and Blondel) would differ in two ways. First, for both thinkers the "necessity" to believe (in, say, the graciousness of God or the cosmic role of the Incarnation) is more fundamentally an ontological necessity than it is a propositional necessity. It belongs to an order constituted by the radical needs of the created spirit. The truth value of the propositions which its statement involves turns on subsequent confirmation from revelation. In Anselm's language in the *Monologion,* the necessary conclusions at which the thinker arrives by exploring the rationality of faith, are not *omnino necessarium,* "altogether necessary," absolutely necessary. The Christian philosopher must await such time as the object of these conclusions (the graciousness of God, the cosmic role of the Incarnation) is confirmed by a higher *auctoritas.* And this "authority" turns out to be Scripture read in tradition. If that is so, one can hardly hold that Anselm is a rationalist *tout court,* making faith's deepest mysteries available to pure ratiocination.

Indeed, enough speaks to that conclusion for some commentators to find him, on the contrary, a fideist: witness Karl Barth's *Anselm: Fides Quaerens Intellectum.*[24] Not surprisingly, then, some historians discover here a desire to have their cake and eat it, bending both ways so to do. According to Gillian Evans: for Anselm, "to prove"

---

the concrete which proclaims the contingency and uniqueness of created being and the true reality of the phenomenon."

24. K. Barth, *Anselm: Fides Quaerens Intellectum* (English translation, Richmond, VA, 1971).

is to make something plain in a fashion which leads people to recognize the satisfying fittingness of some argument (so less than rational demonstrability), while "the ultimate form of a necessary reason lies not in the formal exactness of its structure but in its compelling appeal to the minds of reasonable men" (but how is this essentially different from just such demonstrability?).[25] One answer is furnished by both a medieval disciple of Anselm and a modern medievalist. In the thirteenth century Saint Bonaventure, and in the twentieth the French scholar A. M. Jacquin, sum up the Anselmian position as follows: while there are indeed objectively necessary arguments for the mysteries of the Trinity and the Incarnation, in this life the human intellect does not grasp those arguments with sufficient lucidity to make the act of faith superfluous in this regard.[26]

A second exculpation of Anselm—and Blondel—from the charge of *Güntherianismus* is that the presentation of necessary conclusions about the mysteries of faith (Anselm) or appropriate philosophical analogues for dogma (Blondel) does not suffice to communicate what we might call a "filled out" knowledge of divine realities. Only the experience of faith fully actualizes the understanding of faith. The *ratio fidei* is not the full *intellectus fidei*.[27] We saw in the opening chapter of this study how in Letter 120 Saint Augustine distinguishes between the understanding that leads to faith and the faith that leads to a further stage of understanding. Such higher understanding, mystically penetrated, theologically elaborated, is unavailable (for both Anselm and Blondel) without the act of faith, and this means in the last analysis abidingly unavailable without the act of ecclesial faith, saying "I believe" by self-identification with the corporate *Credo*, the corporate "I believe," of the Church.

---

25. G. R. Evans, *Anselm and Talking about God* (Oxford, 1978), p. 149. Saint Thomas escapes from the dilemma set (unwittingly?) by Professor Evans when he transforms Anselm's necessary arguments into "suitable" arguments, arguments from *convenientia*.

26. See A. M. Jacquin, "Les 'rationes necessariae' de S. Anselme," *Mélanges Mandonnet* (Paris, 1930), pp. 67–78.

27. For the comparison with Anselm, see H. Bouillard, *Blondel and Christianity*, op. cit., pp. 197–202. Bouillard's interpretation of Anselm is drawn from Paul Vignaux, notably the latter's essay "structure et sens du *Monologion*" in *Revue des Sciences philosophiques et théologiques* 31 (1947), pp. 192–212, and from the relevant section of the same author's *Philosophie au Moyen-Age* (Paris 1958). See too idem., "Nécessité des raison dans le *Monologion*," *Revue des Sciences philosophiques et théologiques* 64 (1980), pp. 3–25.

Chapter 9

The Dispute over Apologetics: From Blondel to Balthasar

Introduction

The importance of the topic of apologetics should be fairly clear from what we have seen in this study so far. Highlighting that offers me an opportunity to rehearse the main lessons of the story up to this point. Introducing the theology of faith—the theological study, namely, of what faith is—I said that, beginning as early as the New Testament letters and the early Greek-speaking Apologists of the immediately sub-apostolic period, Christianity had emphasized the importance of being able to give a reasonable justification of one's adherence to the Gospel, to the historic revelation as found in Bible and Church. Although divine grace is the beginning of faith, the *initium fidei* in the words of the Second Council of Orange, divine action targeting the fundamental spiritual powers of the human being—intellect and will—is not to be seen as replacing the normal human functioning of those powers but as assisting that functioning in such a way that the will is drawn to the supreme Good manifested in revelation, the will thereby moving the intellect to give assent to the Word of God, and the Word of God in turn testifying to that manifestation. Because what is involved is assistance, not suppression, the assent of intellect and will, mind and heart, has to be properly human, which means in this context reasonable and prudent. The revelation offered man must be, at the ordinary human level, then, credible.

In the course of the nineteenth-century disputes over the faith-reason relationship, the magisterium of the Catholic Church had to adjudicate both minimalizing and maximalizing statements of such credibility. We investigated one minimizing figure, namely Bautain, whom I described as, at any rate, a semi-fideist, and two maximalizing figures, Hermes and Günther, in whose cases I saw no reason to dispute the standard textbook description: they are semi-rationalists, albeit of remarkably different kinds. As we found, it is characteristic of semi-fideism to hold that revelation respecifies the manner of operation of human rationality, in such a way that to say "revelation is reasonable" becomes in every possible context a tautology. No matter what your original philosophical point of departure, if your manner of exercising reason has been decisively altered by the reception of revelation, it is hardly surprising to hear you now consider revelation the most reasonable thing in the world. That was the position of Bautain. By contrast, it is characteristic of the semi-rationalists we looked at to say that the proposition "revelation is reasonable" is true if we understand "reason" here in one of two ways, corresponding to the two historic figures concerned, Hermes and Günther. Hermes considered he could show revelation to be reasonable so long as we confine our use of the word "reasonable" to the limits set by Immanuel Kant's concept of practical reason, whose concern is with what we need to postulate if we are to reach our goal as moral agents. Günther considered he could show revelation to be reasonable by redefining rationality along Idealist lines of his own devising in such a way that the truths contained in the principal revealed mysteries of the Incarnation and the Trinity become philosophical axioms of an anthropological and cosmological kind.

Both minimalizing and maximalizing accounts of the sense in which the acceptance of revelation by the act of faith may be held to be reasonable were found wanting by the mid-nineteenth century papacy of Gregory XVI and Pius IX, as indeed by a general council, Vatican I, 1869–1870 in its dogmatic constitution on faith and reason, *Dei Filius*. The First Vatican Council, we saw, emphasized that human intelligence is naturally capable of metaphysical exercise in such a way that some truths pertinent to faith, such as the existence and perfection of God, are rationally available, whereas for other truths pertinent to faith, truths which belong exclusively to the supernatural order, the most Christian philosophers can hope to show is that these truths are at any rate not contrary to reason. These were the main themes in *Dei Filius* which explain why in his encyclical *Aeterni Patris* Leo XIII singled out for commendation the contemporary beginnings of revival of interest in the thought of Saint Thomas Aquinas, of which revival

Etienne Gilson's work is one of the best examples, if not indeed the best.

Dei Filius also stated, however, that reasonable people are able to discern the probative force of certain signs of credibility attaching to divine revelation—and this theme, though not much touched on by Gilson, could be found in Thomas's corpus, too.[1] While, as I put it in the opening chapter, for Thomas the act of faith is "prompted" by the desire or appetite for what the will obscurely apprehends as a promised Good that embodies the ultimate goal of human striving, and Thomas, moreover, highlights the "interior instinct and attraction for doctrine," nevertheless he recognizes the concomitant importance for coming to faith of *humanae rationes*, "human reasons," which could be, for example, confirmatory miracles on the one hand, and, on the other, arguments for the congruence or at least the non-impossibility of the dogmas themselves. Up to a point there can be a natural certitude of the fact of revelation, even though only the intervention of grace in the workings of a person's mind and will can procure the kind of transformative assent that belongs with the certainty of faith.

Blondel's Intervention

The effect of Blondel's intervention in the faith-reason debate was to open up this entire issue to new or at any rate better integrated treatment. The basic claim of his massive *L'Action,* so we saw in the last chapter, is that human action has its own characteristic development, the motive-power of which is the lack of adequate correspondence between our particular, limited, choices, on the one hand, and the unlimited character of our "will" or basic spiritual dynamism on the other. Nothing we can choose to do is so comprehensively fulfilling that it exhausts the *élan,* the "onward and upward thrust," of that dynamism. In this way the human condition, for Blondel, inevitably confronts us with the supernatural, which is the "one thing necessary," *L'Unique nécessaire.* I explained that for Blondel, "the supernatural" is not as such the Christian God of grace and glory. The concept of the

---

1. Compare the First Vatican Council's canon 3, *de fide*: "If anyone says that divine revelation cannot be made credible by external signs and that therefore men should be drawn to the faith only by their personal internal experience or by private inspiration, let him be anathema." That canon was cited in full in *Pascendi,* Pope Pius X's 1907 encyclical on Modernism, section 6.

supernatural, as reached by an autonomous philosophy—albeit one initially indebted to a "directing hypothesis" taken from revelation—is too undetermined a notion for Blondel to make any such claim, even supposing he wished to. All that can be said, and all he does say, is that the idea of the Christian God of grace and glory is congruent with the philosophical supernatural: the philosopher, qua philosopher, even if he or she is also a Christian cannot assert that the goal of life is participation in the inner exchange of the Blessed Trinity—though that is indeed, for the theologian, the concrete content of the supernatural fulfillment Blondel describes.

A clerical review which, so it was noted in Chapter 8, described the purpose of *L'Action* as to bring apologetics into the realm of psychology not only moved Blondel to explain how his book was not psychology at all but philosophy. It also caused him to write his *Letter on Apologetics* where he gave his own opinion about the form that should be taken by the Catholic apologetics the mid-nineteenth century papacy and the First Vatican Council had asked for. So in the present chapter I want to consider first of all how, by writing the *Letter on Apologetics,* Blondel set the terms of this debate; second, how his appeal was answered, with varying degrees of disagreement and consent, by two major interlocutors, the Dominican Ambroise Gardeil and the Jesuit Pierre Rousselot; and third, how in the later twentieth century the theological aesthetics of Hans Urs von Balthasar sought in turn to correct *them.*

Blondel's View of Apologetics

To situate correctly the thesis of Blondel's *Letter* we have to bear in mind his conviction that in *L'Action* he had provided a new proof of the existence of God. The necessity of the supernatural was not a logical necessity in the sense of a necessary deduction from propositions already admitted. But nor was it merely a moral necessity in the sense of Kant's postulates of God and immortality as required for the good life. The necessity of the supernatural was, rather, an ontological necessity—a necessity for the life of finite spirit. If truth be, as he argued, an adequation of mind and life, *adequatio mentis et vitae,* then the affirmation of the supernatural was inescapable to anyone who has followed, and accepted, the dialectic exhibited by Blondel's study of action. In this light, it is hardly surprising that Blondel will find unsatisfactory both Scholasticism (whose starting point is the very different one of a realist metaphysics and an ethics of natural law) and its offshoot in apologetics. Indeed, at any rate in his early work (the situation will look different in the 1930s) he renews, if in more moderate language, Günther's *gravamen* against the School.

> When we examine the principles or postulates on which scholastic philosophy is based and the type of problems which it discusses, we see that it is first and foremost an adaptation of the thought of the ancient world and a sort of inheritance from the free spirit of Greek speculation, no doubt recast and gaining in wisdom and completeness, but not essentially renewed in the light of a new teaching which has a quite different origin.[2]

But his own, non-Scholastic, concept of philosophical theory and practice gives Blondel no desire whatsoever to go down the Güntherian road:

> Since it is not the business of philosophy to provide us with the absolute of truth, the truth which is substantial and salutary, whereas its duty is to investigate the conditions in which this truth can be made known to us, it follows that it is not its business to elaborate the principles of faith as if these were, in the ultimate analysis, nothing but the discoveries of the reason.[3]

And when we hear him finish that sentence by adding the words "or more or less symbolic and mythical intuitions," we realize that neither does he show any tendency to go down the road of the sort of Modernism, at once sentimentalist and symbolist, which suffered ecclesial condemnation ten years or so later by means of Pius X's encyclical *Pascendi*.

Against this background, then, in the *Letter on Apologetics* Blondel investigates the way contemporary Catholic apologias for revelation have, in recent times, functioned. He finds that characteristically they fall into two parts. The first is negative and consists of showing rationalist objections to the idea of revelation to be ill-grounded. Blondel has no objection to that. The second part is positive, and it consists in marshalling historical evidence for the fact or

---

2. M. Blondel, *The "Letter on Apologetics" and "History and Dogma,"* op. cit., p. 172.
3. Ibid., p. 191.

alleged fact that a revelation has taken place. It is the value of this second, historical part of a typical apologetics that Blondel disputes. Historical facts relevant to Christian or Judeo-Christian claims for a revelation in history do not demonstrate the truth of those claims, says Blondel, either for reason or for faith. How so?

To the philosopher, argues Blondel, the question of a historical validation of the supernatural—as distinct from inferring the supernatural on the basis of the general structural situation of man, the enduring subject of action—simply fails to arise. It is not a philosophical *type* of question. To the believer, if the historical facts *could* demonstrate revelation, then the act of faith would cease to need the help of divine grace. Faith's reference to reality would be secured scientifically, granting the study of history to be a "soft" or "human" science. By the same token, i.e., if historical facts could demonstrate the occurrence of revelation, the act of faith would also cease to be meritorious, since how could a scientific conclusion—there *was* a revelation in this or that segment of history—be the object of a freely given consent in an act which, accordingly, possessed special or even outstanding moral worth?[4]

> If one tried to begin with the supernatural, treating it as a factual datum, one would be abandoning philosophy. If one tried to produce the supernatural from natural premises as an apodeictic conclusion, an undertaking which has been condemned under the name of semi-rationalism, one would be abandoning orthodoxy. And if one simply brushed aside these difficulties and tried to produce a really convincing proof by this method, one would abandon both philosophy and orthodoxy.[5]

Thus the *Letter* confronted theologians with a mega-question. Should historical data, scientifically assembled, be deleted from Christian apologetics? Ought they to accept this contention, for the reasons Blondel gives? If the answer to the mega-question is No, and Blondelianism be rejected in this regard, then it had to be shown in what sense historical considerations relevant to revelation are probative and how they are compatible with ascribing to faith a gracious quality which elicits free personal response. If the answer to the mega-question was Yes, and Blondel's *Letter* taken as a charter for the

---

4. M. Blondel, *The "Letter on Apologetics" and "History and Dogma,"* op. cit., pp. 133–135.
5. Ibid., pp. 138–139.

future, then it had to be shown in what fashion, though not a scientific fashion, historical considerations could still in some way be appealed to apologetically, since the nineteenth-century magisterium of the Church had made plain that historical arguments for a *de facto* revelation—to Israel, in Jesus, and to the apostolic generation—were a non-negotiable aspect of the preamble of faith. Compare, for instance, the questions put to Bautain by Rome in 1844.

Though Blondel would modify his position under criticism, and admit that he had not given enough weight to the voice of tradition on the question of miracle and prophecy as signs of the credibility of revelation,[6] when writing the *Letter* his mood was very much that of Samuel Taylor Coleridge in his treatise *Aids to Reflection* where Coleridge remarks:

> I more than fear the prevailing taste for Books of Natural Theology, Physico-Theology, Demonstrations of God from Nature, Evidences of Christianity, &c &c. *Evidences of Christianity*! I am weary of the Word. Make a man feel the *want* of it; rouse him if you can, to the self-knowledge of his need for it, and you may safely trust it to its own Evidence.[7]

In a Catholic context, where *Dei Filius* and the papal magisterial tradition were taken seriously, Coleridge's expostulation would not suffice. Turning back from Coleridge to Blondel, could the word "proof" stand when Blondel uses it in the somewhat Pickwickian sense we find, for example, in the following sentence: "The proofs are valid only for those who are thoroughly prepared to accept and to understand them; that is why miracles which enlighten some only blind others."[8]

Blondel did not hold—with a true "Modernist," Edouard Le Roy, against whom he wrote—that miracles did not engender faith for

---

6. In his *Le problème de la Philosophie catholique* (Paris, 1932), Blondel was severe on his "Letter" of some thirty-five years before. But even in the pseudonymously produced *Qu'est ce que la foi?* (Paris, 1908), he noted that miraculous events are credibly significant insofar as they are "visible analogues of God's gracious condescension and refer the mind to God's saving intentions. Miracles can be seen as religious signs because they announce the good news for which our hearts are restless. By making us aware of the gifts of God, these signs give valid rational motives for accepting the solicitations of grace:" thus the reading of this work furnished by A. Dulles, sj, in *The Assurance of Things Hoped For*, op. cit., p. 108.

7. S. T. Coleridge, *Aids to Reflection*, ed. H. H. Coleridge (4th edition, London, 1839), pp. 308–309.

8. M. Blondel, *The Letter on Apologetics*, op. cit., pp. 134–135.

miracles were what faith engendered. To Blondel, the Gospel miracles were objectively real events. But they were likely to lead on to faith only in those who were already responding to the inner prompting of God's grace.[9]

I may say, incidentally, that Blondel was no better impressed by the other range of argumentation customary in nineteenth-century apologetics: namely, the congruence of revelation with the moral and social requirements of man. As he objects, this sort of argument is not capable of showing that Christianity is a translation of the *super*natural. All it shows is Christianity's *natural* excellence.[10] And in tones that anticipate the theological line of Hans Urs von Balthasar vis-à-vis Rahnerianism later in the twentieth century, Blondel warns against speaking: "as if Revelation only confirmed and fulfilled nature without bringing with it any new element, any heterogeneous datum, any unhoped for and unsuspected gift."[11]

The task of the theologian is simply to "let the sun's light shine," by exhibiting the "coherence of dogma" in its "organic synthesis."[12] Theologians have "nothing to gain," he told them, by "covering up or complicating their proper function, by humanizing their teaching."[13]

The Response of Gardeil and Rousselot

The two most influential responses to the challenge Blondel had set came from one Dominican theologian, Ambroise Gardeil, born in 1859, two years before Blondel, dying in 1931, eighteen years before Blondel's death in 1949, and his younger Jesuit counterpart Pierre Rousselot whose dates are 1878 to 1915. Rousselot's early death is easily explained. He fell in one of the battles of the First World War.

Gardeil's response to the *Letter on Apologetics* is found chiefly in his 1907 book *La Crédibilité et l'apologétique* which was thoroughly rewritten in 1912 and reprinted minus various appendices in 1928.

---

9. See on this issue the study of F. Rodé, *Le Miracle dans le controverse Moderniste* (Paris, 1965).

10. M. Blondel, *The Letter on Apologetics*, op. cit., pp. 137–138.

11. Ibid., p. 143.

12. Ibid., p. 190.

13. Ibid., p. 189.

Gardeil was well prepared for this task: the "Regent" (director) of Studies of the Dominican study-house of the Province of France, he was generally recognized as its outstanding speculative theologian, and from 1894 onwards he regularly taught courses to young Dominicans on both apologetics and the treatise *de fide*—much of this work in exile, incidentally, owing to the anti-clerical legislation put in place by the Third French Republic from 1880 until the Great War.[14] Gardeil's study was intended (within definite limits) to retrieve the valid elements in Blondelianism and adapt them to a Scholastic framework. As we shall see, Rousselot sought the same but went considerably further in the direction of Blondelianizing Scholastic thought.

According to Gardeil, the proper object of apologetics is the natural credibility which must attach to the historic revelation if the act of specifically Christian faith—a more determined concept than Blondel's broadly conceived "the supernatural"—is to be legitimate from the point of view of human reason.[15] In principle, says Gardeil, in order to legitimize faith from the rational standpoint, at any rate for the Church as a whole, as distinct from any one generation within it, or any one individual within any one generation, the evidence favoring such natural credibility *should* be demonstrative in character, fully "scientific." That was verified, he thinks, in the experience of the Apostles who could testify personally to such evidence in its maximal form: eyewitnesses to the miracles of the public ministry of Jesus, they had seen one of their number touch the risen Lord, watched the tongues of flame descend on each other's heads at the coming of the Holy Spirit at Pentecost, and so forth. But at the level of individuals in any *post*-apostolic generation, it suffices to have a practical certainty of the duty to believe based upon an accumulation of probable arguments, especially if this is combined with what Gardeil termed *suppléances*, "supplements," gracious helps from God which are either moral or mystical in character, or both. Indeed, for simple people, who can

---

14. R. Garrigou-Lagrange, OP, "In Memoriam. Le Père A. Gardeil," *Revue Thomiste XIV*, 68 (1931), pp. 797–808; "Le Père Ambroise Gardeil (1859–1931)," in *Bulletin thomiste. Notes et communications* 1 (1931), pp. 69*–92*, with full bibliography, and a short biography by Henri-Dominique Gardeil. See more fully H. D. Gardeil, *L'oeuvre théologique du Père Ambroise Gardeil* (Etiolles, 1956).

15. I follow here the exposition in the first edition: A. Gardeil, OP, *La Crédibilité et l'apologétique* (Paris, 1908). A parallel account is his article "Crédibilité" in the *Dictionnaire de Théologie catholique III* (Paris, [1907] 1938), cols. 2201–2309.

hardly grasp the probable arguments or have little or no opportunity to study them and duly "accumulate," the *suppléances* have to do instead.[16] Such supplements set up in each individual what Thomas had called an "interior attraction towards doctrine."[17]

As Gardeil was aware, to demand, at any rate in principle, a scientific demonstration of revelation's credibility might be construed as Hermesianism. And in the light of Blondel's criticism of contemporary apologetics, to say that—once again, in principle—scientific demonstration of credibility would be better than reliance on either mere probability or divine sweeteners seems to imperil the essentially supernatural and therefore free and meritorious character of faith. Gardeil was able to rebut both criticisms since, as he pointed out, to say that revelation is credible is *not yet to make the act of supernatural faith*. Comparably to those Tridentine theologians who posited a still unsupernaturalized *fides humana*, "natural faith" which in the Gospels even the demons possess ("What have you to do with us, O Son of God? Have you come here to torment us before the time?" [Matthew 8:29]), is not *fides divina*, divine faith, which consists in placing the human mind under the sovereignty of the Word of God, or what Thomas termed the authority of the First Truth, *Prima Veritas* being for Aquinas a favored way of referring to God. The testimony on which supernatural faith rests is not human testimony at all, whether demonstrative, probable or what you will. Rather, it is divine testimony. Only an *analogy* relates the rational judgment of credibility, or its equivalent for simple folk, to the act of faith proper. "Only an analogy"; that means, there is significant unlikeness as well as likeness between the two, and in the space located by that unlikeness the qualities of freedom and merit can make their dwelling.

In the second edition of *La Crédibilité et l'apologétique* Gardeil emphasizes that in all cases, including sophisticated critical intelligences studying historical data, and people, like the Apostles, exposed at first hand to the maximum density of reasons for believing, there is

---

16. Idem., *La Crédibilité et l'apologétique*, op. cit., pp. 70–73.

17. But there were no grounds in Thomas's writings for Gardeil's assumption that mystical supplements though normal for the believer who already has the virtue of faith may well be exceptional in the case of someone coming to faith for the first time, as was pointed out by a Benedictine critic, Dom Anselm Stolz in his *Glaubensgnade und Glaubenslicht nach Thomas von Aquin* (Rome, 1933).

at work throughout this process an implicit, grace-supported, orientation towards the object of faith.[18] Every human being, even when totally ignorant of revelation, has the assistance of grace in ordering himself or herself towards his or her own proper end or goal, and thus by implication has the help of grace to orient them towards the acceptance of the revelation that is necessary for fully attaining that goal—even though they are not aware of it. By adding that refinement—which in its concern for holistic process could be called, at a pinch, Blondelian—Gardeil was able to argue that the stages in the process of coming to a reasonable faith which was nonetheless divine supernatural faith, *fides divina,* were organically interrelated. Even the rational judgment of natural credibility, made with minimal *suppléances* or perhaps no *suppléances* at all, has the grace of God behind it, just as it has the grace of God in front of it, awaiting its transformation from a rational judgment based on human testimony to a supra-rational act of faith in the content of revelation on the authority of God revealing.

Gardeil gave a place, albeit a limited one, to what he termed "subjective apologetics"—a portmanteau term which includes not only Blondel's "apologetics of action," moving people to faith by exhibiting their inability to beatify themselves, and the "moral apologetics" of Blondel's teacher, Léon Ollé-Laprune, which turns on the harmony between faith and man's moral aspirations, but also the "fideist apologetics" of the influential Catholic literary critic Fernand Brunetière which "prompts men to act on the hypothesis that faith is valid and thereby makes them more susceptible to the impulses of grace."[19] But in Gardeil's eyes (and as its name suggests) such "subjective apologetics" was unable to furnish an objectively adequate set of reasons for believing. What it *could* usefully do, however, was to investigate the subjective conditions that can "better dispose untutored persons or those confused by modern agnostic philosophies to receive the gift of faith."[20]

> Whatever be the truth of its philosophical departure-point, one sees from the very structure of immanentist apologetics that its practical claim is only to *prepare* the act of faith, by removing obstacles from the heart and

---

18. A. Gardeil, OP, *La Crédibilité et l'apologétique* (2nd ed., Paris, 1912, reprinted 1928), pp. 19–31.
19. I take this summary from A. Dulles, SJ, *A History of Apologetics* (London, 1971), p. 209.
20. Ibid.

spirit, leading them to regard the religious problem as the *unum necessarium,* making them desire the response [of revelation] with a perfect good faith, *une parfaite bonne foi*. When all that is in place, there still remains the task of an objective apologetics which determines the true faith in regard to good faith, or, if that cannot be achieved, for it seems very difficult to coordinate a rational doctrine with an immanentist one, there remains the grace of God and the divine *suppléances* of credibility.[21]

Some *blondeliens* accepted this adjudication. Theirs was *une apologétique du seuil,* "an apologetics of the threshold." Others considered that if an architectural metaphor were sought a better one would be "an apologetics of the crypt," because a crypt supports the entire superstructure of a building—in this case, an objective apologetics of the signs of credibility.

Broadly speaking, Gardeil's answer to Blondel's chief objections to classical apologetics is clear. We shall not be imperilling the economy of grace and the meritoriousness of faith when we seek to establish the rational credibility of revelation and that for three reasons. First and foremost, the rational judgment of credibility is not yet the act of divine faith. Second, for many people even the judgment of credibility has divinely furnished *suppléances* to bolster their feeble awareness of the rational evidences. And third, the entire process of reaching the rational judgment of credibility and moving beyond it to the act of divine faith is underpinned by the way God graciously sustains in each person's life a right orientation towards the goal of human existence.

Moreover, still on Gardeil as respondent to Blondel, the accumulation of probable arguments for the historicity of revelation produces a practical certitude which itself can count as rational certainty, and so Blondel's claim that the philosopher as such can have nothing to do with assessing the value of historical argumentation falls to the ground. In 1911 Gardeil published an entire book entitled *La Certitude Probable* lamenting the fact that philosophers after Aristotle had taken insufficient interest in the notion of probable certainty (in English we usually say "moral certainty") which is so often the guide to life. He was aware in this connection of an English exception:

---

21. Idem., "Crédibilité," art. cit., col. 2307.

Newman's *Essay in Aid of a Grammar of Assent*, of which a key idea is practical certitude generated by convergent arguments and identified by what Newman called "the illative sense."

Rousselot, who was forced by the anti-clerical laws to enter the Society of Jesus, the Jesuits, at Canterbury of all places, was able—unlike Gardeil for most of the time—to teach in France itself. After taking his doctorate in philosophy at the Sorbonne he was given employment by the Parisian *Institut Catholique*. The *Institut*, since it was under the control of the bishops and diocesan clergy rather than a religious order, escaped the full rigor of the law. Like Gardeil, Rousselot was responsible for giving a course *de fide*, "on faith." Rousselot's response to Blondel is best found in a lengthy two part essay, "Les Yeux de la foi," which appeared in the Strasbourg *Recherches de science religieuse* in 1910 and in English translation in book form in 1991.[22] Independent of Gardeil's treatment, it differs from it in at least one crucial respect. Concerned that the signs of credibility (miracle, the fulfillment of prophecy) were treated by more conventional Scholastics (including Gardeil) as essentially extraneous to the revelation to which they testified, Rousselot insisted that *the revelation was itself the significance of the signs* which were, therefore, not extraneous to its content but intrinsically related thereto. The signs of credibility are guides not only to the historical actuality of the fact of revelation but to the meaning of its content. In this, the extraordinary signs are solidary with the more ordinary signs or indicators embedded in the Gospel narrative: the meals the Messiah took with public sinners as an expression of divine charity, for instance, and not just the miraculous meals of the Feeding of the Four Thousand and the Five.[23]

Notice that Rousselot, like Gardeil, has no difficulty with the *historicity* of the miracles: writing in the midst of the Modernist crisis as both men were, they would doubtless have underwritten, had they known it, the *magnum opus* of the German Capuchin Hilarin Felder,

---

22. P. Rousselot sj, *The Eyes of Faith and Answer to Two Attacks*, op. cit., pp. 21–81.

23. I concentrate here on the second of the two essays that make up "Les Yeux de la foi" where the signs in question come from the Gospel narrative; in the first, Rousselot was considering a wider, though for Christianity less obviously crucial, range of signs, "the holiness of a good priest, the healing of a sick person, the impression produced by a religious feast, and so on," ibid., p. 33.

Jesus Christus, (1911–1914), in its day the most learned Catholic response to historical skepticism of a radical kind.[24] The question was, rather, how to extract from the miracles (and the rest of the Jesus narrative) an appropriate content. The Gospels, after all, like the Church Fathers, often praise those who manage to discern divine agency in tenuous indicators, rather than simply waiting around in expectation of extraordinary signs and portents. Such indicators, though not customarily invoked in apologetics, need factoring into any adequate account. And they call for more delicate antennae of interpretation than those required to register a breach in laws of nature. Moreover, when "ordinary" and "extraordinary" signs are brought together, they require for overall understanding the exercise of an appropriate sensibility. As a later twentieth-century Jesuit theologian, Avery Dulles, remarked, "scientific history" is not "capable of settling the question of religious interpretation," for the simple reason that "such interpretation lies within the competence of a man committed, or at least open, to religious values."[25]

Rousselot took a strong line on the lessons to be learned. To acknowledge these points entails rethinking the entire relation between the judgment of credibility and the act of faith. On Rousselot's account, the light of faith has the effect of granting new "eyes," that is, a new manner of understanding, which finds its specificity precisely in the capacity to see in the signs of revelation—whether extraordinary or ordinary—what the signs signify. In accord with the title of his study of Aquinas—*L'intellectualisme de saint Thomas*[26]—Rousselot was more "intellectualist" than Gardeil. He appealed to Thomas's conviction of the inherent tendency of mind towards truth, as well as to the medieval doctor's appreciation of the

---

24. H. Felder, OFM CAP., *Jesus Christus: Apologie seiner Messianität und Gottheit gegenüber der neuesten ungläubigen Jesus-Forschung* (Paderborn, 1911–1914; English translation, *Christ and the Critics. A Defense of the Divinity of Jesus against the Attacks of Modern Skepticism,* London, 1914). Albert Schweizer, whose 1906 *Von Reimarus zu Wrede. Eine Geschichte der Leben-Jesu-Forschung,* Englished in 1910 as *Quest of the Historical Jesus*, was a very different kettle of fish, "paid tribute," it seems, to Felder's prodigious command of the modern literature about Jesus: thus A. Dulles, SJ, *Apologetics and the Biblical Christ* (London, 1963), p. 19.

25. Ibid., p. 28.

26. P. Rousselot, SJ, *L'intellectualisme de saint Thomas* (Paris, 1908). For Rousselot's Thomas, the fact that the human intellect has its fulfillment in the intuitive vision of God necessarily relativizes all forms of rational thinking. In this work, Rousselot likes to repeat the maxim, "the necessity of reason comes from the deficiency [here and now] of the intellect."

role of connaturality in moral and spiritual matters. The sympathetic intelligence can do wonders. Or, in the case of Gospel apologetics, it can coincide with wonders. "One selfsame certitude," wrote Rousselot, is achieved when a "supernatural illumination" combines with the "genuine efficacy of external signs."[27] But in that case, the judgment of credibility *is* the act of faith: the relation of the two is one of what we might call "dynamic identity." In a later generation, Dulles exemplifies Rousselot's approach in what the American writer terms a "confessional apologetic" which would "exhibit concurrently the credibility of the essential facts and of their Christian interpretation. It would invite the inquirer to assent to both in one indivisible act."[28]

Gardeil's *suppléances* (in the plural) were now superfluous. A divinely originated moral-cum-mystical aid to the mind's ability to certify the basic credibility of revelation is now the selfsame divine act as the illumination of the mind and the confirmation of the will in supernatural faith. In words of Rousselot, a writer much given to italicization: "*Perception of credibility and belief in truth are identically the same act.*"[29]

But where did this leave the magisterial claim that the act of faith must be shown to be reasonable? For Rousselot, "reasonable" does not have to mean "accessible to human reason left to its own powers." It can also mean, he proposed, that which is opposed to "a blind acceptance, inspired by a coup d'état of the will." If a new subtlety of

---

27. Idem., *The Eyes of Faith and Answer to Two Attacks*, op. cit., p. 27.

28. A. Dulles, SJ, *Apologetics and the Biblical Christ*, op. cit., p. 62. In his contributions to the American edition of "Les Yeux de la foi," Dulles explains that in 1920, owing to the reactions, both favorable and unfavorable, to Rousselot's doctrine in the Society, the General, Wlodimir Ledochowski, forbad Jesuits to follow Rousselot's theology, and instead, to adhere to the safer positions represented by the more common opinion in the Church, a view maintained by his successor John Baptist Janssens, after the promulgation of Pius XIII's encyclical *Humani generis* in 1951. In a rather surprising note, Dulles gives as ground for demurral that the Second Vatican Council did not reaffirm the pertinent passages of *Humani generis* on the rational character of the credibility of the faith. Thus P. Rousselot, SJ, *The Eyes of Faith and Answer to Two Attacks*, op. cit., p. 113. Dulles explored that more fully in *The Assurance of Things Hoped For*, op. cit., p. 140. While admitting that the Council did not intend "to deny all that it did not assert," he considered that at its hands "certain traditional theses lost their previous importance." In *Dei Verbum* (1–4) the Council Fathers left the impression that the genesis of faith is not "inquiry and reasoning" but "confident proclamation of the mighty acts of God in salvation history." They treated the natural knowledge of God after the revealed knowledge of him, thus reversing the order adopted at the First Vatican Council (6). They also referred to the signs of revelation as though they were not so much extrinsic signs of credibility as integral parts of revelation itself (2 and 4).

29. *The Eyes of Faith and Answer to Two Attacks*, op. cit., p. 31.

intellectual understanding, precisely, is conferred by "les yeux de la foi," that can hardly be called blind acceptance. Unfortunately, whatever magisterial documents mean by "reason," this does not seem to be it. Still, Rousselot argued his position was not fideist, and he defended himself by comparing his theology of faith to the issue of induction in philosophy.

In inductive knowledge, the "index"—that is, the relevant instance, the pertinent fact—say, for example, the sun rising every morning of my life so far, is the cause of the assent I give to the conclusion, Yes, the sun will rise tomorrow as everyday hitherto. Yet this conclusion also throws light on the index, and gives it the meaning pertinent to its status *as* index. It shows what I take to be the index is the index *of*. As Rousselot writes: "The law is seen through the clue, but it is only *in* seeing the law that the clue is seen as clue. The fact cannot be known *as* a clue unless we affirm the law."[30]

There is, then, a reciprocal priority of fact and conclusion, conclusion and fact. Such a reciprocal priority enables us to assess what the principle is that the fact or facts exemplify.[31] So with faith: the act of faith (compare the inferred conclusion in induction) may condition the perception of credibility (compare the registering of the relevant fact in induction); but then the perception of credibility (compare the relevant fact) can also just as well be said to condition the act of faith (compare the inferred conclusion). Invocation of reciprocal priority, so Rousselot evidently thought, would differentiate his case from that of Bautain. In an article of 1914, he sought to place a goodly quantity of blue water between his epistemology of revelation and Bautain's, though, rightly enough, he complained of the merely approximative character of conventional summaries of Bautain's thought.[32]

Others wondered, apart from Thomas, who else was Rousselot's real *maître à penser*, his true intellectual inspiration? Rousselot had appealed to Newman—notably to Newman on the cognitive value for the right determination of the signs of credibility

---

30. Ibid., pp. 29–30. Italics are original.

31. Rousselot was able to point out that *some* notion of "reciprocal conditioning" was in play among stricter Neo-Thomists than himself, specifically R. Garrigou-Lagrange, OP, in *Intellectualisme et liberté chez S. Thomas* (Kain, 1910).

32. P. Rousselot, SJ, "La vraie pensée de Bautain," *Recherches de Science religieuse* 5 (1914), pp. 453–459.

of an antecedent sympathy with the idea of divine purpose. In his sermons, in the *Essay in Aid of a Grammar of Assent* and elsewhere Newman had pointed out how someone already disposed to see in history indications of the hand of God is far more likely to respond positively to the signs of the historic revelation. In a somewhat comparable fashion, for Rousselot, the eyes of faith give us a sympathetic or, in his more characteristic word, *loving* gaze on the signs of revelation, and such love brings with it a cognitive breakthrough in scanning the signs. Rousselot's critics, however, considered him more indebted to Kant: not, as with Hermes, the Kant of the critique of practical reason but the Kant of the critique of pure reason. In any explanation of knowledge, the most important factor for Rousselot, as for Kant, appeared to be not the passively received data but the active spontaneity of mind whereby the subject synthesizes its perceptions and thereby confers a pattern upon the world.[33] Rousselot takes it to be the chief omission of the established apologetics that its representatives "overlook the *synthetic activity of the intelligence*, whether natural or supernaturalized."[34] From a Scholastic standpoint, it is not only reason that is in danger here but objectivity, too.

Balthasar's Critique

This was precisely Hans Urs von Balthasar's objection to Rousselot's teaching in his otherwise favorable account of Rousselot's work in his theological aesthetics: *Herrlichkeit*, or, in the English translation, *The Glory of the Lord*. Of all the figures discussed in this book, Balthasar will be the most familiar to anyone who has dabbled in twentieth-century theology.[35] Born into a patrician family in Lucerne (in central Switzerland) in 1905, he studied *Germanistik* (German literature and philosophy) before entering the Society of Jesus a generation and a half after Rousselot.[36] Balthasar was deeply influenced by the Greek

---

33. Kant was duly praised in this regard in idem., "Amour spiritual et synthèse aperceptive," *Revue de Philosophie* XVI (1910), pp. 238–239.
34. Idem., *The Eyes of Faith and Answer to Two Attacks*, op. cit., p. 26. Italics are original.
35. I offer a fuller overview of the man and his work in the first volume of my "Introduction to Hans Urs von Balthasar," *The Word Has Been Abroad. A Guide through Balthasar's Aesthetics* (Edinburgh 1998), pp. ix–xx.
36. I describe the fruits of that early period in my *Scattering the Seed. A Guide through Balthasar's early Writings on Philosophy and the Arts* (London, 2006).

Fathers as well as Augustine and Aquinas, by the "neo-orthodox" and highly Christocentric Protestant theologian Karl Barth as well as by Adrienne von Speyr, an eccentric but profound Swiss convert from Protestantism to Catholicism whose mystical experience he sought to interpret in the light of the Great Tradition.[37] Balthasar's enormous literary energy, which included huge amounts of translating and editing as well as running a publishing house, was chiefly invested in a comprehensive theological project aiming at totality but not system, and expressed in terms of the three "transcendentals" of high medieval Scholasticism: the beautiful (and hence the disclosure of divine glory), the good (and hence the gift of divine salvation), the true (and hence the revelation of divine wisdom).[38] What I have called the "comprehensive" character of Balthasar's vision made it likely he would deal with the role of apologetics in coming to faith, or perduring in faith. More especially, his concept of theological aesthetics made it inevitable that he would touch on this topic, since he needed to decide to what extent "seeing the form" (that title of the first volume of his *The Glory of the Lord* stands for apprehending divine revelation in human facts) is open to the perceiving intellect of anybody and everybody, and to what extent, contrariwise, it requires the illuminating assistance of grace.

Compared with Gardeil, Rousselot, thought Balthasar, was moving in the right direction. Balthasar did not care for Gardeil's presentation, since Gardeil was operating with too disjoined an account of intellect and will. Will for Gardeil is the faculty whose exercise in the act of faith serves to compensate for the lack of sufficient evidence to move the mind. Balthasar, without necessarily convincing us that Gardeil's analysis differs much from Thomas's, called this "an unsatisfactory state of affairs where both faculties are concerned."[39] Rousselot treats intellect and will in a more unified fashion: they are inter-related aspects of the engaged person.[40] (This may be owing to

---

37. These influences are discussed in A. Nichols, OP, *Divine Fruitfulness. A Guide through Balthasar's Writings beyond the Trilogy* (London, 2007).

38. In addition to the study of his aesthetics noted above, see idem., *No Bloodless Myth. A Guide through Balthasar's Dramatics* (Edinburgh, 2000), and *Say It Is Pentecost. A Guide through Balthasar's Logic* (Edinburgh, 2001).

39. H. U. von Balthasar, *The Glory of the Lord. A Theological Aesthetics. I. Seeing the Form* (English translation, Edinburgh and San Francisco, 1982), p. 166.

40. J. M. McDermott, SJ, *Love and Understanding. The Relation of Will and Intellect in Pierre Rousselot's Christological Vision* (Rome, 1983) has, as its title suggests, a full account of this subject.

Blondel's influence if we can suppose Rousselot to have read Blondel's pseudonymous study of faith which appeared in two different forms in the years 1906 to 1908.[41]) But Rousselot remained too close, says Balthasar, to the Kantianism he was trying, in his own way, to overcome. The synthesis or pattern that faith finds in the signs of revelation belongs too unilaterally with the spiritual dynamism of the human subject—even if it be conceded that, in this context, such "dynamism" is impelled by grace. As Balthasar writes: "[Rousselot] does not sufficiently attribute this synthesis to the efficacy of the objective evidence of the form of revelation itself."[42]

And he explains:

> It is, indeed, right to say that this objective evidence can enlighten only a spirit prepared for it and proportionate to it, and to assert that the subjective conditions of the possibility of such illumination can be described in Kantian categories. But the active-constructive synthetic power ought not to be over-estimated to the detriment of God's own power, which expresses and imposes itself in its historical witness. In the Gospel, the strength of the disciples' belief is wholly borne and effected by the person of Jesus, the locus of revelation. Here we no longer detect the slightest trace of a creative, myth-projecting capacity on the part of man. The discoverability of the objective, synthetic point is reduced to nil, while Jesus' non-inventability, his overwhelming originality has become infinite and of itself demands assent and effects submission.[43]

Balthasar is against everything—including literary, philosophical, or theological presuppositions or methods—which might in any way eclipse or occlude the epiphanizing to human faculties of the unique phenomenon of Jesus Christ: the sign par excellence of divine

---

41. F. Mallet, *Qu'est-ce que la foi?*, op. cit., originally articles in the *Revue du clergé français* 53 (1906), pp. 257–285. As Dulles interprets this work, "Blondel finds it necessary to say with Augustine and Newman that in faith, as a movement of the whole person toward the divine, knowledge and love are inextricably interwoven. As against the logic of rationalism, Blondel proposes a logic of circumincession, in which the priorities of will and intellect . . . are reciprocal," *The Assurance of Things Hoped For*, op. cit., p. 108.

42. H. U. von Balthasar, *The Glory of the Lord. A Theological Aesthetics* I., op. cit., p. 177.

43. Ibid. As Dulles remarks: "Without denying what Rousselot and others have said about the subjective light of faith, von Balthasar seeks to supplement it from the biblical and classical doctrine that the light of faith is also, and indeed primarily, objective. The light is present first of all in God, whose radiance . . . shines from the face of Christ," *The Assurance of Things Hoped For*, op. cit., p. 149.

revelation in act.⁴⁴ The Savior's *Gestalt* is of course especially clearly visible to the loving contemplation of faith—itself an attunement to revelation's own love-content.⁴⁵ But that is not to say that it fails to register on the pre-dogmatic sensibility and mind.⁴⁶ Fulfilled prophecies and miracles "can all play a part" in the "theo-pragmatic" context of divine loving action the splendor of which strikes home and converts.⁴⁷ *Pace* Kant, if the human mind is the source of all phenomenal order, epiphanies are hardly feasible. Balthasar thus leaves us with a question. Is it, then, *aesthetic* reason—registering the sublimity of revelation's form at its midpoint, the incarnate Word, and registering too its wonderful internal harmonics and the splendid proportion into which all other dimensions of reality to fall, we should *really* be looking at when we seek to consider "faith and reason in modern Catholic thought"?

On the more modest stage of theological apologetics, how might a suitable adjudication of the cases of Blondel and Gardeil, Rousselot and Balthasar proceed? From Blondel's account of the inescapable character of the question of the supernatural one might take an "antecedent expectation" of some more-than-natural divine involvement in human history. From Gardeil's account of the need to establish by normal processes of human inquiry the credibility of a revelation whose ultimate epistemic demands are, however, those of the sovereign divine Word in its gracious approach to man, one might draw a conviction of the pertinence (yet, in the last analysis, insufficiency) of historical evidence for assessment of the claims of faith. From Rousselot's account of the "eyes of faith" one might borrow an emphasis on the need creatively to discern pattern in such evidence—a pattern whose outlines are available through the corporate believing activity of the Church in which the individual seeker after

---

44. As has been brought out by several fine monographs: see, for instance, G. Marchesi, sj, *La cristologia di Hans Urs von Balthasar: La figura di Gesù Cristo espressione visibile di Dio* (Rome, 1977); J. Godenir, osb, *Jésus l'Unique. Introduction à la théologie de Hans Urs von Balthasar* (Paris, 1984).

45. Thus H. U. von Balthasar, *Glaubhaft ist nur Liebe* (Einsiedeln, 1963); English translation, *Love Alone: The Way of Revelation* (London, 1968), pp. 43–50.

46. For the notion of an "apologetics of form," see J. P. Disse, "Apologetik der Gestalt: Zur Fundamentaltheologie Hans Urs von Balthasars," in U. Fink—R. Zihlmann (ed.), *Kirche-Kultur-Kommunikation: Peter Henrici zum 70. Geburtstag* (Zurich, 1998), pp. 75–86.

47. H. U. von Balthasar, *Love Alone: The Way of Revelation*, op. cit., pp. 7–8.

truth may, through imaginative effort under grace, have their own share. From Balthasar's account of the epiphanic nature of the Christ-event in the stunning figure of the Jesus of the Gospels, on his way as divinized humanity from crib through Cross to crown, one might take a conviction of the non-invented character of this pattern, its self-presentation to human faculties. This was no synthetic product of those faculties. Rather, echoing C. S. Lewis's celebrated dictum, here myth became stupendous fact.

Meanwhile, it may be relevant to our next chapter to note how combining reason and spiritual experience, objectivity and the creativity of subjects, was the self-set philosophical mission of Karol Wojtyła, better known as Pope John Paul II.

Chapter 10

A Synthetic Outcome? John Paul II's Letter

Fides et Ratio Preamble

John Paul II's letter *Fides et ratio* constitutes a synthesis all its own of the constructive elements investigation of the history of the faith-reason relationship in nineteenth- and twentieth-century European Catholicism can identify—at any rate of the figures I have considered in this book, and I assure the reader that I did not first choose the 1998 letter and then found the thinkers to match! Without too much straining, I hope to show that my claim for *Fides et ratio* is well-grounded. But first of all let me briefly fill in some background for this figure.

Biographical Introduction

The career of Karol Wojtyła, otherwise Pope John Paul II, is, owing to his dramatic role in later twentieth-century events, rather well-known. Born in 1920 in what had been till two years previously the Austrian portion of Poland, the son of an army officer who doubled up as a tailor, his teenage years were dominated by a passion for acting which was at that point his chosen career. Partly to forward it, he studied philology and Polish literature at the University of Cracow, an education rudely interrupted by the German invasion in 1939: in November of that year, the nearly two hundred university lecturers were deported to Sachsenhausen concentration camp. For the rest of the war, Wojtyła worked by day as a laborer in a local quarry. Until 1942, he gave his evenings to the cultural resistance, chiefly through mounting clandestine performances of plays, some of which he wrote himself. In the autumn of 1942 he was secretly accepted as a seminarian, and ordained priest four years later. From 1946 to 1948 he was in Rome, at the Dominican college—later university—of St. Thomas there, writing a dissertation on the theology of faith in the writings of the sixteenth-century Spanish mystic Saint John of the Cross.[1] He did so under the supervision of the principal Roman Neo-Thomist of the period, Réginald Garrigou-Lagrange. After a year as a curate in a rural parish, he combined student chaplaincy work in Cracow with writing more plays and poetry and a second doctorate, this time on the possible usefulness for Catholic moral philosophy of the ideas of the German phenomenologist Max Scheler.[2]

In 1956 Wojtyła was given the Chair of Ethics at the University of Lublin, the only Church-run university in Communist Eastern Europe. In 1958 he was made assistant Bishop in Cracow, and in 1963 became Archbishop of that See, thanks to a misjudgment by the State authorities who had vetoed a series of older and more experienced candidates in the hope that a philosopher-poet would prove an ineffective dreamer. In 1969 he published a major phenomenological study, *Osoba i czyn*, the English translation of which, *The Acting Person*, is generally regarded, unfortunately, as tendentious and unreliable.[3] In 1978, by recognition of his intellectual, spiritual and physical vigor (the previous pope, a chain smoker, had died after only thirty-five days in office) he was elected pope and took the name John Paul II.

His pontificate was chiefly marked by his efforts to ensure a peaceful end to Communism, the defense of human rights in other countries, and the stabilization of the post-Conciliar Catholic Church on the basis of a series of doctrinal encyclicals, as well as two Codes of Canon Law, one for the Latin Church in 1983, the other for the Eastern Catholic Churches in 1990, and the promulgation of a very comprehensive Catechism in 1992. He was the first pope ever to travel widely, in journeys which have been calculated to add up to 2.8 times the distance from the earth to the moon.[4] He died in March 2004.

---

1. K. Wojtyła, *Faith according to Saint John of the Cross* (English translation, San Francisco, 1981).

2. Idem., "Evaluation of the Possibility of a Christian Ethics upon the Assumptions of Max Scheler's Philosophy" [in Polish] (Lublin, 1959).

3. Idem., *Osaba i czyn* (Lublin, 1969); English translation, *The Acting Person* (Boston, 1979).

4. This brief sketch is based on the compendious G. Weigel, *Witness of Hope. The Biography of Pope John Paul II* (New York, 1999).

His Philosophical Formation

Before sinking our teeth into the meat of *Fides et ratio* it seems worth saying a little more about the pope's philosophical background. His background is Thomism transformed by the infusion of phenomenological personalism. Putting first the Thomist contribution to his philosophical outlook must be true chronologically; whether it is also true substantively is more of a moot point. Some interpreters would prefer to say, his philosophy is a phenomenological personalism which has borrowed further elements from Thomas, thus placing the emphasis on the non-Thomasian ingredients.

We already have some awareness of the character of modern Thomism from considering Leo XIII's project and its embodiment in Etienne Gilson—though the sort of Neo-Thomism John Paul learned in Rome would be closer to the other major exemplar of the Leonine project I mentioned: Jacques Maritain, himself much in tune with the future pope's Roman thesis director, Garrigou-Lagrange.[5] It is a Thomism which, over against nineteenth century fideism and a semi-rationalism with its roots in Idealism, emphasized the objective nature of the reality of things, the capacity of mind to mirror that objective nature—to reflect its truth, goodness and beauty (the "transcendental determinations of being," or "transcendentals" for short), and on that basis to proceed by philosophical argumentation of a broadly cosmological kind to the affirmation of the existence of God and his perfection.[6]

But we must also reckon with the influence of a distinctively Polish tributary of the Thomist river: "Lublin Thomism," not only because the future pope wrote his second thesis there but also because he taught there as well.[7] In Poland, Thomists were found in the universities of Warsaw and Cracow in addition to Lublin, but the latter, which acquired a faculty of "Christian philosophy" in 1946, was preeminent. Edward Nieznański has identified five distinct

---

5. For a charming introduction to Maritain's life and writings, by a fellow philosopher, see R. McInerny, *The Very Rich Hours of Jacques Maritain. A Spiritual Life* (Notre Dame, IN, 2003).

6. See A. Nichols, OP, *Reason with Piety. Garrigou-Lagrange in the Service of Catholic Thought* (Naples, FL, 2008).

7. R. Duncan, "Lublin Thomism," *The Thomist* 51. 2 (1987), pp. 307–324.

philosophical currents in twentieth-century Polish Thomism.[8] Except for the third, a cosmologically inclined scientific Thomism (writing in German, Nieznanski uses the more pejorative term "szientistisch") and the fifth, concerned chiefly with the logical analysis and formalization of Thomasian texts, these schools, though differing among themselves, have in common a concern with anthropology and ethics, and this would be a hallmark of Wojtyła's writing as well. An apologetically oriented "fundamental" Thomism included, in the Dominican Jacek Woroniecki, Rector of the University of Lublin in the 1920s, an opening to personalism, an interest in "characterology" and the educational elements in the Thomist ethic.[9] An "assimilative Thomism," stimulated by the dialogue with modern philosophy in the Louvain school, took an interest in phenomenology, notably for the light the latter might throw on the relation between the transcendental and *values*. While the aesthetician Władysław Stróżewsk, who taught at Lublin from 1957 to 1967 is perhaps the purest example of the tendency, Wojtyła certainly fits well in this context.[10] The remaining school is more or less Gilsonian in character: its *forma mentis* is "existential Thomism." In its Lublin embodiment seen, for instance, in Stefan Swieżawski, professor at Lublin from 1946 to 1956 before transferring to Warsaw, this Polish Gilsonianism stressed the link between philosophical anthropology and metaphysics, treating ontology as a "kind of contemplation of being, necessary for the education of the human being and the attainment of an appropriately human culture."[11] Among the interlocutors of these anthropologically and ethically attuned varieties of Thomism was the phenomenologist Max Scheler, whose study *Formalism in Ethics and Non-Formal Ethics of Values*[12] Wojtyła is known to have kept on his desk while writing his own *The Acting Person*. Clearly, a word needs saying on this score.

All phenomenologists study how things are present to the "intentional" mind: the mind at work in its environment as focused

---

8. E. Nieznanski, "Polen," in E. Coreth, W. M. Neidl, G. Pfligersdorffer (ed.), *Christliche Philosophie im katholischen Denken des 19. und 20. Jahrhunderts. 2. Rückgriff auf scholastiches Erbe*, op. cit., pp. 804–823.

9. Ibid., p. 812.

10. Ibid., p. 815.

11. Ibid., p. 818.

12. M. Scheler, *Formalism in Ethics and Non-Formal Ethics of Values* (English translation, Evanston, IL 1973).

on this or that element in its life-world. More especially Scheler belonged with a group of thinkers of that school—sometimes known as the "Munich Phenomenologists"—who parted company with the founder of phenomenology, Edmund Husserl, when the latter appeared to be abandoning his early concern with "essences," how things present themselves in experience in a holistic way, and reverting to some kind of Kantianism for which experience tells us more about ourselves, and notably how our minds are structured, than about the world. Scheler's particular interest was ethics or, as he would put it, the status of values which for him are neither simply subjective nor simply objective (he distinguishes them in this latter respect from "goods," which are things that *possess* value). Instead, values are something in between, in which regard Schelerian values have been compared with the status, in Scholasticism, of universals once abstracted from the concrete individuals that embody cathood or humanity or whatever. This is Scheler's ethical "formalism." His ethical "non-formalism," on the other hand, derives from his assertion that each value has an intrinsic essence, a given content—a bit like the virtues in Aristotle or Saint Thomas—and from his conviction that the comparison of value contents enables us to rank values on a scale of importance. Though Scheler considered that all the main levels of cosmic reality—thus being, life, sense, reason, spirit—are present in man, he made a very sharp distinction between human nature and the human person. He saw the person not so much as an individual substance but rather as a mode of action. This mode is not initiated until a human individual unifies all his or her relevant powers in moral agency. For this reason, relationship to others in community, an essential aspect of moral activity as presumably everybody would agree, is in Scheler's thought actually constitutive of the person—which not everybody would agree.[13] According to Scheler: humanly, I exist as an I, but personally I only exist as an "I-We." Wojtyła will go on to echo this in a more Christian idiom when he calls the "I" an acting person *in communion*.

---

13. See R. Harvanek, sj, "The Philosophical Foundations of the Thought of John Paul II," in J. M. McDermott, sj (ed.), *The Thought of Pope John Paul II. A Collection of Essays and Studies* (Rome, 1993), pp. 1–21. Harvanek draws a persuasive comparison with the thought of John Macmurray (*The Self as Agent*, London, 1969, and *Persons in Relation*, London, 1970)—not that there is any reason to think John Paul II was aware of these works.

The Phenomenon, the Person, and the Moral Act

In, then, *The Acting Person,* John Paul is chiefly concerned with the expression of personhood in moral action, and, as befits one phenomenologically trained, he approaches this matter by a reflective description of the experience of being a personal subject engaged in free activity. By way of contrast to Scheler, Wojtyła emphasizes the unity, not the disjunction, of person and nature, and notably of bodily nature; furthermore, he stresses the cognitional character of personal agency: it opens the person to the order of truth, something Scheler does not really mention. What is highly Schelerian, however, in *The Acting Person* is the way Wojtyła links emotions to values—emotions are, for him, references to values or their rejection, and the way too that, as already touched on, Wojtyła takes a person is to be essentially a communicator or respondent, who only becomes an isolated ego by alienation, that is: withdrawal from communion.[14] That contrast of person with individual could also be found in Maritain, notably in his short study *The Person and the Common Good.* But at Wojtyła's hands it is warmer, more affective. As he himself explained, with reference not so much to *The Acting Person* as to his essay on sexual ethics, *Love and Responsibility*:

> I formulated the concept of a personalist principle. This principle is an attempt to translate the commandment of love into the language of philosophical ethics. The person is a being for whom the only suitable dimension is love. We are just to a person if we love him.[15]

Scheler had claimed that knowledge of persons is not "objective" but must pass through love.

Phenomenology helps to explain John Paul's meandering style which some would regard as prolix. He is a writer who makes his points at seemingly unnecessary length. For the phenomenologist, "grasp of truth . . . only slowly emerges through extensive rumination

---

14. Ibid., pp. 10–11. Again, Harvanek makes a useful cross-reference, this time to the convergent account of the person as respondent in Lublin Thomism, as classically represented by M. Krapiec, OP, *I-Man: An Outline of Philosophical Anthropology* (English translation, New Britain, 1983).

15. John Paul II, *Crossing the Threshold of Hope* (English translation, London, 1994), pp. 200–201.

on the multiple appearances [compare the word "phenomenon"] of the question," as one perspective after another is analyzed until the most comprehensive version emerges.[16] For a Christian phenomenologist, this may well entail intertwining a theological with a philosophical approach, in which case, of course, John Paul could also call on the resources of his first doctorate, notably Saint Thomas and Saint John of the Cross as well as, naturally, the Scriptures, the Church Fathers and the other monuments of tradition such as Conciliar definitions whose role is normative in the making of Catholic theology.

The American Jesuit philosophical theologian John McDermott summed up John Paul II's intellectual style in these words:

> He is orthodox in theology, considering himself a guardian of the Church's spiritual heritage, the gospel message, which has been proclaimed through the centuries. Yet one does not find the categories of the traditional Thomistic orthodoxy that dominated Catholic theology in the century before Vatican II and that was taught to him at the Angelicum in Rome by Garrigou-Lagrange, his doctoral director. The traditional doctrine has been clearly re-thought by a very perceptive, active mind in touch with the concrete reality of faith, fascinated by the experience of the mystics, and trained in a personalist philosophy. Out of that lived matrix of experience and thought the Pope seems to draw the inspiration for his spiritual doctrine.[17]

Without rejecting a philosophy of being as such, Wojtyła had found that a metaphysics able to "underpin an *effective* theology today" must find its "starting point" in "man as a unique free subject." His would be, in the words of another Jesuit commentator, a "metaphysics of concrete subjectivity which nonetheless remains unquestionably a metaphysics of being."[18] As the same writer explains, what this means is that "subjectivity" here is "not to be equated with the pure consciousness of idealistic phenomenology." Rather, "subjectivity" means for John Paul "man's awareness of his own subsistent being revealed in its activity through what Saint Thomas would call an immediate act of *intellectus* . . ."[19] "understanding," or, as the contemporary Thomistic

---

16. J. J. Conley, SJ, "The Philosophical Foundations of the Thought of John Paul II: A Response," in J. M. McDermott, SJ (ed.), *The Thought of Pope John Paul II*, op. cit., p. 25.

17. J. M. McDermott, SJ, "Introduction," in ibid., p. xiii.

18. G. A. McCool, SJ, "The Theology of John Paul II," in ibid., pp. 36–37.

19. Ibid., p. 38.

epistemologist Bernard Lonergan translates the word, "insight."[20] It seems worth noting that the conjunction of those terms "*intellectus*," "being," and "activity," furnishes an advance indication that my claim for a "synthetic outcome" of the contributions we have looked at in this book has *something* to it. "Understanding," in different senses of the word (*Vernunft* or constructive reason, *intelligence* or transempirical apprehension), was key to, respectively, Günther and Bautain; "being" to Gilson; "activity," again, in a different sense of the word (practical reason, action), to Hermes and Blondel.

The question inevitably arises, Which, if any, of these factors —insight, being, action—has priority? Examination of a study of the documents of the Second Vatican Council Karol Wojtyła wrote when Archbishop of Cracow suggests the answer may be: well, actually, none of them. In *Sources of Renewal. The Implementation of the Second Vatican Council*,[21] Wojtyła linked the proper structuring of the conscious fundamental attitudes required for the authentic life of faith to the proper ordering of revealed truths [as] demanded by the logic of the Church's faith.

In the Creed, so he pointed out:

> [T]he Church's confession of her own divine origin followed upon her confession of the prior truths on which her own nature rested. In proper order, these prior truths were the creation, the incarnation and redemption, and finally the sending of the Holy Spirit.[22]

That would seem to mean, then, giving *revelation* priority vis-à-vis whatever consciousness of insight, being and action are attained by other routes. In point of fact, *Fides et ratio*—which, as a document of the papal magisterium does not reflect *simply* Wojtyła's personal

---

20. B.J.F. Lonergan, *Insight. A Study of Human Understanding* (New York, 1957); a useful guide to this labyrinthine work is E. McKinon, "Understanding according to Bernard J. F. Lonergan, SJ," *The Thomist* 28 (1964), pp. 97–132, 338–372, 475–522. It is an epistemological metatheory of cognition, claiming to find a fourfold pattern in all acts of knowledge (the experience of data, the understanding of their meaning, the assessment of their value and lastly an evaluative decision).

21. *Sources of Renewal. The Implementation of the Second Vatican Council* (English translation, San Francisco, 1980).

22. G. A. McCool, SJ, "The Theology of John Paul II," art. cit., p. 44.

philosophy and theology—will somewhat correct that impression by invoking the image of a "circular" relationship between revelation and these other resources.

Fides et Ratio

After an introduction, placed under the rubric of the words written above the entrance to the temple of Apollo at Delphi, "Know yourself," *Fides et ratio* consisted in seven chapters. To sum up in advance, the first chapter, entitled "The revelation of God's wisdom," gave the priority to the Word incarnate as revealer of the Father. This is in line with what has just been said of John Paul's view of the foundation of the Church's consciousness in the Trinitarian gift of her being. Only secondarily did that chapter consider what John Paul calls reason "before," i.e., in relation to, "the mystery." The next two chapters investigated those two key phrases from Augustine's Letter 120 to which I drew attention in the introduction to this study: first, "Credo ut intellegam," "I believe that I may understand," and then following it the maxim to which Anselm, followed implicitly by Blondel, gave such attention, "Intelligo ut credam," "I understand that I may believe." Chapter four of *Fides et ratio*, dispensing with Latin formulae, considers in so many words, "the relationship between faith and reason," namely our topic in this book. Chapter five, like my own Chapters 5 and 6, looked at the "interventions of the magisterium in philosophical matters." Chapter six of the encyclical concerned the interaction between theology and philosophy, which could be paraphrased: "the interaction between faith and reason once intellectually elaborated." The pope's last chapter was a forward-looking portmanteau finale entitled "current requirements and tasks."

So let us now consider the sections in turn (not only for greater vivacity but in recognition of the contemporaneity of this document, verbs will be in the present tense). The introduction manifests John Paul's desire to synthesize objectivity and subjectivity, world and self. He understands the pagan imperative "Know yourself" to mean, Set off on a journey (subjective) to meet truth more deeply (objective). The two dimensions are inescapably inter-related. As he puts it:

> [T]he more human beings know reality and the world [objective], the more they know themselves in their uniqueness [subjective], with the question of the meaning of things [objective] and of their existence [subjective] becoming ever more pressing.[23]

The philosophical tradition at its best, the pope records, seeks to do justice to these inter-related issues. Philosophies that content themselves with merely linguistic or hermeneutical analyzes suffer, in this perspective, from false modesty; those that eschew metaphysics, like, one supposes, the "cognitive science" favored at the University of Edinburgh, sell people short, while philosophies that embrace radical pluralism (presumably, Postmodernism is in mind) merely engender skepticism. The Church's "service of the truth" forbids her from accepting such options. The Church, "sure of her competence as the bearer of the Revelation of Jesus Christ," as John Paul more assertively puts it,[24] wishes to recall philosophy to its vocation of, as he writes, "shaping thought and culture" by reference to truth. There is an analogy here, surely, with Leo XIII's wake-up call in *Aeterni Patris*. One obvious difference, however, is that John Paul addresses philosophers beyond the Church, and not just within it. He puts himself, in other words, in the civil setting occupied by Blondel, and not just the ecclesial one of, say, Gardeil and Rousselot. As Alasdair MacIntyre has written: *Fides et ratio* is not only an encyclical about philosophy, as was *Aeterni Patris*, but is also, as *Aeterni Patris* was not, itself

> a contribution to philosophy, inviting philosophical scrutiny of its arguments and assertions in a way that is rare, perhaps unique, among encyclicals. It does so just because the questions which are central to it are in part philosophical questions and the Encyclical insists that in pursuing them "philosophy must remain faithful to its own principles and methods."[25]

Turning to chapter one of *Fides et ratio*, we see how such a universal appeal can be made by one speaking precisely as pope. True,

---

23. *Fides et ratio*, 1.
24. Ibid., 6.
25. A. MacIntyre, "Truth as a Good," in J. McEvoy and M. Dunne (eds.), *Thomas Aquinas: Approaches to Truth* (Dublin, 2001), cited in J. McEvoy, "Commentary," in L. P. Hemming and S. F. Parsons (eds.), *Restoring Faith in Reason* (London, 2002), p. 184. The internal citation is of *Fides et ratio*, 49.

as he remarks, "underlying all the Church's thinking is the awareness that she is the bearer of a message which has its origin in God himself," a supernaturally communicated message, then.[26] But, as he points out on the basis of the constitution *Dei Filius* of the First Vatican Council, this in no way nullifies the claim of philosophy to access of its own to worthwhile truth, since the natural order and the supernatural order, and their corresponding modes of knowledge, are distinct, not mutually exclusive. Moreover, these orders intersect. In John Paul's words, "this [supernatural] truth which comes to [people] as gift . . . urges reason to be open to it and to embrace its profound meaning." His account of how such encounter between the gifted divine truth and human reason comes about is highly reminiscent of Blondel's story of the way the option for the supernatural unfolds in the pages of *L'Action*. As *Fides et ratio* has it:

> [T]he Church has always considered the act of entrusting oneself to God to be a moment of fundamental decision which engages the whole person. In that act, the intellect and the will display their spiritual nature, enabling the subject to act in a way which realizes personal freedom to the full . . . [F]reedom is not realized in decisions made against God. For how could it be an exercise of true freedom to refuse to be open to the very reality which enables our self-realization?[27]

For this "opening" to take place in a Christian context, reason has for its assistance the signs provided by revelation history: here we are in the area of the "Apologetics Debate" we looked at in Chapter 9 of this book. When John Paul says that these "signs" "urge reason to look beyond their status as signs in order to grasp the deeper meaning which they bear" he is, we can say, mediating that debate. The signs bear a deeper meaning than their status as signs: this indicates agreement with Rousselot that the content of revelation is the meaning of the signs. Nonetheless, it is reason which initially establishes their status as signs: this corresponds to the emphasis of Gardeil. Finally in this chapter, Wojtyła echoes Gilson on the capacity of revelation to set new tasks for philosophy when he writes:

---

26. *Fides et ratio*, 7.
27. Ibid., 13.

> Revelation . . . introduces into our history a universal and ultimate truth which stirs the human mind to ceaseless effort; indeed, it impels reason continually to extend the range of its knowledge until it senses that it has done all in its power.[28]

at which point he introduces a favorable reference to Saint Anselm who, as we saw, charges philosophy with the task of discovering the *ratio fidei* though not the *intellectus fidei* which only theology—or, let us say, a wisdom based on a theologically elaborated faith—can provide.

In chapters two and three, which I deal with more briefly —justifiably, since John Paul's literary technique means each chapter flags up much of what follows in his text—we see the two sides of the coin: "I believe that I may understand; I understand that I may believe." When we looked at Augustine's Letter 120 we saw that for Augustine believing in order to understand is not only for the sake of profounder penetration of the faith. Believing may also be a moral necessity to humble the mind by the assent of faith before even a rudimentary grasp of faith's content is possible. John Paul II links such epistemically relevant humility to the Cross of Christ, which humbles the pride of systematic rationalists. As he writes:

> Of itself, philosophy is able to recognize the human being's ceaselessly self-transcendent orientation towards the truth; and, with the assistance of faith, it is capable of accepting the "foolishness" of the Cross as the authentic critique of those who delude themselves that they possess the truth, when in fact they run it aground on the shoals of a system of their own devising.[29]

Doubtless Bautain would approve of this Pauline contrast, based on Saint Paul's Letters to Corinth, between the "wisdom of the Cross" and the "wisdom of the world."

What, then, of the other side of the coin: "I understand that I may believe"? This time it is the Paul of the Acts of the Apostles who catches the pope's eye, and specifically Paul addressing the Athenian philosophers on the Areopagus. Here John Paul commends pure philosophy for its disinterested search for truth in the form of the objective reality of things, over against falsehood (this would please

---

28. Ibid., 14.
29. Ibid., 23.

Neo-Scholastics, including Gilson). But he also commends practical philosophy, or ethics, for seeking in its turn "true values" which alone can "lead people to realize themselves fully, allowing them to be true to their nature," thus putting a spin on Scheler's thought which, no doubt, would have satisfied Hermes in *his* focusing on rationality as practical reason. However, John Paul insists that neither mode of reason, pure or applied, must be made to stop short of ultimates. As he explains:

> Every truth—if it really is truth—presents itself as universal, even if it is not the whole truth. If something is true, then it must be true for all people and at all times. Beyond this universality, however, people seek an absolute which might give to all their searching a meaning and an answer—something ultimate, which might serve as the ground of all things. In other words, they seek a final explanation, a supreme value, which refers to nothing beyond itself and which puts an end to all questioning.[30]

It is towards this ultimate repose, the quieting of desire, whether of mind seeking truth or will seeking the good, a repose faith can identify as the vision of God, that philosophy drives.

In chapter four, then, the author of *Fides et ratio* can come to the heart of the matter, the faith-reason relation. Like in their different ways Günther, Bautain and Leo XIII, John Paul devotes a good deal of attention to the history of this relationship: what went right, and what went wrong. What went right entails looking at the Fathers and Saint Thomas (here Bautain and Leo are in agreement, but not Günther). The Fathers could enter into a "fruitful dialogue" with ancient philosophy because the latter, starting out from what the pope calls "ancient traditions" (compare the traditionalist element in Bautain), had "allowed a development satisfying the demands of universal reason."[31] The Fathers established a valid model for the future when they sought to engage critically with philosophy, while at the same time infusing it with "the richness drawn from Revelation."[32] After the Fathers, if Anselm had charged reason with finding "explanations which might allow everyone to come to a certain understanding [note the qualification there] of the contents of faith,"[33] it was Thomas who gave "pride

---

30. Ibid., 27.
31. Ibid., 36.
32. Ibid., 41.
33. Ibid., 42.

of place to the harmony which exists between faith and reason."[34] Wojtyła shares the concerns of Gardeil when he writes:

> Although he made much of the supernatural character of faith, the Angelic Doctor did not overlook the importance of its reasonableness; ... human reason is neither annulled nor debased in assenting to the contents of faith, which are in any case attained by way of free and informed choice.[35]

What went wrong, historically, with the faith-reason relationship was the later medieval, Renaissance and early Modern "drama," as John Paul puts it, of their separation. Here all the writers we have looked at would agree with him, though not always from the same motives; exceptions would be the Louvain Neo-Thomists to whom I have made occasional allusion. John Paul sees the culmination of this process in not only philosophical varieties of atheistic humanism, in which category he places Marxism, but also in the great Idealist systems though the way he describes these—"various ways to transform faith and its contents ... into dialectical structures which could be grasped by reason" would actually cover the thought of a pious man like Günther who considered he was *unifying* faith and reason not disjoining them.[36] Positivism, for which reason is merely instrumental in finding technical applications of science, and nihilism, for which every assertion is provisional, are also among the evil fruits of the separation of faith and reason. Deprived of the resources of revelation, reason has gone up cul-de-sacs, or at least side-tracks. Deprived of the discipline of reason, faith has emphasized feeling and experience, "and so runs the risk of no longer being a universal proposition."[37]

This separation, moving onto chapter five, is among the main reasons why the magisterium has found itself compelled to enter into the arena. Though reason is autonomous (Blondel would approve)

---

34. Ibid., 43. It is noteworthy that Thomas is the only individual figure from the history of Christian thought to be given a section all his own, under the heading "The enduring originality of the thought of Saint Thomas Aquinas." Writing personally rather than officially, Wojtyła called Thomas "the master of philosophical and theological universalism," thus John Paul II, *Crossing the Threshold of Hope*, op. cit., p. 31. For an exploration of this Pope's relation to Thomism, see M. Dauphinais and M. Levering (ed.), *John Paul II and Saint Thomas Aquinas* (Naples, FL, 2007).

35. *Fides et ratio*, 43.

36. Ibid., 46. John Paul II's singling out of the Death and Resurrection of Christ as key to these "contents" thus dialectically transformed shows it is really Hegel he has in mind.

37. Ibid., 48.

since of its nature it is ordered to truth and equipped to acquire truth, and the Church of herself has no philosophy of her own (but what about Leo XIII then?), it is nonetheless, says *Fides et ratio*, "the Church's duty to indicate the elements in a philosophical system which are incompatible with her own faith,"[38] doing so not, insists John Paul, in a spirit of negativity, but rather to "encourage [further] philosophical inquiry.[39] More widely, and this fits somewhat uneasily with the claim that the Church has no philosophy of her own, the magisterium has the further duty of stressing the "basic principles of a genuine renewal of philosophical inquiry, indicating as well particular paths to be taken.[40] (So up to a point at least, *Aeterni Patris* is vindicated after all.[41])

Thomism, says Wojtyła, has given the Church enormous service in this area, not least philosophically, though she is also indebted to — and then a number of descriptions follow to which no names are added. Thus we read "some devised syntheses so remarkable that they stood comparison with the great systems of idealism." That could hardly be Günther, but it might be members of the Catholic Tübingen school like Bautain's correspondent Möhler who shared Günther's debt to the classical German philosophers, though Möhler's colleagues Johann Sebastian Drey and Franz Anton Staudenmaier showed a more marked systematic bent.[42] "Others," still citing *Fides et ratio*, "established the epistemological foundations for a new consideration of faith in the light of a renewed understanding of moral consciousness." That could scarcely be Hermes, granted the forcefulness of the

---

38. Ibid., 50.

39. Ibid., 51.

40. Ibid., 57.

41. It could be argued that a degree of ambivalence on this topic was needed so as to capture the sense of the document of the Second Vatican Council which bears most closely on the theme, *Optatam totius* at paragraphs 15 and 16. There: "Saint Thomas is recommended as a teacher. He is not only the master who formulated in his time the contents of revelation in the intellectual and linguistic forms of Aristotelianism (which was then modern) and hence became a model of the adaptation of theological research and language to contemporary life and culture—this was conceded by all, and many required that the Council should limit itself to recognizing this method—but he is also a teacher inasmuch as he arrived at permanent insights which have to be taught in theological instruction," J. Neuner, "Decree on Priestly Formation," in H. Vorgrimler (ed.), *Commentary on the Documents of Vatican II*, vol. 2 (English translation, New York, 1989), pp. 398–399.

42. For an excellent English-language survey of these writers, see D. J. Dietrich, *The Goethezeit and the Metamorphosis of Catholic Theology in the Age of Idealism*, op. cit., pp. 75–197.

nineteenth-century condemnations, but it might be a figure worth comparing with him, John Henry Newman.[43] "Others again produced a philosophy which, starting with an analysis of immanence, opened the way to the transcendent." That can only be Blondel.[44] And finally there were "those who sought to combine the demands of faith with the perspective of phenomenological method." That surely refers to those indebted to the Munich Phenomenologists like Edith Stein whom John Paul beatified and later canonized.[45] All these are valid examples of Christian thought uniting faith and reason.[46] "*Fides et ratio,*" wrote the North America historian of ideas Wayne J. Hankey, "may perhaps be an act of reparation in so far as it recommends thinkers condemned or dismissed in the nineteenth-century turn to Neo-Thomism."[47] (The word "condemned" refers to the mid-nineteenth century Italian priest, Antonio Rosmini-Serbati, earlier judged guilty of "ontologism"—the confusion of an intuition of being with an intuition of God—rather than any of the figures studied here; "dismissed" is another matter.) And the pope ends chapter five by anticipating chapters six and seven: this union is so key that Catholic theology must never be pursued without the concomitant study of philosophy.

In the penultimate chapter, chapter six, on the interaction of theology and philosophy, Wojtyła distinguishes between on the one hand the "hearing of faith," *auditus fidei,* the concern of which is simply to grasp what the revealed message is—for this, philosophy is *relatively* necessary, because reflection on biblical language and a knowledge of the original meanings of the concepts used in first formulating the faith, e.g., at the early Councils, is desirable, and, on

---

43. Compare these words: "Now certainly the thought of God, as Theists entertain it, is not gained by an instinctive association of His presence with any sensible phenomena; but the office which the senses directly fulfill as regards creation, that devolves indirectly on certain of our mental phenomena as regards the Creator. Those phenomena are found in the sense of moral obligation;" thus J. H. Newman, *An Essay in Aid of a Grammar of Assent* (London 1882, 5th edition; New York, 1947), p. 79. For a discussion, see D. A. Pailin, *The Way to Faith: An Examination of Newman's "Grammar of Assent" as a Response to the Search for Certainty in Faith* (London, 1969).

44. P. Henrici, "The One Who Went Unnamed: Maurice Blondel in the Encyclical *Fides et ratio,*" Communio 26 (1999), pp. 609–621.

45. S. Borden, *Edith Stein* (London, 2003), pp. 20–45, 90–116.

46. *Fides et ratio,* 59.

47. W. J. Hankey, "Practical Considerations about Teaching Philosophy and Theology Now," in L. P. Hemming and S. F. Parsons (ed.), *Restoring Faith in Reason,* op. cit., p. 199.

the other hand, the *intellectus fidei* or deeper understanding of faith, for which philosophy is *absolutely* necessary. Speculative dogmatic theology cannot do without a philosophical anthropology, cosmology and ontology if it is to expound the wider significance of the revealed message; fundamental theology cannot show the credibility of revelation and the reasonableness of the act of faith without philosophy; moral theology cannot do without a philosophical inquiry into the foundations of ethics.[48]

The relation between theology and philosophy, declares the pope, is best construed as a circle. As he explains:

> Theology's source and starting-point must always be the word of God revealed in history, while its final goal will be an understanding of that word which increases with each passing generation. Yet, since God's Word is Truth (cf John 17:17), the human search for truth—philosophy, pursued in keeping with its own rules—can only help to understand God's Word better.[49]

Moreover, a philosophy which shuns revelation damages itself. As the Washington philosophical theologian David Schindler comments on the important paragraph 75 of *Fides et ratio* which falls within this sixth chapter, the pope limits a "Gospel-independent" philosophy to times and places where the Gospel has not been preached, and even then such a philosophy always remains open *at least* implicitly to the supernatural, such that its autonomy, rightly conceived, precludes an anterior closure to the truth offered by divine revelation.[50] "The historical appearance of the fullness of truth," namely, the event of divine self-disclosure in Christ, cannot be for philosophy a "matter of indifference."[51] Readers of the remaining sections of chapter six will see that John Paul in effect espouses Gilson's concept of Christian philosophy: a "philosophy consonant with the Word of God" which can nonetheless be "a place where Christian faith and human cultures may meet, a point of understanding between believer and nonbeliever."[52]

---

48. Ibid., 66–68.

49. Ibid., 73.

50. D. L. Schindler, "God and the End of Intelligence: Knowledge as Relationship," *Communio* 26 (1999), p. 512.

51. Ibid., p. 513.

52. *Fides et ratio*, 79. "The pope seems clearly to accept the main lines of Gilson's lifelong argument that there is such a thing as a Christian philosophy: a positive influence—subjective

And that is why, in the concluding chapter of *Fides et ratio* on current needs, he rejects:
- philosophies that are functional, formal or utilitarian, rather than sapiential, focusing on the overall meaning of life;
- philosophies that are radically phenomenalist or relativist, rather than those which "verify" the human capacity to know truth, understood as the correspondence of mind and thing;
- philosophies that are merely empiricist, rather than those which have a "genuinely metaphysical range," able to transcend empirical data in the direction of attaining foundational ultimates.[53]

Opposing these deficient philosophies will mean, says John Paul, unmasking particular errors of method, notably eclecticism, historicism, scientism, pragmatism and nihilism, with which he equates much Postmodernism.

The task thus set is enormous. Indeed, so much is it so that it seems hardly surprising when the encyclical ends with a request for supernatural assistance. This the pope does through his closing reference to the Virgin Mother of God whom a Byzantine writer, here cited, calls "the table at which faith sits in thought." "To philosophize in Mary," *philosophari in Maria*, is John Paul's final counsel since:

> [J]ust as in giving her assent to Gabriel's word, Mary lost nothing of her true humanity and freedom, so too when philosophy heeds the summons of the Gospel's truth its autonomy is in no way impaired. Indeed, it is then that philosophy sees all its inquiries rise to their highest expression.[54]

---

and objective—of faith and revelation on philosophy which nonetheless leaves philosophy, precisely in its receipt of this influence, its rightful autonomy": thus D. J. Schindler, "God and the End of Intelligence: Knowledge as Relationship," *Communio* 26 (1999), p. 514.

53. *Fides et ratio*, 81–83.

54. Ibid., 108. See on this D. V. Meconi, sj, "*Philosophari in Maria: Fides et ratio* and Mary as the Model of Created Wisdom," in D. R. Foster and J. W. Koterski, sj, (ed.), *The Two Wings of Catholic Thought. Essays on* Fides et ratio (Washington, 2003), pp. 69–87.

Chapter 11

From Cracow to Regensburg: Benedict XVI

Background and Life

John Paul's successor, Benedict XVI, was born Joseph Ratzinger in 1927 in Marktl-am-Inn, a village in the foothills of the Bavarian Alps. He was the son of a rural policeman. Owing to his father's terms of employment, his family moved a number of times in his childhood but always (in his own words) "in the triangle formed on two sides by the Inn and Salzach rivers, whose landscape and history marked my youth."[1] What appears to have been a lyrically happy childhood was overshadowed, however, by the rise of National Socialism. The age-old Catholic culture of rural Bavaria now faced twin enemies. Government sought to overthrow the Church's hegemony in its parochial schools and make life difficult for priests who criticized the State ideology. Influential individuals like, Ratzinger recalled, a local schoolmaster, took the initiative in attempts to introduce neo-pagan ceremonies as an alternative to the feasts and fasts of the liturgical year, intertwined as these were with countryside rhythms.

At Easter 1939 he followed his elder brother Georg in entering minor seminary, intending to become a priest. In the circumstances, this could not be an easy path. In 1943, with a pressing shortage of manpower, boys of his age were required to serve by manning anti-aircraft batteries—in Ratzinger's case, located on the edge of Munich. In 1944 he came of age for full military service, which took the form of digging trenches on the Reich's frontier with Hungary, which had just surrendered to the Russians. With the American advance into Germany he was taken prisoner but released in June 1945.

---

1. J. Ratzinger, *Aus meinem Leben. Erinnerungen* [1927–1977] (Stuttgart, 1998); English translation *Milestones. Memoirs 1927–1977* (San Francisco, 1998), p. 7.

Ratzinger's seminary training resumed at Freising where his increasingly omnivorous intellectual appetite was stimulated by notably wide reading in philosophy, as well as in twentieth-century literature. He already felt a strong attraction to Augustinian wisdom, which he admired for its passionate personalism, over against the admittedly much more impersonal formulations of Scholastic thought as found among Thomas Aquinas and his successors. (Unsurprisingly, Ratzinger would elect a theme from Augustine as the topic of his first post-graduate thesis.[2]) He also found in Cardinal Michael Faulhaber, the Archbishop of Munich, a stalwart opponent of the Nazis, not just, as he put it, an "accessible" bishop but someone who had become deeply identified with a great mission in Church and world.[3] This lifted his sights.

The transition from philosophical studies to theological brought him to the Munich Theology Faculty, where a distinguished tradition of historical and speculative theology dated from the beginnings of the post-Revolutionary Catholic revival in southern Germany.[4] Though the Faculty was closed down by the Nazis on the eve of the Second World War (a consequence of Faulhaber's brave stand), its reopening, with professors drawn from all over Germany, was evidently marked by a determination to recreate its earlier ethos—a predominantly historical approach to theology emphasizing Scripture and the Fathers of the Church but open to speculative development thanks to the interplay of dogma, exegesis and philosophy. This was not the narrow intellectual outlook ascribed in stereotype to the "pre-Conciliar" Catholic Church.

> All of us lived with a feeling of radical change that had already arisen in the 1920s, the sense of a theology that had the courage to ask new questions and a spirituality that was doing away with what was dusty and obsolete and leading to a new joy in the redemption. Dogma was conceived, not

---

2. Idem., *Volk und Haus Gottes in Augustins Lehre von der Kirche* (Sankt Ottilien, 1954, reprinted with a new preface in 1992). That this theme was ecclesiological should have deterred later critics who found in his Augustinianism a pessimism about the corporate which deflected him into a mistaken piety of "God and the soul." As he wrote in 1968, "God and the soul —nothing else is impracticable; and it is also unchristian": J. Ratzinger, *Introduction to Christianity* (English translation, San Francisco, 2004), p. 95.

3. Idem., *Milestones*, op. cit., p. 45.

4. A. Nichols, OP, *The Thought of Benedict XVI. The Theology of Joseph Ratzinger* (London, 2007, 2nd edition), pp. 11–14.

as an external shackle, but as the living source that made the knowledge of the truth possible in the first place. The Church came to life for us above all in the liturgy and in the great richness of the theological tradition.[5]

Ordination to priesthood by Faulhaber in 1951 led to a first pastoral assignment in a Munich parish. He was already earmarked, however, for an intellectual apostolate of teaching and writing. That apostolate unfolded in one sense effortlessly: through the writing of the two theses required by the German educational system for acquisition of a doctorate, and then a series of appointments in faculties of Catholic theology attached to State universities in Münster, Bonn, Tübingen and, finally, Regensburg. Any crises were of a strictly academic nature. Thus, on finishing his second thesis or *Habilitationsschrift*, a study of the medieval Franciscan theologian Saint Bonaventure, disagreement with a much-respected teacher, Michael Schmaus, over whether, or to what extent, revelation was for Bonaventure an intersubjective divine-human exchange rather than (simply) an objective content found in Scripture (and Tradition), threatened to bring his academic career to a premature end.[6] Yet thinking pertinaciously through these issues would equip him for his main contribution at the Second Vatican Council which he attended as a peritus (theological adviser) to the Archbishop of Cologne. That contribution concerned precisely the interrelation of the ideas of revelation and of revelation's media of transmission in Scripture and Tradition in the Dogmatic Constitution on Divine Revelation, *Dei Verbum*. In a second troublesome episode, his time at Tübingen was marred by the disruption of classes, and even more of tone, by students converted to Neo-Marxism: a common phenomenon in Western European, British and North American Universities in or around 1968. The encounter with a Marxism careless of civility in intellectual exchange confirmed what had already emerged from his inquiry into Bonaventure's theology. It was necessary to distinguish between the authentic eschatology of Bible and Church on the one hand, and a utopianism which could easily degenerate into totalitarianism on the other. There is a

---

5. J. Ratzinger, *Milestones*, op. cit., p. 57.

6. The thesis was eventually published as *Die Geschichtstheologie des heiligen Bonaventura* (Munich, 1959; 2nd edition, Saint Ottilien, 1992), translated into English as *The Theology of History in Saint Bonaventure* (Chicago, 1971; 2nd edition, 1989).

difference between, on the one hand, a super-rationality where *logos,* the principle of intelligibility, is crowned by union with love, and, on the other, a descent into the sub-rationality of intellectual violence. Ratzinger's perceived enemies on the hard Left were those of the New Left, for whom the "masters of suspicion" had rendered rational interchange of dubious value. This was in contrast to Wojtyła's experience. Wojtyła had faced down ideologists of the Old Left, which, albeit in the increasingly sclerotic form of official Marxism-Leninism, was at any rate argumentative. The proposal that history ends not in the resolution of a dialectic (whether socioeconomic or intellectual) but in the free divine gift of a kingdom of justice, love and peace, would be highly pertinent to Ratzinger's own adjudication of the faith-reason relationship. The central feature of that adjudication is the convergence of the (mainly philosophical) disclosure of *logos* and the (chiefly theological) revelation of love.

In 1977 Ratzinger was made Archbishop of Munich and Freising by Pope Paul VI. Two years later, amid the doctrinal near-chaos of post-Conciliar Catholicism, a new pope, John Paul II, called him to Rome as Prefect of the Congregation for the Doctrine of the Faith. In his wanderings among the German University faculties he had, after all, taught almost all the theological "tractates" in which Catholic doctrine is subdivided for study purposes, and had shown an impressive capacity to combine theological orthodoxy with acute awareness of contemporary questions. His work as Prefect should not be identified with his own writings. This is not to say that his official work went against the grain of his personal convictions. In a religiously minded man of such integrity that is hardly likely. The books and articles he put out under his own name, while Prefect and, after 2005, Pope, were often related, moreover, to the issues with which his official duties had faced him. Those considerations warrant referring to him indifferently as "Ratzinger" and "Benedict" in what follows.

BENEDICT XVI ON FAITH AND REASON

Ratzinger's concern with the issue of the faith-reason relation was signaled comparatively early, in the 1968 *Introduction to Christianity.* In the new edition of this book, from the year 2000, Ratzinger went out of his way to underline the importance of the question—not only in itself but for revelation as well. In a programmatic statement, he wrote:

> Ever since the Prologue to the Gospel of John, the concept of *logos* has been at the very center of our Christian faith . . . The God who is *logos* guarantees the intelligibility of the world, the intelligibility of our existence, the aptitude of reason to know God and the reasonableness of God, even though his understanding infinitely surpasses ours and to us may so often appear to be darkness.[7]

After an initial historical claim about the centrality of the concept of the Logos for Christian theology, the bulk of this citation links a fundamental ontology ("the intelligibility of the world, . . . of our existence") with an epistemology open to the divine ("the aptitude of reason to know God"). Taken overall, Ratzinger's words signify that both fundamental ontology and an epistemology appropriate to the human being need to be informed by distinctively Christian faith in God as the *logos*. And he continues, in a breathtakingly brief expansion of this claim: "The world comes from reason, and this reason is a Person, is Love."[8]

That "the world comes from reason" is, or should be, a statement that philosophy can, once clarified, defend. It is an assertion about the origination of the world in creative divine rationality. But when we hear further that, for the New Testament understanding, this same rationality is fully personal—not so much a *what* as a *who*—and is so *because it "is Love,"* we realize we have crossed the threshold from philosophy into theology, or, as Ratzinger prefers to put it, into the realm of "biblical faith." As we shall see, the convergence of the accelerating self-disclosure of an implicitly or explicitly divine principle of intelligibility to reason in the history of philosophical thought with the self-manifestation of the God of love to Israel and the Church in the history of revealed faith is, for Ratzinger, the key to a harmonious equilibrium in the relationship, so often stormy, of reason and faith *tout court*. Among the magisterial interventions of the mid-century popes I recorded in Chapter 5 the claim of Pius IX in *Singulari quidem* that reason and faith, rightly understood, enjoy a happy collaboration. At Pius's hands that was sheer—if, in context,

---

7. J. Ratzinger, "Preface to New Edition," *Introduction to Christianity*, op. cit., p. 26.
8. Ibid.

useful—assertion. What Ratzinger offers is one way in which to make for it an argued case.

Introduction to Christianity is framed as a commentary on the Apostles' Creed. So Ratzinger is dealing with a text governed by the word *credo* and can hardly avoid giving some account of the act of faith. He begins from the assertion that for human living, openness to a reality that exceeds the visible and tangible is an existential desideratum—nay, imperative. And that is so even if there is something "adventurous" about regarding the empirically unavailable as the fundamentally real.[9] Yet until the early modern period, rational thought assisted, rather than inhibited, the act of faith in the invisible. For ancient and medieval ontology, being is true—intelligible, meaningful, apt for apprehension—because it is creatively thought by God, who (in a formula indebted, surely, to Idealism) is absolute spirit. So long as this presupposition is in place, we can describe human thinking as the "rethinking of being" or the "rethinking of the thought that is being itself." Man can rethink the *logos*, the meaning of being, because his own *logos*, his own reason, is *logos* of the one *logos*, thought of the original thought, of the creative spirit that permeates and governs his being.[10]

This (healthful) assumption was abandoned, highly influentially, by the eighteenth-century Neapolitan philosopher Giambattista Vico who put in its place an alternative preface to thought. According to Vico, understanding is or should be of the humanly initiated. Now the maxim runs: not *verum quia ens*, "true because being," but *verum quia factum*, "true because made." The insistence that what is humanly initiated is the properly intelligible governs for Ratzinger all succeeding philosophy in the European West. That philosophy takes in one way or another the form of a reflective history of human things—ideally with Hegel, sociologically with Comte, biologically with Darwin, economically with Marx. Eventually, this line of intellectual development produces the technological rationality which Ratzinger takes to be normative today.[11] The true is now *the feasible*. Here we

---

9. Ibid., p. 52.
10. Ibid., p. 59.
11. He refers here to Martin Heidegger's distinction between calculating thought and reflective thought to indicate the contemporary noetic fall. Of course both are necessary—and precisely this should forbid one from absorbing the other.

have a further definition of truth, *verum quia faciendum*: something is "true because it can be done." Whether our philosophy is Vico-esque or merely a commitment to technology, in either case it will disable us from coming to terms with the affirmation *credo*. That is so above all when the context of our self-opening to the wider reality in which our lives are set is not simply that of ancient thinking, or the philosophical element in medieval thinking, but is, rather, the context of the Bible for which faith is "taking a stand trustfully on the ground of the word of God."[12] That word is meant to clear a path to the totality of reality in a way commensurate with man's need to situate himself vis-à-vis that wider whole. Such a total meaning cannot be made. It can only be received. That enables Benedict to make a link with New Testament concepts of faith. In the words of the Letter to the Romans with a vigrand history before them in the Latin tradition (compare the introduction to the present study), Christian faith is a faith that is *ex auditu*: it comes "from hearing."[13] Or to put this in a more "Benedictine" way, typical of revealed faith is that "[such faith] is the reception of something that I have not thought out, so that in the last analysis thinking in the context of faith is always a thinking over of something previously heard and received."[14]

This emphasis on the *reception of a total meaning* is what enables Ratzinger to say that the development of the philosophical *logos*—which in partial ways can adumbrate that total meaning and also clarify the conditions of its reception—converges with the progressive unfolding of such meaning in the story of God's self-revelation in Israel, Christ and the Church. Between the Greek word *logos* and the Hebrew word *Amen* there is already a fundamental affinity: these words "embrace the indivisibility of meaning, ground and truth."[15] In Christian Hellenism, indeed, the Gospel, as the climactic message of Judeo-Christianity, merged with an inquiry into understanding. For Ratzinger, this was "no mere accident." The episode in Acts 16 when Saint Paul sees in a night vision a man bidding him "come over to Macedonia and help us"[16] hints at a "divinely arranged

---

12. J. Ratzinger, *Introduction to Christianity*, op. cit., p. 69.
13. Romans 10:17.
14. J. Ratzinger, *Introduction to Christianity*, op. cit., p. 91.
15. Ibid., p. 76.
16. Acts 16:9.

necessity," whereby the Gospel left the shadows of Asia and entered the luminosity of Greece.[17] "Before the Age of Reason," an Australian philosopher remarks:

> God was generally accorded both an ontological and an epistemological function, as the *fons et origo* of all that is and as the guarantor of determinate meaning. Thereafter, God's epistemological function passed to man, initially by means of the Cartesian *cogito*, and subsequently by means of the Kantian transcendental subject.[18]

Benedict is proposing that the "function" had no need to pass: man is *pontifical man*, from the Latin *pons* or bridge and *facere*, to make.[19] He is the bridge maker, indeed he is the living bridge between God and the world. The analogous senses of *logos* show how.

But Benedict needs to go further. He has to come more fully to terms with the *Christologically formed* character of this *logos*-related faith. The affirmation *credo in* typically ends, for the Church's discourse, not with a ground but with a person: the incarnate Word, in whose life "the meaning of the world is present before us." This is where Ratzinger places, besides the language of *logos*, the language of *love*. With the Incarnation, for man's sake, of One who is God, the meaning or *ratio* of the world vouchsafes itself to us as love that loves even me and makes life worth living by this incomprehensible gift of a love free from any threat of fading away or any tinge of egotism.[20]

Or, in a memorable summary, "Meaning knows me and loves me."[21]

Benedict's investigation of that key text for biblical theology, Exodus 3:14—at the "burning bush," the God of the patriarchs reveals himself to Moses as "I Am"—confirms what has just been said. God bears a name, because he revealed to Israel's ancestors his personal invocability, and such self-bestowal is, as it were, the first act of the drama of loving kindness to which the Incarnation forms the climax. But by this name the Lord of Israel can also be understood in the

---

17. Ibid., p. 78, footnote 16.
18. K. Hart, *The Trespass of the Sign. Deconstruction, Theology and Philosophy*, op. cit., p. 29.
19. See A. Nichols, OP, *Epiphany. A Theological Introduction to Catholicism* (Collegeville, MN), p. 22.
20. J. Ratzinger, *Introduction to Christianity*, op. cit., p. 79.
21. Ibid., p. 80.

language of philosophical ontology as plenary Being. He is so utterly different from the myriads of other gods that the Hebrew Bible can fairly describe them as "naught."[22] The self-communicative fullness of being (a philosophical description) is identical with the self-donation of the God of love. Plotting key moments of this convergent identity (absolute Being, unsurpassable love) will involve reference to the Wisdom literature, Second Isaiah and the Gospel of John where Jesus uses for himself the divine formula, "I Am" or "I am He."

The God of the Philosophers, and the God of Faith

Are we to say, then, that the God of faith is identical *simpliciter* with the God of the philosophers? No. The biblical revelation could not leave the philosophical concept of God as it stood. In the light of Christ, it had to factor into that concept the notion of all-sustaining love which, left to its own resources, philosophical reflection could not have attained. In this sense the God of the philosophers is quite different from what the philosophers had thought him to be, though he does not thereby cease to be what they had discovered.[23]

The attributes of divine being uncovered on the trajectory of philosophical reason are amplified, enhanced, transformed—not truncated or denied—once that trajectory meets, and merges with, the trajectory of biblical faith. Being revealed as love: this is henceforth the only adequate formula for the divine. It has the further advantage, in Benedict's eyes, that it constitutes a starting point for specifically *Trinitarian* faith.[24] In words from a later study which, however, encapsulate the doctrine of *Introduction to Christianity* on this point:

> The primacy of the Logos and the primacy of love proved to be identical. The Logos was seen to be, not merely a mathematical reason at the basis of all things, but a creative love taken to the point of becoming sympathy, suffering with the creature. The cosmic aspect of religion, which reverences

---

22. Ibid., pp. 116–136.
23. Ibid., p. 144.
24. Ibid., p. 148.

the Creator in the power of being, and its existential aspect, the question of redemption, merged together and became one.[25]

Judging by this seminal text (and its later echoes), it would seem that, unlike John Paul II, Benedict may prefer to unite philosophy and theology in a single, internally differentiated but also internally cohesive, intellectual act. On the basis of what I have been speaking of as the "convergence of trajectories" he wishes (like Bautain) to re-create, at any rate in large part, the mindset of the early Church for which Christianity was *vera philosophia*, the "true philosophy." Elsewhere he draws his readers' attention to the portrayal of the figure of the philosopher in early Christian iconography, that philosopher whom some art historians interpret as "the *homo christianus* who has received the revelation of the true paradise through the Gospel."[26]

Much of what he says sounds highly Gilsonian. As his 1984 essay "Faith, Philosophy, and Theology" makes clear, he takes the view that theology does not only make use of philosophy, as the Septuagint translation of the word of the Lord to Moses in the book of Exodus made use (doubtless) of Hellenic thought. Theology also serves philosophy by saving it from both triviality and gnosis. Philosophy becomes trivial when, through over-approximation to the exact sciences, it ceases to ask the existentially most heavyweight questions: those that concern the meaning of human life and its destiny. Philosophy can do that, of course, in various ways: by shrinking itself to the dimensions of formal logic, for instance, or by reinventing itself as, in effect, a philosophy of natural science. (This is a well-known trap for analytic philosophers, illustrated in Bertrand Russell's expression of doubt that the idea of philosophy "as a study distinct from science and possessed of a method of its own, is anything more than an unfortunate legacy from theology."[27]) Philosophy becomes gnostic when it transmutes

---

25. J. Ratzinger, *Glaube, Wahrheit, Toleranz Das Christentum und die Weltreligionen* (Freiburg, Basle, Vienna, 2003); English translation, *Truth and Tolerance. Christian Belief and World Religions* (San Francisco, 2004), p. 182.

26. F. Gerke, *Christus in der spätantiken Plastik* (3rd edition, Mainz, 1948), p. 7, cited J. Ratzinger, *Wesen und Auftrag der Theologie. Versuche zur ihrer Ortsbestimmung im Disput der Gegenwart* (Einsiedeln, 1993); English translation, *The Nature and Mission of Theology. Essays to Orient Theology in Today's Debates* (San Francisco, 1995), p. 14.

27. B. Russell, *Logic and Knowledge: Essays 1901–1950*, ed. R. C. Marsh (London, 1956), p. 325.

into a kind of religion of its own, where all major questions (and minor as well) are already answered and, in a would-be totally comprehensive system of thought, questions are no longer asked (except for pedagogical purposes). The perils of the "self-limitation of reason" are likewise a major theme of the 2003 *Glaube, Wahrheit, Toleranz* put into English the following year as *Truth and Tolerance*.[28]

Yet not only in *Introduction to Christianity* but also in "Faith, Philosophy, and Theology" Ratzinger seems to have gone further than Gilson in the direction of a synthesis of philosophy and theology. Gilson's "Chalcedonian" model, which we considered in Chapter 7, stresses the essential distinctness as well as the inseparability of the two disciplines. While Ratzinger accepted that the clarification of their respective methods by the thirteenth-century schools was an inevitable consequence of a sharper distinction between the natural and the supernatural, he also considered that later commentators exaggerated the extent to which Thomas—by adopting this clarification and distinction—departed in this regard from the more holistic tradition of the Fathers.[29] Thus he passed beyond hailing distance of the Louvain school, who criticized Gilson for, if anything, insufficient attention to philosophy's need for wholly independent existence within the Church. Inevitably, then, the Ratzinger of the 1960s, 1970s and 1980s, made *some* movement towards *bautainisme* which, owing to its inheritance from traditionalism, considered faith to be an indispensable auxiliary to reason if reason were ever to attain fundamental truths. Among the writers discussed in this book, perhaps his position bore closest resemblance to that of Franz Jakob Clemens (touched on in Chapter 6), for whom reason, which is always culturally formed, remains reason—and highly penetrating reason—when it has been formed in a Christian way.[30]

---

28. J. Ratzinger, *Glaube, Wahrheit, Toleranz. Das Christentum und die Weltreligionen*, op. cit.

29. Idem., *The Nature and Mission of Theology*, op. cit., pp. 16–17.

30. Among writers not discussed, since they belong to non-Catholic traditions of Christianity, there is a distinct family resemblance to Paul Tillich's discussion of the faith-reason relation, not least in his *Dynamics of Faith* (New York, 1957). "Under the conditions of actual existence, Tillich believed, reason is estranged from the ultimate reality that is its ground. Having lost contact with its true ground, it becomes superficial and distorted. Revelation is needed to reunite reason with its own depth. Faith is the act by which reason, healed by revelation, 'ecstatically' reaches beyond itself, overcoming its estrangement," thus A. Dulles, sj, *The Assurance of Things Hoped For*, op. cit., p. 123. Tillich's counter-position of ontological reason to (merely) technical reason, and his insistence that faith is the fulfillment of reason seem distinctly Ratzingerian.

Yet his standpoint was all his own. In the 1984 essay he described in three stages the kind of synthesis of philosophy and theology he wanted to see.
- First, the "prior givens" of faith, studied in theology, consist of answers to a series of ultimate questions, questions philosophy needs *for its own sake* to be kept alive.
- Second, the universal destination of faith (the Gospel is for all men) means that theology has to appeal to the "common reason of mankind."[31] Reciprocally, philosophy must "open itself to faith's claim on reason," *or else it will cease to be a (comparably universal) search for wisdom.*[32]
- Third, and appealing to Saint Bonaventure, Christian love (whose primacy among the virtues theology recognizes) includes the desire to bring one's neighbor to the truth. *Only if such love includes "eros for truth" (and therefore a strong philosophical component)* does it "remain sound as agape for God and man."[33]

Regensburg and Rome

These themes recur (but with, as we shall see, a "touch on the tiller" by the captain of the ship) in the two, highly publicized, lectures Ratzinger has given on faith and reason since becoming pope. The first, "Faith, Reason and the University. Memories and Reflections," was actually delivered, with unexpectedly tumultuous effects, to a University audience at Regensburg on September 12, 2006. The second, "The Truth Makes us Good and Goodness is True," should have been given on January 17, 2008, at Rome's Sapienza University. But owing to hostility among a minority of staff and students, it was thought inadvisable for the pope to appear in person and the text was made available in written form instead.

The main point of the Regensburg lecture was lost to view in the turbulence aroused among Muslims by a merely illustrative reference to the 1391 "dialogue" of the emperor Manuel II Palaeologos with a Persian scholar, a dialogue in which the Byzantine partner

---

31. J. Ratzinger, *The Nature and Mission of Theology,* op. cit., p. 25.
32. Ibid.
33. Ibid., p. 27.

criticized Islam for spreading the prophet's teaching by the sword. Benedict's actual message was rather different. He stressed that faith in the divine Logos enjoys a profound harmony with the philosophers' conviction of the rationality of ultimate reality.[34] God is reasonable, and so should religion be. Moreover, religion, along with ethics, belongs among philosophy's legitimate concerns. To sever religion from philosophy is to reduce reason to less than fully human proportions. Reason should be religious.

At Regensburg, Benedict called the alternatives "pathological." If reason and religion do not mesh, reason will end up with a debased anthropology which seeks to spin whatever moral substance it can from the webs of evolutionary science, psychology or sociology. And religion in turn will become fundamentalist. A "theology grounded in Biblical faith," by contrast, so far from denying reason's "grandeur," will have, rather, "the courage to engage the whole breadth of reason" instead. For philosophy, moreover:

> Listening to the great experiences and insights of the religious traditions of humanity, and those of the Christian faith in particular, is a source of knowledge, and to ignore it would be an unacceptable restriction of our listening and responding.

Reason and faith need each other in order to purify each other from the pathologies that threaten them when they go each their own way.

In the text of the aborted lecture at La Sapienza Benedict's concern was principally with ethics or moral rationality, and most notably the justification of moral norms as reasonable. His question was: How, if at all, can the Church's faith elucidate this topic? He appealed to two secular thinkers: the American John Rawls, the most noted theoretician of modern Liberalism in political theory, and the

---

34. We can call this the foundational conviction of Christian Hellenism, of which Ratzinger is as much a devotee as is any Greek Orthodox (if at the same time he is also open to possible *praeparationes evangelicae* elsewhere, notably in the high cultures of Asia). His view of that unique moment is the same as that of the Irish historian of philosophy James McEvoy, commenting on *Fides et ratio*: "The Christian mind met Greek and Hellenistic culture, not in the purely particular features of the latter but at the point where it was moving beyond itself in the direction of universality": see "Commentary," in L. P. Hemming and S. F. Parsons (ed.), *Restoring Faith in Reason,* op. cit., p. 191.

German Jürgen Habermas, a post-metaphysical philosopher whose most influential concept is that of "communicative rationality."[35]

Benedict notes of Rawls that while he denies to "comprehensive religious doctrines" (such as Catholicism evidently is) the character of "public reason," he nevertheless holds that secular rationality should not simply disregard "nonpublic reason."[36] Rawls' argument is that, over a long period of time, good (though not demonstrative) argumentation has emerged to support the traditions of religious ethics involved. And Benedict draws from Rawls' words the following conclusion:

> In the face of an a-historical reason that tries to construct itself through a-historical rationality, the wisdom of humanity as such—the wisdom of the great religious traditions—is to be valued as a reality that cannot be with impunity thrown into the dustbin of the history of ideas.

And bravely—or at least it would have been brave had the lecture gone ahead as scheduled—the pope offered himself as a representative of ethical reason inasmuch as he represented a "believing community in which, over the centuries of its existence, a determinate wisdom of life has matured," containing within it a "treasury of ethical knowledge and experience" of importance for all humanity.

This claim, says Ratzinger, asks of the university some response, for truth (with which, it may be supposed, a university is concerned) means more than knowing. "Knowledge of the truth has knowledge of the good as its scope." In faculties of jurisprudence so much is obvious: the concern of law is with "giving the right form to human freedom," and "right" there can only mean a form that is in accord with the good. At this juncture Benedict turns to Habermas, with whom, as Cardinal Ratzinger, he had debated in Munich just four years earlier, in January 2004.[37] What had worried both men was

---

35. J. Habermas, *Theorie des kommunikativen Handelns* (Frankfurt, 1982, 2nd edition) is the best known of his wide-ranging works. A concise version of his central idea is found in *Kommunikatives Handeln und detranzendentalisierte Vernunft* (Stuttgart, 2001).

36. See J. Rawls, *The Law of Peoples: with "The Idea of Public Reason Revisited"* (Cambridge, MA, and London, 1999).

37. J. Ratzinger, "Was die Welt zusammenhält. Vorpolitische moralische Grundlagen eines freiheitlichen Staates (Gesprächsabend mit Jürgen Habermas am 19. 1. 2004 in der Katholischen Akademie in Bayern, München)," *Zur Debatte. Themen der Katholischen Akademie in Bayern* 34.

the difficulty pinpointed by another German thinker, Ernst-Wolfgang Böckenförde, for whom "the secularized Liberal State lives by presuppositions it cannot guarantee." Habermas proposed two pillars as the foundation of a democratic order serving an objective common good: the first was the egalitarian political participation of all citizens; the second the "reasonable form" in which political conflicts are resolved.[38] It is the second, notes Benedict, that is problematic. Modern parties, which "have the charge of the formation of the political will" are concerned with gaining majorities. But Habermas plainly denies that possessing such a majority could *count as* imposing "reasonable form." Reasonable form has to include "a process of argumentation that is sensitive to the truth." Precisely because truth enters in there, Rawls' (limited) commendation of the wisdom traditions of the religions becomes pertinent. Benedict points to the significance in this connection of the structure of the medieval university. Alongside a faculty of law, that university had faculties of philosophy and theology. To these faculties "was entrusted the study of man's being in its totality and, along with this, the task of keeping the sensitivity to truth alive." What Benedict is saying is that modern politics need philosophy and theology for their own good.

We can note, however, that by this date, 2008, he has adopted a fully Gilsonian picture of how philosophy and theology interrelate, appealing explicitly, in fact, to Gilson's comparison with Chalcedon. They should be united "without confusion and without separation." In the conclusion to this lecture the pope reiterates much of what he had said as Joseph Ratzinger in, not least, *Introduction to Christianity*, "Faith, Philosophy and Theology" and *Truth and Tolerance*. For instance, he repeats his warning that philosophy, shorn of theology, will become humanly truncated, though now his caveat that theology without philosophy may become fundamentalist has mutated into the claim that such an unphilosophical theology will turn out to be "confined to the private sphere." (Post-Conciliar Catholicism in Western Europe hardly betrayed many signs of incipient fundamentalism; it

---

1 (2004), pp. 5–7. The lecture was subsequently published alongside Habermas' in J. Habermas, J. Ratzinger (eds.), *Dialektik der Säkularisierung: Über Vernunft und Religion* (Freiburg, 2005).

38. Habermas had earlier laid out the main lines of his own political philosophy in *Faktizität und Geltung. Beiträge zur Diskussion des Rechts und des demokratischen Rechtsstaats* (Frankfurt, 1992).

showed numerous signs of accepting that relegation to the private to which secularism would condemn it.) But the *principles* on which the pope bases these admonitions are now fully Gilsonian.

The key Chalcedonian adjectives have become all-determining. Thus on "without confusion," we read:

> Philosophy must truly remain an undertaking of reason in its proper freedom and proper responsibility; it must recognize its limits, and precisely in this way also its grandeur and vastness. Theology must continue to draw from the treasury of knowledge that it did not invent itself, that always surpasses it and that, never being totally exhaustible through reflection, and precisely because of this, launches thinking.

And on "without separation":

> Philosophy does not begin again from zero with the subject thinking in isolation, but rather stands in the great dialogue of historical wisdom, that again and again it both critically and docilely receives and develops; but it must not close itself off from that which the religions, and the Christian faith in particular, have received and bequeathed to humanity as an indication of the way.

Surprisingly, Benedict does not draw a comparable lesson for theology under the rubric of *achôristos*, "unseparated." Instead, he reverts to a theme of his own apologetics. If what is sought is the empirical validation of Christianity then we can find it in the lives of the saints which here he calls "the history of the humanism that grew up on the basis of the Christian faith," and declares to "demonstrate the truth of this faith in its essential nucleus," making it an "example for public reason."

That is of course a challenge to the shade of Rawls. As to Habermas, he had responded positively to the Regensburg lecture by an article of February 2007 in the noted Swiss newspaper, *Neue Zürcher Zeitung*. The need of the hour, thought Habermas, was for an alliance between enlightened reason, or what he called the "clarified consciousness of modernity," on the one hand and, on the other, "the theological consciousness of the world religions." That puts in interreligious terms what Ratzinger was seeking for the relations of Catholicism and philosophy, faith and reason. That is so whether he was applying the model of the "convergence of trajectories" or simply using the Gilsonian paradigm which may now have become more prominent in his doctrine, perhaps because his interests are, as supreme pastor rather than official theologian or academic, less historical and more contemporary in focus. Or perhaps again—who can say?—it is under the influence of a Petrine "charism of truth."

Conclusion

As the closing remarks of the previous chapter suggest, the present writer is inclined to the view that, of all the mediations of faith and reason—and thus theology and philosophy—set out in this study, Etienne Gilson's is the most satisfying. From the point of view of the construction of Christian doctrine, the most important reason for so saying is the congruence of Gilson's approach with the Christologically founded faith of the Church. Precisely because Gilson's picture of the relationship is "Chalcedonian"—modeled on the interrelation of divine and human natures in the incarnate Word—it takes its cue from the supreme disclosure of the possibilities of collaboration between the Uncreated and the created, divine knowledge and human exploration. This "collaboration," as the Fathers of Chalcedon insisted, involves perfect mutuality without either confusion or separation. As David Schindler explains:

> [T]he divine and human do not need to be *juxtaposed* or *separated* in order to retain their mutual integrity as divine and as human . . . It is precisely the hypostatic *unity* of divine and human in Jesus Christ that alone affords the *right sort of distinctness* between the divine and the human—even as the distinctness of each, within their unity, remains "perfect" . . . adding the rider (sometimes overlooked in Western Christologies of a Leonine type) that this "simultaneous order of unity and 'perfect' distinctness is asymmetrical, with divinity having priority, since the single hypostasis is divine."[1]

Applying this model to the issue which has concerned us in these pages, Schindler continues:

> It is in the anterior unity between faith and reason in the God of Jesus Christ, as the origin and end of both, that the rightful distinctness between

---

1. D. L. Schindler, "God and the End of Intelligence: Knowledge as Relationship," art. cit., p. 516.

faith and reason occurs. The rightful distinctness of faith and reason, and of their respective formal objects, in other words, cannot be conceived first in terms of juxtaposition, as though in the first instance they lay side by side with each other—and, *a fortiori*, not first in terms of opposition. On the contrary, . . . "each is found in the other"—differently—and each one's rightful scope for action occurs precisely within this mutual if asymmetrical penetration.

The massive intelligibilities found within faith can shape the rational enterprise in productive ways. But the vast range of that enterprise is not of itself shapeless. Its ontological scanning—which can be done in various manners, by Platonism as an exploration of the transcendentals, by Aristotelianism as an account of the causes whereby things (including human action) are understood, by Idealism as a philosophy of history, by existentialism and phenomenology as an integral anthropology—points the student in the direction of faith.

> Faith "contains" reason, and reason, in the one historical order of existence, is always-already—albeit implicitly—open from within to the order of faith. In a word, the relation between faith and reason is mutual and asymmetrical, analogous to the way in which the relation between divine and human in Jesus is mutual and asymmetrical. In neither case is the relation first extrinsic and "additive," much less inverse.[2]

That is a theological case for what in Pius IX's *Singulari quidem* was a bare assertion (the mutual help reason and faith offer each other) and in John Paul II's *Fides et ratio* a metaphor (the two wings of Catholic thought, philosophy and theology, which keep the bird in flight). It seems a solution capable of integrating many of the diverse "solutions" discussed in this book—always assuming their supporters can lay aside the inveterate human habit of intellectual unilateralism (for G. K. Chesterton the essence of heresy).

On such a Chalcedonian model, reason can be, in relation to revealed truth, both responsive *and* originative. Reason will be *responsive* insofar as it seeks to respond to, and thus lay out with greater fullness, the massive intelligibilities found in the doctrine of faith. On a Chalcedonian view of the faith-reason relation, this corresponds to the divine nature which enters into union with the human in the

---

2. Ibid., pp. 516–517, with the internal citation of a phrase from *Fides et ratio*, 17.

hypostatic union in Christ. By contrast, reason will be *originative* insofar as it seeks, by its own legitimate autonomy, to lay out pathways for philosophical thought, ways that can be brought into relation with the intelligibility found in revelation as registered by faith. In Chalcedonian terms, that corresponds to the human nature which enters hypostatically into union with the divine. Such originative reason will always be, however, even in its autonomy a dependent reason. It does not originate itself in any absolute or unconditional sense—any more than human nature does. Originative reason has its own foundation in the eternal Logos who at the beginning established the world, just as he also established human subjectivity in the origins of *homo sapiens*. All new beginnings for reason—new beginnings which make possible that variety of differentiated but not (we trust) ultimately competitive rationalities to which allusion was made, with MacIntyre's help, in the opening chapter of this book—are comprehended in the One who is their Alpha. So too, when human thought has exhausted in history its own modalities, will those beginnings be comprehended in him as their Omega, at the end—and this is so whether or not any philosopher ever establishes epistemic foundations in a manner calculated to satisfy representatives of all traditions of rationality.

Thanks to its high doctrine of creation, and the human rationality that follows from humankind's making in the image of God, the tradition of Thomism is at ease with what I have called, in the wake of a distinguished representative of *Communio* theology, "originative reason." (Schindler is editor of the American edition of the inspirationally Balthasarian journal of that name.) Philosophy so conceived can shape a natural wisdom well-placed to say much of value about the nature of God, world, soul, and the human good. "Originative reason" makes possible that truth common to all cultures, epochs and individuals that enjoy mental health, intellectual sanity, or what the Germans call *das GemeinWahre* with, at its heart, surely, a metaphysics of being. If a philosophy sustained by originative reason happens to have the benefit of a Catholic Christian context for its work, it can, moreover, go on to reconcile human reason to the Word of God, and elicit reason's testimony to the credibility of the founding events of the Gospel.

Furthermore, in exploration of revelation, through analogy and the *nexus mysteriorum*, philosophy, as the school of Thomas conceives it, will also be happy with what I am terming, again in Schindler's footsteps, "responsive reason," too. The deployment of philosophical reason in the theological explication of the revealed mysteries renders theology's presentation both clearer and richer, thus enabling it to unfold the virtualities of the Word, the riches of wisdom and knowledge that lie hid in Christ Jesus, revelation's center. Philosophy, operating in the fashion of responsive reason, has its own contribution to make to the understanding of faith (compare Blondel's project, and, standing behind him, the figure of Anselm).

Yet the *language* of "responsive" and "originative" reason is not, it must be said, Thomism's chosen idiom. In our era, though, this neo-idiolect commends itself. In an age often called—indeed, self-proclaimed—post-metaphysical, it is well that the Church confirms her hold on philosophical reason by means theological. An example may instruct. If any name from the beginnings of modernity stands for modern philosophy it is the name of Immanuel Kant. Yet in the fashionable world of postmodern thinking, where Friedrich Nietzsche is the preferred household god, the figure of Kant sways on his throne. Our opening investigation of Georg Hermes showed that business could be done with Kantianism—up to a point. That point was sufficient, at any rate, for a magisterial intervention in a debate to make sense to both sides. In the eyes of philosophers of being, Kant is perilously situated between realism and idealism, between phenomenology and constructivism. And yet at least, for him, the proper exercise of reason depends upon what can be experienced, while for Nietzsche reason has no foundation other than the play of the non-ground of interpretation.[3]

The postmodern conviction that universal canons of reason cannot be developed sits uneasily with the Catholic emphasis on the unity of the human species, the availability of natural law, the possibility of a natural knowledge of God, and the accessibility of the "transcendentals"—the one, the true, the good, the beautiful—as lamps lighting up all minds. For the sake of intelligibility, communication and coherence in culture and society, rationality requires more than endless playful deferrals of meaning. Something fuller and more definite needs to be said. The writers surveyed in this study, and the issue of their thought in the teaching of two great popes, suggest that the revelation carried by Catholic Christianity may help one to say it.

---

3. K. Hart, *The Trespass of the Sign*, op. cit., p. 73.

Revelational thinking assists both conceptual amplitude and argumentative solidity, desirable qualities of philosophical reason as such.[4]

But are amplitude and solidity to be achieved only at the price of submission to the straitjacket of a single philosophical methodology? Despite (or because of) the passion with which he was committed to Thomas's sense of being ("the *ultima Thule* of metaphysics, the foundation of metaphysics for all periods"[5]), Etienne Gilson appears to have been clear that the reason he and Thomas sought to serve was pluriform. That is not a matter of which philosophical conclusions are arrived at, though of course such decisions are vital: philosophical conclusions, as already noted, frequently have theological implications, some of them crucial for the construction of doctrine, which requires, for instance, "metaphysical and epistemological realism."[6] Rather it is a question of the *manner* whereby the conclusions arrived at are reached or entertained. As Gilson put it, intelligence is a "simple light," yet if it is to "move among beings" that light must be refracted into "reasons."[7] I take "reasons," *raisons,* to mean in that passage: not merely a plurality of argumentative steps, but, more compendiously, a number of argumentative modes, a variety of ways of rational proceeding, so long as these are—at least prospectively—complementary and convergent rather than competitive.[8] *Pace* MacIntyre, to *show* the latter may not be fully feasible now, but it will be eventually. Whether that "eventually" is at the Eschaton, or in some "para-eschaton" of thought at the hands of a second Thomas, a master of integrative thinking, is another matter. The first Thomas, by his combination of generosity and firmness, points the way.

---

4. An example: the assistance the doctrine of the divine image in man gives to philosophical anthropology when it seeks to assert "human rights": see R. Ruston, *Human Rights and the Image of God* (London, 2004).

5. E. Gilson, *Le philosophe et la Théologie*, op. cit., p. 211.

6. F. A. Murphy, *Art and Intellect in the Philosophy of Etienne Gilson*, op. cit., p. 4; cf. idem., *God Is Not a Story: Realism Revisited* (Oxford, 2007), an expansive treatment of this crucial instance.

7. E. Gilson, *Le philosophe et la Théologie*, op. cit., p. 154.

8. In Thomas's case, one could think, for instance, of the coexistence in his thought of demonstrative argumentation, modeled on Aristotelian noetics, with *ex convenientia* thinking, which can be called an aesthetic mode of reason: see G. Narcisse, OP, *Les raisons de Dieu. Argument de convenance et Esthétique théologique selon saint Thomas d'Aquin et Hans Urs von Balthasar* (Fribourg, 1997). In a modern example, one might think of the compatibility of phenomenological description and the analysis of causal relations (material, formal, efficient, final) in the work of Karl Wojtyła. In terminology drawn from Anglo-American philosophy, these could be called different ways of specifying truth-conducive grounds.

Bibliography

J. Alfaro, "Faith," *Sacramentum Mundi*, 2 (English translation, New York and London, 1968), pp. 313–322.

B. d'Amore (ed.), *Tommaso d'Aquino nel I. centenario dell'enciclica "Aeterni Patris"* (Rome, 1981).

R. Aubert, "Aspects divers du néo-thomisme sous le pontificat de Léon XIII," in G. Rossini (ed.), *Aspetti della cultura cattolica nell'età di Leone XIII* (Rome, 1961), pp. 133–227.

Idem., *The Church between Revolution and Restoration* (English translation, New York, 1981).

Idem., *Le pontificat de Pie IX* [1846–1878] (Paris, 1952).

Idem., *Vatican I* (Paris, 1964).

Idem., *Le problème de l'acte de foi. Données traditionelles et controverses récentes* (Louvain, 1969, 4th edition).

H. U. von Balthasar, *Herrlichkeit. Eine theologische Ästhetik*. I. Schau der Gestalt (Einsiedeln, 1961); English translation, *The Glory of the Lord. A Theological Aesthetics* I. Seeing the Form (Edinburgh and San Francisco, 1985).

Idem., *Glaubhaft ist nur Liebe* (Einsiedeln, 1963); English translation, *Love Alone: The Way of Revelation* (London, 1968).

B. Bastgen, *Forschungen und Quellen zur Kirchengeschichte Gregors XVI* (Paderborn, 1929).

L. Bautain, *La morale de l'Evangile comparée à la morale des philosophes* (Strasbourg-Paris, 1827).

Idem., *De l'enseignement de la philosophie en France au XIXe siècle* (Strasbourg, 1833).

Idem., *La philosophie du Christianisme* (2 vols, Strasbourg–Paris, 1835, reprinted Frankfurt, 1968).

Idem., *Philosophie morale* (2 vols, Strasbourg–Paris, 1842).

Idem., *Les Choses de l'autre monde. Journal d'un philosophe* (Paris, 1868).

K. Beck, *Offenbarung und Glaube bei Anton Günther* (Vienna, 1967).

U. Betti, *La costituzione dommatica "Dei Filius"* (Rome, 1961).

L.-M. Billé (ed.), *Foi et raison: Lectures de l'encyclique* Fides et ratio (Paris, 1998).

M. Blondel, *L'Action. Essai d'une critique de la vie et d'une science de la pratique* (Paris, 1893; 3rd edition reprinted Paris, 1973; English translation *Action: Essay on a Critique of Life and a Science of Practice,* Notre Dame, IN, 1984).

Idem., *De vinculo substantiali et de substantia composite apud Leibnitium* (Paris, 1893); French translation as *Le Lien substantiel et la substance composée d'après Leibniz* (Louvain–Paris, 1972).

Les premiers écrits de Maurice Blondel (Paris, 1956; includes "Lettre sur les exigences de la pensée contemporaine en matière d'apologétique" (1896), pp. 5–95; "L'Illusion idéaliste" (1898), pp. 97–122; "Principe élémentaire d'une logique de la vie morale"

(1903), pp. 123–147; "Histoire et dogme. Les lacunes philosophiques de l'exégèse contemporaine" (1904), pp. 149–222; "De la valeur historique du dogme" (1905), pp. 229–245; English translation *The Letter on Apologetics and History and Dogma* (London, 1964, reprinted Grand Rapids, Michigan, 1994, and Edinburgh, 1995).

H. Bouillard, *Blondel et le Christianisme* (Paris, 1961; English translation, Washington and Cleveland, 1969).

Idem., *The Logic of the Faith* (English translation, New York, 1967).

V. B. Brezik (ed.), *One Hundred Years of Thomism*, "Aeterni Patris" *and Afterwards: A Symposium* (Houston, Texas, 1981).

A. Bunnell, *Before Infallibility. Liberal Catholicism in Biedermeier Vienna* (London and Toronto, 1970).

R. Buttiglione, *Karol Wojtyła: The Thought of the Man who became John Paul II* (English translation, Grand Rapids, Michigan, 1997).

O. Chadwick, *The Popes and European Revolution* (Oxford, 1981).

Council of the Vatican, Dogmatic Constitution *Dei Filius* (1869), Latin original in H. Denzinger, *Enchiridon symbolorum, definitionum et declarationum de rebus fidei et morum* (Freiburg, 1991, 37th edition), 3000–3045.

R. Crippa—P. Henrici (ed.), *Attualità del pensiero di Blondel* (Milan, 1976).

K. Deufel, *Kirche und Tradition bei Joseph Kleutgen. Ein Beitrag zur Geschichte der theologischen Wende im 19. Jahrhundert am Beispiel des kirchlich-theologischen Kampfprogramm P. Joseph Kleutgens sj* (Munich and Paderborn, 1976).

P. Dezza, *Alle origini del neotomismo* (Milan, 1940).

A. Dulles, sj, *The Splendor of Faith. The Theological Vision of Pope John Paul II* (London, 1979).

Idem., "Faith" in F. S. Fiorenza and J. P. Galvin (ed.), *Systematic Theology. Roman Catholic Perspectives* (Dublin, 1992), pp. 89–128.

Idem., *The Assurance of Things Hoped For* (New York and Oxford, 1994).

H. Duméry, *Raison et religion dans la Philosophie de l'action* (Paris, 1963).

R. Echauri, *El pensiamento de Etienne Gilson* (Pamplona, 1980).

K. Eschweiler, *Die zwei Wege der neueren Theologie. Georg Hermes—Matthias Joseph Scheeben. Eine kritische Untersuchung des Problems der theologischen Erkenntnis* (Augsburg, 1926).

R. Fisichella, *Hans Urs von Balthasar: Dinamica dell'amore e credibilità del cristianesimo* (Rome, 1981).

T. Fliethmann, *Vernünftig glauben. Die theorie der Theologie bei Georg Hermes* (Würzburg, 1997).

D. R. Foster and J. W. Koterski, sj, (ed.), *The Two Wings of Catholic Thought. Essays on "Fides et ratio"* (Washington, 2003).

A. Gardeil, *La Crédibilité et l'apologétique* (Paris, 1908; 2nd edition, 1912).

Idem., "Crédibilité," *Dictionnaire de Théologie Catholique* (Paris, 1907; 1938), cols. 2201–2310.

H.-D. Gardeil, "Le Père Ambroise Gardeil (1859–1931)," in *Bulletin thomiste. Notes et communications* 1 (1931), pp. 69°–92°, with full bibliography, and a short biography.

Idem., *L'oeuvre théologique du Père Ambroise Gardeil* (Etiolles, 1956).
R. Garrigou-Lagrange, OP, "In Memoriam. Le Père A. Gardeil," *Revue Thomiste* XIV. 68 (1931), pp. 797–808.
L. Gilen, "Kleutgen und der hermesianische Zweifel," *Scholastik* 33 (1958), pp. 1–31.
E. Gilson, *Being and some Philosophers* (Toronto, 1949; 2nd edition, Toronto, 1961).
Idem., *The Christian Philosophy of Saint Augustine* (London, 1961).
Idem., *Elements of Christian Philosophy* (New York, 1960; 1963), *Introduction à la Philosophie chrétienne* (Paris, 1960; English translation, *Christian Philosophy: An Introduction*, Toronto, 1993).
Idem., *L'esprit de la Philosophie médiévale* (Paris, 1948, 2nd edition; English translation of the 1st edition, *The Spirit of Mediaeval Philosophy*, London, 1936).
Idem., *God and Philosophy* (New Haven and London [1969], 2002).
Idem., *The History of Christian Philosophy in the Middle Ages* (New York, 1955).
Idem., *Introduction à l'étude de saint Augustin* (Paris, 1929; English translation, *La philosophie au moyen âge, des origines patristiques à la fin du XIV siècle* (Paris, 1944, 2nd edition).
Idem., *Jean Duns Scot. Introduction à ses positions fondamentales* (Paris, 1952).
Idem., *La philosophie de saint Bonaventure* (Paris, 1943, 2nd edition; English translation of the 1st edition, *The Philosophy of Saint Bonaventure*, London, 1938).
Idem., *Le philosophe et la Théologie* (Paris 1960, 2002; English translation, *The Philosopher and Theology*, New York, 1962).
Idem., *Le Réalisme méthodique* (Paris, 1936).
Idem., *Le Réalisme thomiste et la critique de la connaissance* (Paris, 1939; English translation, *Thomist Realism and the Critique of Knowledge*, San Francisco, 1986).
Idem., *Saint Thomas d'Aquin* (Paris, 1925, republished as *Saint Thomas moraliste*, Paris, 1974).
Idem., *Reason and Revelation in the Middle Ages* (New York, 1938).
Idem., *Le Thomisme. Introduction au système de saint Thomas d'Aquin* (Strasbourg, 1919; English translation of the 3rd edition, *The Philosophy of Saint Thomas Aquinas*, Cambridge, 1924).
Idem., *Le Thomisme. Introduction à la philosophie de saint Thomas d'Aquin* (Paris, 1965, 6th edition; English translation, *Thomism: the Philosophy of Thomas Aquinas*, Toronto, 2002).
Idem., *The Unity of Philosophical Experience* (London, 1938).
J. Godenir, OSB, *Jésus l'Unique: Introduction à la théologie de Hans Urs von Balthasar* (Paris, 1984).
Dr. Anton Günther's gesammelte Schriften (9 vols, Vienna, 1882, reprinted Freiburg, 1968).
A. Günther, *Späte Schriften, Lentigos und Peregrins Briefwechsel und Anti-Savarese*, ed. J. Reikerstorfer (Vienna, 1978).
T.J.A. Hartley, *Thomistic Revival and the Modernist Era* (Toronto, 1971).
J. J. Heaney, SJ (ed.), *Faith, Reason and the Gospels* (Baltimore, 1961).
G. Hermes, *Untersuchung über die innere Wahrheit des Christentums* (Münster, 1805, reprinted Freiburg, 1967).

Idem., *Einleitung in die christkatholische Theologie,* I. Philosophische Einleitung (Münster, 1819, 2nd edition, 1831, reprinted Freiburg, 1967); II. Positive Einleitung (Münster, 1829, 2nd edition, 1834, reprinted Freiburg, 1967).

Idem., *Christkatholische Dogmatik,* ed. H. Achterfeldt (3 vols, Münster, 1834).

L. P. Hemming and S. F. Parsons (ed.), *Restoring Faith in Reason. A New Translation of the Encyclical Letter* Faith and Reason *of Pope John Paul II together with a commentary and discussion* (London, 2002).

A. E. van Hooff, *Die Vollendung des Menschen. Die Idee des Glaubensaktes und ihre philosophische Begründung im Frühwerk Maurice Blondels* (Freiburg, 1983).

John Paul II, *Faith and Reason* (English translation, 1998).

Idem., *Faith according to Saint John of the Cross* (English translation, San Francisco, 1981).

Idem., *Love and Responsibility* (English translation, London, 1981).

Idem., *Sources of Renewal: The Implementation of Vatican II* (English translation, San Francisco, 1980).

Idem., *Crossing the Threshold of Hope* (English translation, London, 1994).

A. Kenny, *Faith and Reason* (New York, 1983).

J. Kleutgen, *Die Philosophie der Vorzeit verteidigt* (2 vols, Münster, 1860–1863).

Idem., *Die Theologie der Vorzeit verteidigt* (4 vols, Münster, 1853–1870; 2nd edition, Münster, 1867–1874).

C. Kopp, *Die Philosophie des Hermes* (Cologne, 1912).

G. Larcher, *Modernismus als theologischer Historismus. Ansätze zu seiner Überwindung im Frühwerk Maurice Blondels* (Frankfurt–Berne, 1985).

Leo XIII, *"Aeterni Patris,"* in *Acta Sanctae Sedis* 12 (1879), pp. 97–115; English translation in C. Carlen, IHM, *The Papal Encyclicals 1878–1903* (Raleigh, VA, 1990), pp. 17–27.

P. Levillain, J.-M. Ticchi, et al., *Le pontificat de Léon XIII. Renaissances du Saint-Siège?* (Rome–Paris, 2006).

R. Lill, *Die Beilegung der Kölner Wirren, 1840–1842* (Dusseldorf, 1962).

J. M. McDermott, SJ, *Love and Understanding. The Relation of Will and Intellect in Pierre Rousselot's Christological Vision* (Rome, 1983).

Idem., (ed.), *The Thought of Pope John Paul II* (Rome, 1993).

M. McGrath, *Etienne Gilson. A Bibliography* (Toronto, 1982).

A. MacIntyre, *Whose Justice? Which Rationality?* (London, 1988).

E. Mann, *Die Wiener theologische Schule Anton Günthers im Urteil des 20. Jahrhunderts* (Vienna, 1979).

G. Marchesi, SJ, *La cristologia di Hans Urs von Balthasar: La figura di Gesù Cristo espressione visibile di Dio* (Rome, 1977).

G. Martina, SJ, *Pio IX* [1846–1850] (Rome, 1974).

Idem., *Pio IX* [1851–1866] (Rome, 1986).

Idem., *Pio IX* [1867–1878] (Rome, 1990).

F. A. Murphy, *Art and Intellect in the Philosophy of Etienne Gilson* (Columbia and London, 2004).

J. Murphy, *Christ our Joy. The Theological Vision of Pope Benedict XVI* (San Francisco, 2008).
A. Nichols, OP, *The Thought of Benedict XVI*. The Theology of Joseph Ratzinger (2nd edition, London, 2006).
B. Osswald, *Anton Günther. Theologisches denken im Kontext einer Philosophie der Subjektivität* (Munich, 1990).
G. Perini, "Dall' *Aeterni Patris* al Concilio Vaticano II: Le direttive del Magistero delle dottrine di S. Tommaso," *Scripta theologica* 11 (1979), pp. 619–658.
J. Pieper, *Faith* (English translation, London, 1964).
Pius IX, *Qui pluribus* (1846). The crucial sections of the Latin text for the issue of faith and reason are provided in H. Denzinger, *Enchiridon symbolorum, definitionum et declarationum de rebus fidei et morum*, op. cit., 2775–2780.
Idem., *Singulari quidem* (1856).
Idem., *Eximiam tuam* (1857). Key sections of the Latin text are found in H. Denzinger, *Enchiridon symbolorum, definitionum et declarationum de rebus fidei et morum*, op. cit., 2828–2831.
V. Possenti, *Philosophy and Revelation. A Contribution to the Debate on Reason and Faith* (Farnborough, 2001).
H.-J. Pottmeyer, *Der Glaube vor dem Anspruch der Wissenschaft: Die Konstitution über den katholischen Glauben, Dei Filius, des I. Vatikanischen Konzils und der unveröffentlichen theologischen Voten der vorbereitenden Kommission* (Freiburg, 1968).
P. Poupard, *l'Abbé Louis Bautain: Un essai die Philosophie chrétienne au XIX siecle* (Tournai, 1961).
J. Pritz, *Glauben und Wissen bei Anton Günther* (Vienna, 1963).
H. Putnam, *Reason, Truth and History* (Cambridge, 1981).
J. Ratzinger, *Milestones. Memoirs 1927–1977* (English translation, San Francisco, 1998).
Idem., *Introduction to Christianity* (revised edition, English translation, San Francisco, 2004).
Idem., *The Nature and Mission of Theology. Essays to Orient Theology in Today's Debates* (English translation, San Francisco, 1995).
Idem., *Truth and Tolerance. Christian Belief and World Religions* (English translation, San Francisco, 2004).
P. Rousselot, "Les yeux de la foi," *Recherches de science religieuse* 1 (1910), pp. 241–259, 444–475; English translation *The Eyes of Faith and An Answer to Two Attacks* (New York, 1990).
T. Rowland, *Ratzinger's Faith. The Theology of Pope Benedict XVI* (Oxford, 2008).
K. L. Schmitz, *At the Center of the Human Drama: The Philosophical Anthropology of Karol Wojtyła/Pope John Paul II* (Washington, 1993).
H. Schwedt, *Das römische Urteil über Georg Hermes. Ein Beitrag zur Geschichte der Inquisition im 19. Jahrhundert* (Rome-Freiburg-Vienna, 1980).
L. K. Shook, *Etienne Gilson* (Toronto, 1984).
T. L. Smith (ed.), *Faith and Reason* (Chicago, 2001).

F. Topíc, *L'uomo di fronte alla rivelazione di Dio nel pensiero di Hans Urs von Balthasar* (Rome, 1990).

D. V. Twomey, SVD, *Pope Benedict XVI: The Conscience of our Age* (San Francisco, 2007).

R. Virgoulay, *Blondel et le Modernisme. Le philosophe de l'action et les sciences religieuses [1896–1913]* (Paris, 1980).

L. P. Wallace, *Leo XIII* (Durham, NC, 1966).

C. Weber, *Aufklärung und Orthodoxie am Mittelrhein* (Münster-Paderborn, 1973).

G. Weigel, *Witness to Hope. The Biography of Pope John Paul II* (New York, 1999).

P. Wenzel, *Das wissenschaftliche Anliegen des Güntherianismus* (Essen, 1961).

G. H. Williams, *The Mind of John Paul II*. Origins of his Thought and Action (New York, 1981).

Index

Abraham 4
Adam 20, 46, 54, 65, 86, 147
Anselm 8n, 64, 85, 107, 149–150, 150n, 180, 183, 184, 210
Apollo 180
Aquinas, *see* Thomas Aquinas
Aristotle 6, 16, 56–57, 72, 115, 122, 143, 143n, 162, 176
Aubert, R. 2n, 3, 7n, 15n, 93n, 96n, 97n, 98n
Augustine vii, 6–10, 6n, 13n, 14n, 19, 30, 45n, 51, 64, 66n, 71, 100, 125–6, 133, 150, 168, 169n, 180, 183, 191

Bacon, F. 69
Balthasar, H. U. von iv, 132, 151, 154, 158, 167–171, 169n, 209, 211n
Baltzer, J. B. 100
Barth, K. 149, 168
Basil 30
Bautain, L. iv, 60–72, 73, 81–86, 95, 98, 100, 102, 104, 105, 106, 112, 113, 124, 126, 151, 152, 157, 166, 179, 183, 184, 186, 199, 200
Benedict 58, 93
Benedict XIV 119
Benedict XVI iv, ix, 190–206, 191n, 200n, 202n
Bentham, J. 17
Bergson, H. v, 122, 128n
Berkeley, G. 35
Bernard 143–144, 144n

Blondel, M. iv, 132, 133–150, 136n, 142n, 148n, 153–171, 157n, 169n, 179, 180, 181, 182, 185, 187n, 210
Böckenförde, E.-W. 204
Bonald, L. G. A. de 51, 59
Bonaventure 107, 115, 123, 126, 133, 150, 192, 201
Boniface II 9
Bonnetty, A. 65n, 94
Bosses, B. des 136
Bouillard, H. 141, 145n, 150n
Brunschvig, L. 145, 146
Bruno, G. 111
Bucer, M. 119
Bunnell, A. 44n, 92n, 93

Cajetan, *see* Thomas de Vio
Capellari, M., *see* Gregory XVI
Chesterton, G. K. iv–v, ix, 131, 131–132n, 208
Clemens, F. J. 110–111, 200
Clement VI 120
Clement of Alexandria 30, 104
Coleridge, S. T. 157
Comte, A. 195
Consentius 6
Cousin, V. 61–62

Darwin, C. 57n, 132n, 135, 195
Denzinger, H. 9n, 10n, 95
Descartes, R. iv–vi, 56–57, 57n, 62, 64, 70, 108, 110, 122, 129, 130
Drey, J. S. 186

Droste zu Vischering, C. A. von 76, 80
Dulles, A. 2n, 3, 5n, 8–9n, 16n, 40n, 73n, 99, 100n, 157n, 161n, 164, 164n, 165, 165n, 169n, 200n

Eckhart, M. 63, 64n
Eliot, G. 40, 65
Elvenich, J. P. 100
Evans, G. 45n, 144n, 149, 150n

Faulhaber, M. 191–192
Felder, H. 163, 164n
Fichte, J. G. 27, 28n, 29n, 32, 35, 43, 47
Firrao, A. 118
Förster, H. 93
Francis 123
Franz Joseph 90–91, 92
Franzelin, J. B. 96, 97

Gardeil, A. 154, 158–163, 160n, 164, 165, 168, 170, 181, 182, 185
Garrigou-Lagrange, R. 57n, 131n, 159n, 166n, 173, 174, 178
Geissel, J. von 94
Gilson, E. v, 57, 59, 72, 106, 114, 120, 121–132, 122n, 123n, 126n, 127n, 128n, 131n, 133, 135, 139, 144, 153, 174, 175, 179, 182, 184, 188, 188–189n, 199–200, 204–206, 207, 211
Gorner, P. 35–36
Gregory XVI 59n, 73–86, 87, 100, 152
Gregory Nazianzen 8n, 30, 85
Günther, A. iv, 42–59, 42n, 44n, 46n, 56n, 57n, 60, 67, 68, 72, 73, 90–95, 92n, 94n, 95n, 97–100, 102, 105, 106, 110–119, 124, 140, 149, 150, 152, 155, 179, 184, 185, 186
Guéranger, P. 95

Habermas, J. 203–205
Haldane, J. 133–134, 134n
Hankey, W. J. 187
Harnack, A. von 31
Hart, K. 36, 197n, 210n
Hegel, G. W. F. iv, 27, 43, 45, 45n, 55, 57, 58, 62, 63, 92, 130, 185n, 195
Heidegger, M. 36n, 127, 195n
Henrici, P. 139, 170n, 187n
Hermes, G. iv, 14n, 22–41, 10n, 27n, 29n, 31n, 33n, 34n, 35n, 38n, 40n, 49, 60, 72, 73, 74, 75–80, 81, 83, 83n, 85, 86, 89–90, 93, 95, 98, 99n, 100, 102, 105, 110, 112, 114, 116, 117, 124, 152, 160, 167, 179, 184, 186, 210
Hirscher, J. B. 116, 117, 117n
Hofbauer, C. M. 44, 91
Hohenlohe, K. von, see Hohenzollern, K. von
Hohenlohe-Schillingsfürst, C. A. 93
Hohenzollern, K. von 118
Humann, M.-L. 63–66
Husserl, E. 176

Isaiah 198

Jacquin, A. M. 150
James, W. 129
John 4–5, 7, 11, 13, 55n, 99, 188, 194, 198
John of the Cross 173
John Damascene 107

John Paul II iv, x, 171, 172–189, 190, 193, 199, 208, 211n
Joseph II 42
Justin Martyr 6, 30, 66

Kant, I. iv, v, vi, 17, 20n, 22–23, 26–27, 28, 28n, 29, 31, 32, 33, 34, 34n, 35, 35n, 36, 37, 39, 41, 43, 49, 57, 62, 65, 71, 74, 76, 90, 98, 114, 129, 130, 131n, 135, 143, 146n, 147, 152, 154, 167, 167n, 169, 170, 176, 197, 210
Klee, H. 77
Kleutgen, J. iv, 35n, 97, 102, 111–120, 116n, 121
Knoodt, P. 44n, 100

Lamennais, R. F. de 51, 65, 77, 96n
Le Pappe de Trévern, J.–F. 81–83
Le Roy, E. 157
Leo XIII 101, 102–111, 102n, 114, 118, 119–120, 121, 123, 124, 125, 126, 127, 128, 132, 133, 134, 134n, 152, 174, 181, 184, 186, 207
Leibniz, G. W. von 4n, 25, 62, 113, 135, 136, 136n, 148, 148n
Lewis, C. S. 46, 171
Locke, J. 113
Lonergan, B. 11n, 179, 179n
Louis–Philippe 81
Luigia, M. 118
Luther, M. 24, 49, 80
Lydia 48, 53n, 54n

MacIntyre, A. 16, 17, 19, 61, 68, 181, 209, 211
Maistre, J. de 51, 65
Mandonnet, P. 123, 150n
Manuel II Palaeologos 201

Maritain, J. 121, 112, 126, 126n, 131, 174, 177
Martha 137
Martina, G. 75n, 87, 89, 89n, 91n, 92n, 93n, 95n, 96, 96n, 100, 101n, 102n, 117, 118, 117–118n
Marx, K. 44n, 195
Mary 189
Mastai–Ferretti, G. M., *see* Pius IX
McDermott, J. 168n, 176n, 178
Melzer, E. 100
Metternich, C. W. L. von 87
Möhler, J. A. iv, 83–84, 93n, 186
Moses 82, 104, 197, 199
Müller, A. 44, 44n
Murphy, F. 123n, 126n, 128, 211n

Napoleon 61
Nazianzen, *see* Gregory Nazianzen
Newman, J. H. iv, 14, 85, 109n, 163, 166, 167, 169n, 187, 187n
Nicholas of Cusa 111
Nietzsche, F. 210
Niezńanski, E. 174–175

Origen 8n, 103

Papalettere, S. 93
Parmenides 130
Paul 4–5, 4n, 10, 11, 12, 48, 58, 65, 69, 90, 99, 183, 196
Paul VI 193
Pecci, G. 101, 109
Pecci, V. G., *see* Leo XIII
Perrone, G. 28, 85
Peter 5
Philo of Alexandria 36
Pius VI 88n
Pius VII 87
Pius VIII 74, 75–76

Pius IX 42n, 59, 73, 87–96, 101, 104, 118, 119, 152, 194, 208
Pius X 153n, 155
Pius XI 124, 125
Pius XIII 165n
Plassmann, H. E., 110–111
Plato viii, 56, 71, 111
Poupard, P. 60n, 63n, 66n, 69n, 70, 81n, 83n, 84n, 86n
Putnam, H. 19, 20

Ratzinger, G. 190
Ratzinger, J., see Benedict XVI
Rauscher, O. von 92
Rawls, J. 202–205
Ritschl, A. 31
Roselli, S. 109
Rosmini–Serbati, A. 187
Rossi, P. 88
Rousselot, P. v, 79, 80n, 142n, 154, 158–170, 169n, 181, 182
Russell, B. 199

Sanseverino, G. 109, 111
Sartre, J.-P. 127, 130
Savarese, G. 44–45, 46, 51
Scheeben, M. J. 14n, 95, 95n
Schelling, F. W. 27, 28n, 43, 62–63, 111
Scheler, M. 14n, 173, 175–177, 184
Schindler, D. 188–189, 207, 209
Schleiermacher, F. D. E. 28n, 31, 31n, 76, 111
Schmaus, M. 192
Schopenhauer, A. 139
Schulz, H. 31
Schwarzenberg, F. 93
Scotus, John Duns 30

Sixtus V 107
Solomon 78
Spencer, H. 135
Speyr, A. von 168
Spinoza, B. vi, 62
Staudenmaier, F. A. 47, 93n, 186
Stein, E. 187
Stróżewsk, W. 175
Swieżawski, S. 175
Suárez, F. 25n, 109, 136

Teilhard de Chardin, P. 136
Tertullian 6, 6n
Theodoret 8
Théry, G. 123
Thomas Aquinas iv, 5, 8, 8n, 10–14, 11n, 13n, 15, 18, 29, 30, 50, 56, 69, 85, 107–111, 108n, 113–116, 115n, 119–120, 121–132, 128n, 133–134, 134n, 142, 142n, 150n, 152–153, 160, 160n, 164, 164n, 166, 168, 173, 174, 176, 178, 181n, 184, 185n, 186n, 191, 200, 209, 211, 211n
Thomas de Vio 107

Überwasser, F. 27

Vega, A. de 15
Vico, G. 224
Victor Emmanuel II 93

Watterich, J. 100
Wittgenstein, L. 86
Wojtyła, K., see John Paul II
Wolff, C. 23n, 25, 25n, 108
Woroniecki, J. 175